WORKAHOLICS

The Respectable Addicts

Barbara Killinger, Ph.D.

A FIRESIDE BOOK
Published by Simon & Schuster
New York, London, Toronto, Sydney, Tokyo, Singapore

I dedicate this book with
much love to my children:
Kathy, Michael, and Suzy

FIRESIDE
Simon & Schuster Building
Rockefeller Center
1230 Avenue of the Americas
New York, New York 10020

First Fireside Edition 1992
Published by arrangement with Key Porter Books Limited
Originally published in Canada by Key Porter Books Canada

FIRESIDE and colophon are registered trademarks
of Simon & Schuster Inc.

Manufactured in the United States of America

10 9 8 7 6 5 4 3 2 1 Pbk.

Library of Congress Cataloging in Publication Data
Killinger, Barbara.
    Workaholics: the respectable addicts/Barbara Killinger.—1st Fireside ed.
        p.   cm.
    "A Fireside book."
    "Originally published in Canada by Key Porter Books Canada"—T.p. verso.
    Includes bibliographical references and index.
    1. Workaholism. 2. Workaholics—Family relationships. I. Title.
RC569.5.W67K55   1992
616.85'2—dc20
                                                                91-45419
                                                                CIP
ISBN: 0-671-76984-7

CONTENTS

ACKNOWLEDGMENTS

For their wonderful gifts of unconditional love, faith, and support, I wish to thank my parents, Eva and Cuyler Henderson. Many friends offered love and encouragement as ideas developed into this book. Clients have generously shared many experiences to further the understanding of workaholism. Their journeys to unlock repressed feelings and to find the balance in their lives are a constant inspiration. Maria Quilici tended my garden and home faithfully to free me to write, and Judy Varjas cheerfully offered computer advice. My agent, Beverley Slopen, always enthusiastic; Jennifer Glossop, my editor, most helpful and fair; and Dan McEwen, a friend who asks probing questions — I thank them all for their expertise and sense of humour.

The Workaholic Quiz

Before reading on, stop for a few minutes to take this quiz. Then, guess how your spouse would answer these questions. Better still, ask your spouse to take the quiz as well, then compare notes on how many "yes" and "no" responses each of you came up with.

1. Is your work *very* important to you?
2. Do you like things done "just right"?
3. Do you tend to see things as black or white, not grey?
4. Are you competitive and often determined to win?
5. Is it important for you to be "right"?
6. Are you overly critical of yourself if you make a mistake?
7. Are you afraid of failing?
8. Are you restless, impulsive and easily bored?
9. Do you drive yourself, and have high levels of energy and stamina?
10. Do you suffer periodic bouts of extreme fatigue?
11. Do you take your briefcase home and work nights and/or weekends?
12. Do you feel uneasy or guilty if there is nothing to do?
13. Do you think you are special or different from other people?

14. Do you read work-related material when you eat alone?
15. Do you make lists of things to do, or keep a daily diary?
16. Do you find it harder and harder to take long vacations?
17. Do you often feel hurried, rushed, or a sense of urgency?
18. Do you keep in touch with your office while you're on holidays?
19. Do you "work" at play, and get upset if you don't play well?
20. Do you avoid thinking about planning your retirement?
21. Are you responsible at work, but not in personal matters?
22. Do you try to avoid conflict instead of dealing with it?
23. Do you act on impulse without considering the effect on others?
24. Do you fear rejection and criticism, yet judge and criticize?
25. Is your memory for what others have said getting worse?
26. Do you get upset if things don't work out as you expected?
27. Does being interrupted at work or at home annoy you?
28. Do you create pressure situations with self-imposed deadlines?
29. Do you concentrate on future events instead of enjoying the present?
30. Do you forget or minimize family occasions or celebrations?

Number of "yes" answers: _____

Number of "no" answers: _____

1.
Workaholism:
The "Respectable" Addiction

'Tis a gift to be simple
'tis a gift to be free
'tis a gift to come down
    where you ought to be
And when we find ourselves
    in the place just right
'Twill be in the valley of love
    and delight.
SHAKER SONG

I love this poem because it describes so well the journey my clients and I travel together in search of a simpler, more down-to-earth life. The workaholic's world is one of power, control, success, and prestige; of complexity, responsibility, ambition, and drive. The ideals of simplicity, freedom, spontaneity, humility, love, and delight that are embodied in this poem are foreign to the workaholic's thinking and to his or her current way of life.

Right now, you too may be caught up in that frenzied world. You too may be growing more worried about your performance. Something is terribly wrong at work. Even though you put in longer and longer hours, things aren't going well. Contributing to your stress is the fact that your marriage is in trouble. Your spouse is complaining about rages that you can't remember having. In fact, your memory just isn't what it used to be. The children are acting up, and they often seem anxious. If the truth be told, your whole world appears to be in a state of confusion. Or perhaps you are still in control of your world,

3

but notice that you are becoming more impulsive and impatient and that you often don't take the time to show love or empathy to others. You are more intense than you once were and often feel a sense of urgency. Your feelings are flat, but you experience unexpected flashes of anger. Look at your responses to the quiz on page 1. If you answered yes to twenty or more questions, then you most likely are a workaholic. Chaos is painful, but all the sympathy in the world won't help unless you begin to understand what's wrong! That's when you will start to put your life back together.

The knowledge and insight I have gained from my studies and from working with workaholics and their families are presented in these pages in the hope that you will recognize how devastating this addiction called workaholism really is. For some families, the help offered in this book will come too late; for them, workaholism may be too far advanced to treat. I hope this book will give these families an understanding of the breakdown syndrome, of the dynamics of the addiction, and of how long the process has actually gone on. All family members are caught in the workaholic web and react to the pressures exerted by an unhealthy family atmosphere. No, what has happened to you is not your fault, and you are not crazy. With understanding and compassion, family members can forgive one another in the learning process and go on to establish intimate and healthy relationships of their own.

It is my wish that the information and suggestions presented here will reach you in time to minimize the profound personality changes that workaholism can lead to. If caught in time, workaholism, like other addictions, can be reversed before these personality changes cause permanent damage to both you and your loved ones. Recovery is possible when the walls of denial are dismantled to allow for understanding. Remember, your marriage, your family life, and your job satisfaction depend on *your* psychological health.

WORKAHOLIC? — WHO, "MOI"?

"You must be kidding! Me, a workaholic? No way!" Not many people are comfortable with that label. We all think we know someone who is a workaholic, but few of us are willing to acknowledge our own addiction to work. And yet, workaholism has become part of everyday life and language. The term was coined in 1971 by Wayne Oates, an American minister and professor of the psychology of religion. In his personal story, *Confessions of a Workaholic*, he begins with a light-hearted attempt to josh his readers into chuckling with him over the notion of a compulsion to work. This approach soon gives way to a serious look at his own addiction and its roots.

The term "workaholic" is still used loosely and often in a humorous way — although a note of bitterness sometimes intrudes. One cartoon shows a worried woman standing in front of a perfume counter: "Do you have anything that smells like a desk?" she asks. In reality, there is nothing funny about workaholism. It ruins lives, destroys families, and causes discomfort and unhappiness.

So, who is a workaholic? First, let's consider those the label doesn't fit. A person who works long hours is not necessarily a workaholic. Work is essential for our well-being. Through work we define ourselves, develop our strengths, and take our places in society. Work gives us satisfaction, a sense of accomplishment, and mastery over problems. It provides us with a direction, and gives us goals to reach and hurdles to overcome. When we lose a job, or cannot work for whatever reason, our personalities suffer profound emotional disorganization and disturbance.

Work addiction is different. Ironically, it usually happens to middle-class people who are not driven to overwork by economic necessity. Someone who has to work extra hard to clothe and feed the family is simply facing a stark reality. He or she is not motivated by an obsession or driven by a neurotic addiction. Hard workers who are not workaholics enjoy their work and at times do become passionately devoted to it. They pour great energy and enthusiasm into work and, on such occasions, may perform remarkable feats. These bursts of productivity are not the norm, however. Most of the time, these workers can maintain balance in their lives and are fully in charge of their work schedules. Although their career helps define who they are and is instrumental in supporting their lifestyle, it does not "consume" them. Work is just one part of their lives and is offset by their love for family and friends, by their interest and involvement in many and varied activities, and by their spiritual and social beliefs and concerns. Such people are in touch with their feelings and able to express their love for others through words and deeds, even through troubled times.

Workaholism is not about healthy work, but about addiction and the abuse of power and control. A workaholic is not someone who simply works hard and enjoys what he or she does. For a workaholic, the job is simply the setting for the addiction, a place where approval is sought. Many perfectionistic homemakers are workaholics.

A workaholic is a person who gradually becomes emotionally crippled and addicted to control and power in a compulsive drive to gain approval and success. The obsession with work grows out of the workaholic's perfectionism and competitive nature. Excessive work, with its adrenalin high, hooks the workaholic, and a compulsive need for approval drives him or her to stay busy, be productive, and enjoy the accolades that hard work receives in our society. Work is the "fix," the drug that frees the workaholic from experiencing the emotional pain of anger, hurt, guilt, and fear.

Workaholics cannot *not* work without becoming anxious. The "work persona" (the image they wish others to see) thus begins to dominate their own lives and soon engulfs those of their family members. Emotional turmoil causes confusion and rigidity, and they become self-absorbed and self-centred. Fear, anxiety, and alienation eventually produce anger, which is then projected onto those close to them. Eventually, everything that goes wrong becomes other people's fault. Being *right* becomes extremely important: it allows them to control their external environment and to counteract the inner chaos. Since workaholics lack a balanced psyche, their perspective on the true meaning and value of life and love becomes distorted. Their denial defences and dishonesty do not permit them to acknowledge that they are no longer psychologically or spiritually healthy. Gradually, narcissism and paranoia grow powerful and reshape the personality.

"Work is life itself!" said one client nervously. "I throw myself into my work. What else is there?" Work, for the addict, becomes a *state of mind* rather than a job. It is an escape *to* an overly inflated sense of responsibility, *away from* true intimacy with others. In a conversation with Linda Leonard, who writes about alcoholism, I suggested that workaholism is an escape *to* responsibility, whereas alcoholism is an escape *from* responsibility. We agreed that both addictions serve as a means to avoid personal responsibility to family and others.

Workaholism is a *major source of marital breakdown.* I believe the correlation between the current crisis levels of workaholism and the high incidence of divorce is no coincidence. Workaholics strive to remain responsible at work even when they become more inefficient and insecure, but they gradually become personally irresponsible and lose their capacity to be loving and intimate. Intimacy requires a mutual sharing of feelings and of power, and each partner needs to be empathic and emotionally available to the other person. This is not possible for the workaholic. Tragically, work becomes an avoidance of living, an escape from a full and complete life.

Workaholics typically *work at play.* They think about work strategies and problems on vacations, and even while making love. Such distractions help them avoid the intimacy they fear. One client proudly confessed that he was at his creative high during intercourse, and that the solution to a very perplexing business problem once clicked into his mind just before orgasm. A woman who had lost all her sexual feelings told me she felt numb during intercourse, but coped by concentrating on an important project she was involved with. Both these workaholics were performing intercourse rather than making love, and by doing so they were avoiding facing the problems in their relationship.

Work is a *substitute "religious" experience* for many workaholics. Peak performances are a form of ecstasy, and the accompanying surge of adrenalin acts like a drug. People can become drunk with power. Like cocaine, work is extremely addictive, but unlike drug addictions, overwork has society's blessing. Work is placed in an exalted position because workaholics wish, above all, to be successful, or to be seen to be successful by their peers. It matters not that family and personal values are sacrificed to the goals and drama of the workplace.

Denial is the ultimate defence that protects this addiction, and it is the workaholic's real enemy. Workaholics need help and courage to recognize their addiction. It takes much humility, bravery, and wisdom to know when you need help. Workaholics prefer to think of themselves as hard-working types who are "doing it all for the family," or just pulling their weight for the company. Instead, they are too busy and preoccupied with being the wonderful doctor or making that scientific breakthrough. Some rationalize that they or the companies they work for provide an essential service to the community. Too many work until illness or a crisis at work or in the family breaks through the denial and forces recognition. Others unconsciously create a crisis by "acting out" with unusual, atypical behaviour, or "acting in" with depression or anxiety attacks. Still others suffer a complete breakdown in physical health. "I'm still wrestling with the concept of being a workaholic," admitted one client wryly. "I feel that I wasn't successful enough at work to merit the title. However, this may be part of my problem. I must merit whatever to the nth degree, even if it's an illness!"

Workaholism has *far-reaching consequences*. The long-term damage of this addiction is extremely serious. Whole companies become workaholism hotbeds, encouraging the growth of this addiction in its executives and employees. The work ethic today has never been stronger or more respectable. In this age of global competitiveness and consumerism, how much you earn determines how "successful" you are in your career, and earning top dollar has become a priority, even a necessity, for some die-hards. Since it is so respectable, work dependency is one of the most dangerous of all the addictions. It gives the addict a false sense of self-worth, of power and control, until the obsession becomes so consuming that it takes control of the workaholic, the family, and the company. Work then dictates the family's destiny, and too often the punishing hours previously reserved for dealing with crises or peak periods become the norm. When I asked if there was any activity unaffected by his workaholism, one recovering workaholic client responded: "No, I can make a job of every activity."

THE SOURCES OF WORKAHOLISM

Workaholism manifests itself in a variety of individuals — men and women, young and old. It can happen to those in their twenties or even in their teens, but it usually occurs later, in the forties and fifties. Although male workaholics outnumber female workaholics now, the ratios are changing. Your own husband or wife, your doctor or minister, your boss or secretary, or you yourself may have become a workaholic without realizing it.

But where does it come from? Its roots are in the upbringing of the workaholic-to-be and in our society. Let's look, first, at the family influences.

Dysfunctional Families

Workaholics typically come from dysfunctional families, families whose patterns of behaviour and interactions are not healthy. The members of these families suffer psychological problems as a result. In many dysfunctional families, some form of addiction has distorted the way the family functions. The addiction might have been to a substance — alcohol, drugs, or food — or it might have been an obsession with relationships, sex, perfectionism, or orderliness. Often the addict's family members later form dysfunctional relationships or acquire addictions of their own. In the children, the addiction is often to work. In this way, the pattern repeats itself from generation to generation until someone or something intervenes to block its destructive path.

The children of addicts often become workaholics, not realizing that work is simply their drug of choice. Instead, as adults, they pride themselves on being free of the addiction they grew up in the shadow of. "No way am I going to have that happen to me!" is a familiar statement. Denial and dishonesty, which are rampant in these families, prevent them from confronting or seeing the fact that work has become a neurotic compulsion, a necessity for avoiding negative emotions.

The spouse and children in addictive families are called "co-dependents." They are the caretakers who look after others but not themselves. Melody Beattie, in *Codependent No More*, says co-dependents appear to be depended upon, but are actually dependent on other people. They are controlled by others' moods, behaviour, sickness, or well-being. They seem to be strong and controlling, but in reality they feel helpless and are themselves controlled, sometimes by alcoholism.

Families of workaholics, too, become co-dependents. Work addiction is perpetuated when a co-dependent spouse, child, secretary, friend, colleague, client, or parishioner helps a workaholic maintain his or her closed addictive system. Whereas a workaholic will sneak back to the office to finish a report, but say she is going out to do some shopping, the co-dependent deals in a more subtle kind of dishonesty. A spouse wants to take care of others, to keep harmony in the family at all costs. So, she says the "nice" thing — what she thinks the other person wants to hear. She does not say how she feels; nor does she do what she wants. Her dishonesty is an avoidance of the truth, or a lie by omission.

Dysfunctional and addictive families unconsciously follow a set of oppressive "rules." Robert Subby and John Friel describe these rules in their book *Co-dependency: An Emerging Issue*. Did you grow up with any of these problematic teachings? Most workaholics find that a majority of the rules I describe here applied in their families.

1. *Children are taught that it is not okay to talk about problems.* Not talking about problems promotes secrecy and keeps the family system "closed" to other points of views. It also creates the illusion that family life is harmonious. "Talking back or arguing was never allowed in our house. We just didn't dare stand up to Father. He just had to glare at us, that was enough" is a common summary of familial relations. The children rarely risk the anger and rejection of a volatile, powerful figure. The children may or may not be aware of their own anger at the parent, but they fear driving him or her farther away. Such situations promote the repression of negative thoughts and feelings that will later surface as anxiety. Denial and dissociating — pretending something didn't happen or someone doesn't matter — are encouraged and become defences the children use to ignore negative occurrences in their lives.

2. *The family does not believe that feelings should be expressed openly.* Healthy communication is difficult when healthy role models are absent. When parents are emotionally crippled by workaholism or other addictions, they really no longer know how they feel. Often they are emotionally flat and depressed. Any expressions of emotion by other family members are usually met with anger or are sabotaged. The addicted parent is usually unaware of his or her own faults. Instead, he or she typically lets feelings build up, then blames others. Such volatility discourages further discussion, reinforcing the "rule" about hiding feelings.

3. *Communication between family members is usually indirect, with one person acting as the messenger between two others.* The dysfunctional family always forms "triangles," where one member of the family talks to another about a third member instead of speaking directly with the person with whom they have a problem. These indirect communication patterns are dysfunctional because they rarely lead to problems being solved, but, rather, create new ones. The strong relationship between the husband and wife slowly erodes as control issues and power struggles in the workaholic system begin to dominate. If one parent's work addiction keeps him or her preoccupied, the other parent, by default, often fills the central role in the family circle and is closest to the children. Even in families where both parents are addicts, this situation occurs. One parent, usually the father, often becomes peripheral, and communication triangles form. The children go to Mother to talk about Dad, to send him messages or to ask him questions. Children learn early how to play Mom and Dad off against each other, asking one or the other if they can go somewhere, or buy something, or sleep over at so-and-so's house. Such unhealthy triangles cause havoc, and once established, the lines of communication are hard to change. Habits die hard. Triangles breed secrecy and mistrust, and help keep the family system closed, since truth and reality are not tested.

4. *Children get the message that they should be strong, good, right, and perfect.* Conditional love says: "I will love you *if* you are good, perfect, strong, and responsible." Unconditional love says: "Be who you are; I will support you as your own unique person. I will let you know when I do not approve and support your behaviour, and will try to offer you some guidance and wisdom for your consideration. You can accept or reject this, and I will still love you." In families where perfectionism is an ideal and "nothing is ever good enough," children are expected to succeed. Competing and winning are treasured values. "Why didn't you get all As?" is a typical reaction to a report card. Mistakes are frowned upon, and children are not taught to learn from their errors. Forgiveness for wrongdoing is not part of their experience. Throughout the lives of children of such parents, failure means loss of self-esteem and love.

5. *Parents expect children to make them proud*. In dysfunctional families, children are often seen as extensions of the parents' unmet needs and unfulfilled desires. In healthy families, the child is taught to feel proud if he or she makes a good effort. The parents comment on the quality of the job done, but do not attach labels of "good" or "bad" to the performance. Jill is a "good girl," not because of the work she has done, but because she is a special person who does well sometimes but not always. In dysfunctional families, performance and the essence of the person, the "self," are not kept separate.

6. *"Don't be selfish" is a common admonition from parents.* "Healthy selfishness" means looking after yourself. In dysfunctional families, the children and spouse learn to take care of other people, but often forget their own happiness and health, and even who they are. They are so busy pleasing others that they let other people run right over them. They become victims, martyrs, or doormats. They feel "selfish" if they are assertive about having their own needs and wishes met. They often do not eat properly or are immoderate in their eating and drinking, and have poor sleeping habits. They also tend to hand over responsibility for their own happiness to others. Children learn to give generously of their time and effort to please others, even if it means that their own physical and emotional health are sacrificed. In the workplace, as adults, they think nothing of putting in overtime on a regular basis. They skip lunches and run personal errands — anything to please.

7. *Children are told "Do as I say and not as I do."* In dysfunctional families, the deeds and behaviour of the parents do not always set a good example for the children. Being thoughtful, sensitive, empathic, and loving and considerate of others is not the norm. Honesty and discussion are not encouraged. Instead, self-righteous talk makes the parent look good no matter what is going on. These people like to tell others what is right, what is best for them. They can solve other people's problems at the drop of a hat. The dysfunctional parent often shows poor judgment, or is dishonest or controlling, and is not a good role model. Children grow up believing that being "right" is more important than being honest.

8. *Children learn that it is not okay to play or be playful.* Play is the essence of creativity and joy, of friendship and fun. In the dysfunctional family, play is suspect. Children hear a lot of "shoulds" about what they must do before they are allowed out to play. Work-oriented performance helps ease insecurity, fear, and guilt, and is therefore encouraged. In adulthood, often these people can enjoy play only if they work at it. "Winning," "beating so-and-so," "showing him up" or "putting him down" with sarcasm or ridicule — these are the tactical score-cards. One workaholic mentioned that she had been down all week and couldn't get herself back up. It turned out that her golf swing was off, and she had played abysmally with her peers, not just once, but twice that week. She was kicking herself, and lecturing herself about her lousy concentration. This is fun?

9. *"Don't rock the boat" is a family motto.* If you don't rock the boat, how will you discover there is a leak in the side of it? Only in a storm will you learn that your vessel is not sea-worthy. A family's experience of problems needs to be tested against the reality of how other people survive them. Healthy families stumble and fall, then pick themselves up and dust themselves off. They learn from their mistakes, grow a bit more, and then change so everyone can be happy. In dysfunctional families, parents cannot permit self-analysis or confrontation. Their inner world, and often the outer one as well, is in too much confusion and chaos. These families, set adrift on the sea of life, become isolated, frightened of disapproval, and terrified of the truth. There is no clear internal navigation system, no true spirituality to guide them over rough seas. Children grow up afraid of failure and risks.

Growing up in a dysfunctional family guided by such rules, children learn to value themselves according to what they do, how well they perform, and what tasks or goals they accomplish. Children are not valued or accepted for who they are, separate from what they do. Consequently, they are under constant pressure to perform, to achieve higher and higher goals so that they will feel good about themselves. Perfectionism is encouraged in this world, and good enough is never enough. Anxiety builds; to ease the fears of failure, a greater effort is made; a workaholic is born. As we learn later, anxiety and anger bubble below the surface as these people push, and are pushed, farther up the ladder of success.

However, the family is not the only influence that encourages workaholism. Changing social values in the second half of this century have fostered a climate of materialism and consumerism. Industrial and technological growth and expansion have encouraged a sterile and competitive workplace in which workaholism has flourished. Let's look at some of the contributing societal influences.

Our Workaholic Society

The roots of workaholism lie in the old Calvinistic philosophy that work redeems the believer and that indulging in pleasure, especially the pleasures of the flesh, will bring eternal damnation. Even three hundred years later, this joyless dictum that work is virtue and play is sin still pervades our society. The work ethic encourages the attitude that it is respectable to work hard and put in long hours. Such behaviour is seen as admirable. We say that someone is "devoted" to his work. "But she works so darn hard" is a compliment, and is even used to excuse the workaholic who has been insensitive or thoughtless to others. "Work smarter" loses to "work harder" in Calvinistic thinking; failure is a vice, not one of life's lessons.

In the twentieth century, work has become even more exalted. Prior to the Second World War, work was seen primarily as a means to an end, as a way of supporting the family and providing for its needs and comforts. The war brought women into the labour force, where they found personal and financial satisfaction, working outside the home. War veterans were given the opportunity to further their education and the incentive to rise beyond their prewar social levels. Work was the means of upward mobility, and work as a goal in itself was on its way to becoming a respected reality.

The upwardly mobile 1950s saw men working progressively longer hours to climb the corporate ladder. Their wives mostly stayed at home, took care of the house and the children, and organized the family's social life. They also were responsible for intimacy and closeness. No one thought to complain about this division of responsibility because it was the norm and most families were living the same way. The "nuclear family" moved to the suburbs and left behind the old neighbourhoods with their old values and cultures. Promotions or new job opportunities took the family across the country, away from extended families and social conformity, to live in relative anonymity. However, the nuclear family was intact and exerted a strong influence on its members.

The sexual revolution in the 1960s, brought on by growing feminism and the introduction of The Pill, gave women new freedom. Change became the norm, as social and political unrest spread. As radicals and idealists protested the status quo, a jaded view of work emerged. Student activists began to question the acquisitive values of their parents and their government. Hippies railed against materialism, and the devotion to work was shunned in favour of the values of community. Communes, love-ins, and peace marches had little to do with work or upward mobility. Radicals pushed for reforms in judicial systems, and idealists confronted the military-industrial complex as the support for Vietnam soured. In the 1960s, the assassinations of John and Robert Kennedy and Martin Luther King, Jr., dealt idealism a great blow. Interference in the affairs of other countries was increasingly unpopular after Vietnam, and the focus of America turned back in on itself.

Work had become respectable again by the early 1970s. Women began to work outside the home in ever-increasing numbers, and to have a significant impact on the work-force. At home, the well-defined rules regarding "who does what" were questioned. Resistance to the changing patterns was strong, and many moms became supermoms to preserve harmony and peace. Some families now had two potential workaholics, but Father's job still took precedence. Then, competition between the spouses for power became problematic as individual ambition began to outpace commitment to the partnership.

A growing conservatism and intense seriousness about work marked the 1970s. As the Baby Boomers flooded the job market, young people settled down to the important business of getting a job. Competition for education and for the almighty dollar made material success and security worthy goals. Work and career planning again not only became respectable but, in many cases, began to take precedence over marriage and the family. Large corporations and subsidiaries mass-produced their ideas and products. The corporate world swamped the individual, and the philosophy of "bigger is better" led to expansion, take-overs, conglomerates, and power bases. Consumerism, commercialism, and materialistic values became the foundation of success. People were defined by the kind of work they did and by their material goods. Personal worth and values often got lost in the swirl.

Industry went through a seductive but chaotic expansion, with its share of growing pains. Prosperity encouraged growth and acquisition as the stock market soared and the economy boomed. The worker became a very small cog in the wheel of Big Business; the entrepreneur, with more capital to spend, flourished. Teams of experts were formed to generate winning strategies to stay competitive. Specialization became more important, as each team member was expected to contribute some unique expertise. The pressure to perform and work harder became intense.

When the economy started to lag because of oil embargoes, and European and East Asian competition heightened, business began to "down-size" by weeding out employees. In corporate take-overs as well, many middle-aged top executives came to their offices in the morning and were gone by noon, made redundant by a duplication of jobs and services. The threats of job loss fuelled paranoia in the workplace, and people worked even harder to ensure that this would not happen to them.

As growth slowed, sometimes to a halt, the economy in the early 1980s fluctuated widely. In all the wheeling and dealing, business made some grave errors and found itself in big trouble. "Trouble-shooter" workaholics were brought in to save the day. These executives did manage, at times, to pull a company back from the brink of bankruptcy, but their schemes and strategies were often ruthless. Lacking compassion, they bulldozed their ideas through to completion, and left a path littered with destroyed lives, hurt feelings, paranoid fears. Workaholism created an environment of confusion and secrecy, inefficiency and rigidity. These "trouble-shooters" were then replaced with another type of leader — the "healers." Their job was to restore damaged egos, reassure demoralized employees, and motivate the disillusioned and confused workers who were, themselves, victims of the workaholic system. These peacemakers, by necessity, possessed people skills and were more open and approachable.

In periods of chaos, consolidation, or downturn, where many changes are required, workaholics do not do well. They are often in a confused state and no longer function well enough to be competitive and resourceful. They become incapable of making decisions and show poor judgment. Whereas an effective worker might regain power and confidence by redirecting the company to launch a new product or might amalgamate with a more effective team of workers, a workaholic is in no condition to do this because his or her intuition is not working well. In the late 1980s, we saw the chaos that workaholics caused as businesses went under at an alarming rate.

Business and industry only recently have become aware that workaholism is counter-productive over the long run. Employees are becoming physically ill, and psychotic episodes are not uncommon during prolonged periods of stress. Some changes are taking place as a result. Many personnel departments are beginning to look for well-balanced, healthy individuals. They are interested in people's values, lifestyles, and life experiences, as well as their employment histories. Unhappy, insecure workers are not effective or productive, and companies lose their cohesiveness when discontent reigns. Companies that do not look after the physical and psychological health of their employees lose the staff's trust, respect, and loyalty. Paranoia, suspicion, irritability, and fear do not lead to creativity and productivity. Consequently, more companies are willing to pay for counselling to keep employees and their families intact and well. They recognize that the workaholic's breakdown often results in family breakdown, which, in turn, leads to depression, loss of motivation, and "acting out" behaviour. No one works well when constrained by inner chaos and inefficiency.

The workplace, which once encouraged workaholism, is now beginning to realize that the addiction is not so respectable after all. It damages the individual, the family, the company, and, ultimately, society.

If you recognize the signs of this addiction in yourself — or in your spouse, friend, or colleague — you can begin to do something now. In this book, we will take a journey together through the causes and effects of workaholism, and then explore the path to recovery. Since the first step is awareness, we are well on our way.

2.

The Workaholic Personality:
Mirror, Mirror, on the Wall

"The tension always present in her office . . . accompanied her wherever she went. The demand for perfection, the rapid changes of mood, the towering temper, bound some people closely to her in their desire to please her; others were alienated permanently. To those whom she wished to help she gave generously. . . . But she could be harsh to those who opposed her, in some cases, even threatening to destroy their careers." William French, then the *Globe and Mail*'s literary editor, reviewing Phyllis Grosskurth's biography of Margaret Mead, added his own evaluation: "The overwhelming impression [Grosskurth] leaves [of Mead] is of an arrogant, domineering woman, who is more interested in self-promotion than in serious research. She was a compulsive meddler in other people's lives and was absolutely certain she was right about everything."

Workaholism does this to people. Their public contributions to society are exemplary, but their private lives are a disaster. They are like Dr. Jekyll and Mr. Hyde. This dual personality is a puzzle. The inner workings of a workaholic's behaviour may or may not be obvious to co-workers before the breakdown becomes severe. Family members usually recognize atypical behaviour but do not understand what is happening.

As workaholism begins to control the workaholic's life, three traits — perfectionism, obsession, and narcissism — become exaggerated and dominate the workaholic's thoughts and actions. We will see how perfectionism leads to obsession and, eventually, to narcissism. Consider how far along a continuum line you are for each of these traits. We all slide along the continuum and exhibit neurotic behaviour some of the time, but we need to be alert for the signs that indicate abnormal levels.

PERFECTIONISM — GOOD, BETTER, BEST

As I stepped into the elevator in my office building one morning, my attention turned to a poster on the wall. Under the heading "Steps to a Positive Attitude" was listed: "Go as far as you see, and when you get there you will always be able to see further." What great advice for churning out more budding perfectionists, I laughed.

A perfectionist, ever restless and impatient, strives for perfection, a state of excellence and mastery that exists only in the realm of the gods. Perfectionism shapes a person's lifestyle. In order to fulfil her ambitions and dreams, the individual must become single-minded or one-sided. Any world-class athlete must forgo a normal adolescence and concentrate fully on developing his natural talent. Countless hours of practice and enormous will-power and discipline are required. Throughout history, perfectionists have made their mark on music, politics, science, entertainment, the military and so on, but most paid a high price. They had abysmal personal lives and missed out on the chance for wholeness and a life fully lived.

Perfectionists believe that they are highly intelligent, even superior, and thus capable of great achievements. Although they are, indeed, often quite bright, they are also openly arrogant, ambitious, competitive, and demanding of themselves and others. Although self-sufficient and independent on the surface, they require admiration from others, or demand obedience and want their own way. Underneath this self-confident façade lies an insecurity fed by unconscious inner struggles to overcome unresolved childhood fears of helplessness, dependency, and loss of approval and affection.

The proud perfectionist, torn between arrogance and insecurity, solves the dilemma by consciously identifying with only his positive attributes, those that protect the perfect ideal image. The workaholic will glow over a report that his boss thought was brilliant, but will repress any memories of the short, sharp commands he barked at his poor secretary who loyally worked late into the evening, making endless corrections to it. Her tears of relief when the report was finally finished did not register with him as having anything to do with his prickly behaviour or her resentment at having to work so late. "Her home life is probably a mess," he projected.

Unfortunately, a constant vigilance is needed to falsify reality, to suppress or deny any contradictory negatives. This one-sided polarization, identifying with only the positive aspects of your behaviour, eventually leads to neurotic obsession.

Obsession occurs "when all the psychic energy, which ought to be distributed among the various parts of the personality in an attempt to harmonize them, is focused on one area of the personality to the exclusion of everything else." Marion Woodman, in *Addiction to Perfection*, adds: "To move toward perfection is to move out of life, or what is worse, never to enter it." When the pursuit of perfection becomes an obsession, the personality ceases to develop normally, and fears immobilize psychological growth. It is as though workaholics were trapped in a train, with the window blinds down, chugging along a track headed towards a single destination. They are unable to stop or get off or change tracks. Their goal or ambition is driving the train, and they cannot see the scenery which might reveal other options or alternatives.

Although workaholics have become obsessed with work, they can become cross-addicted to other obsessions as well. Some victims of obsession pursue thinness and become anorexic or bulimic, while others become obese, trying to fill up the emptiness deep inside. Still others smoke or crave caffeine or other drugs, or become shopaholics to ease their pain and distract their attention. Relationship addicts will obsessively talk about nobody else but their lover, think of nothing else but the relationship, and be so preoccupied by the love object that they barely listen to others. Their own thoughts are churning. Their obsessions run them and use up their psychic energy and adrenalin, pumping the system dry. Work addicts, I believe, are often inclined to be addicted to perfection as a reaction against their parents' own addictions to alcohol, smoking, food, or neatness, etc. They are determined that they will never show such weak and self-defeating behaviour.

Perfectionism clearly is not a positive trait but a curse that leads to a compulsive need to be successful and to create a persona that broadcasts success. It is a merciless taskmaster and eventually takes on a life of its own, driving the individual to be ambitious and competitive and to be always "right." "My way or the highway" is an expression often used. Delegating or sharing responsibility would only interfere with perfectionists' single-minded pursuit of excellence. They have no wish to share credit for their accomplishments. However, working hard, doing an excellent job, and striving towards a realistic goal require normal discipline and commitment. Neurotic obsession is not part of this process. The healthy ego is fed and nourished by the genuine pride in a job well done. Self-respect is earned through real accomplishments. The unhealthy ego is driven to perform by an obsessive need to compete, to win, to score, to be "the best," and nothing less.

Conditional Love in Dysfunctional Families

The roots of perfectionism lie in childhood. Some children, for many different reasons, feel they must perform in order to be loved and appreciated. Such children are rewarded for what they do, rather than for who they are. Future workaholics learn early that praise is attached to performance, and that acting responsibly brings rewards. Their emotional stability is dependent on their parents' reactions to what they do. They hear praise — "You're a good boy" — only when the grass is cut perfectly. But, of course, perfect is an ideal, so each time the child must strive harder to get it right. Those who offer conditional love give praise only when the person performs a certain way or meets certain criteria. Sometimes a child will think that parents expect more than they actually do.

Those who offer unconditional love accept the person as a unique individual. The person's behaviour is seen as separate from his or her personality. "The grass looks terrific. You must be very proud of yourself!" teaches the child this separation of "doing" from "being."

"Good girl" is not attached to the job she did on the grass. Instead her self-pride is encouraged when the job is found acceptable. Since the ego develops from this sense of accomplishment, it is important for children to recognize when they have done a job well. It is also important for parents to give a child feedback on what is acceptable, appropriate behaviour. Unconditional love means helping children develop their own moral and ethical standards. It does not mean being permissive or overly protective. Conditional love teaches a child to be dependent on others for approval; unconditional love encourages independent appraisal, objectivity, and self-affirmation in deserved pride.

Ben, the son of a workaholic dentist, was a born naturalist; in his teen years, he loved nothing better than spending hours quietly observing insects and birds and documenting their habits. His hyper-energetic father, used to scheduling every second in his office to achieve a super-efficient assembly-line practice, derided Ben about being lazy and wasting precious time. Ben and his father were on different wavelengths. When they did communicate, Ben never felt understood or accepted. Needing encouragement and love to function well, Ben strove to become a super-efficient scientist in a desperate bid for his father's approval. Gradually his kind and gentle ways gave way to obsessive efforts to publish and to become chairman of his department. Eventually, burned out by the unnaturally frantic pace, Ben suffered a severe breakdown.

In later years, failure, or the making of mistakes, creates a crisis for the perfectionist. She is blocked from "doing," and must fall back on simply "being." She assumes that she has not done as much as she should. Having been found wanting, she often can't forgive herself for errors of judgment. Failures are generalized, and translate into "I am a *bad* person because of what I have done." Sometimes the person becomes totally immobilized and cannot even do what she is good at any longer. She's afraid to just "be," since she has never spent any time discovering and loving herself. When she is told to shape up or, even worse, has lost the job because she has become totally ineffective, the workaholic is paralysed by fear and guilt. At such times, remembered criticisms from parents can heighten the pain of lost self-esteem. Marilyn, unable to work because of exhaustion and self-doubt, remembered an incident that still made her cringe. She had once told her father that one of the dads at the club told her that "I hope my little girl will be as beautiful a skater as you are." Pleased, Marilyn relayed this compliment to her father, who rebuked her sharply: "Young lady, you'll get a swelled head telling me things like that."Marilyn, reliving this hurt, said she had been baffled by this cruel response, and any pride she had felt had dissipated in angry tears. After this, she always rejected compliments as being self-serving.

Belonging and being valued are elusive dreams for the workaholic adult who never felt accepted as a child. Teresa, a theatrical producer, told me she had become a workaholic to avoid dealing with an unhappy reality and to prove her self-worth. "I've been chasing approval, maybe also acceptance, all my life. As a child, I felt left out or on the sidelines or I was the last one to be picked for things. I sense that I need to be seen as successful or uniquely different in order to be noticed or invited to join The Club, so to speak. I feel I've never been asked to join. Perhaps the criteria for membership are such that I don't actually qualify. As if my personal appearance, for example, isn't acceptable. Also that my self or my own way of being isn't normal. I feel that I would have to behave differently in order to be asked to join, but the problem is, I really don't want to behave differently."

Teresa, reflecting on her emerging new self-esteem, added: "I'm not really so bad as I am now. Sometimes, I don't actually care about The Club. It is a conflict I have, though: whether I want to be in or out. I do know I don't want to be a chameleon any more. Trying to blend in is so superficial, and I have no respect for chameleons. I prefer people who are honest and straightforward about their feelings. I'm trying to be true to myself all the time, no matter what, but I can see that I do have to resolve where I belong."

Teresa is sorting through a variety of ambivalent feelings about how she fits into society and why she never felt she belonged. Self-honesty and reality-testing have become very important for her peace of mind. The workaholic may see rejection and disapproval in all the mirrors he looks in to see himself. His own insecurity gets reflected back when the boss scowls or a colleague scuttles away to avoid his pain. At the same time, his wife points out his shortcomings because she is angry at him for what he has or has not done. The faces staring back are all negative reflections. Without external praise or evidence of productivity, the workaholic is thrown back on his own resources and his poorly developed self-concept. Panic sets in. Desperate, he tries to work even harder. Increasingly poor judgment leads him to spend twelve or fourteen hours doing what he used to do in four. Exhaustion and chronic fatigue eventually take over.

Often it is an emotional or physical breakdown or a stress burnout that forces discovery and recognition of the inner chaos. Unfortunately for some, if the damage is severe, it is too late for recovery. We all know tragic tales of corrupt politicians, bankrupt business tycoons, and disbarred lawyers. Often these people were once idealistic, driven perfectionists, but they lost their way. Enough is never enough, so honesty, integrity, and wisdom are sacrificed for greater recognition and power. Wholeness is within our grasp, but perfectionism leads to neurotic obsession.

Rebecca

Rebecca came into my office, looking dishevelled and frumpy. A distraught young woman, she had a fragile air about her. In a high-pitched voice, she quickly let me know that she was totally exhausted and ashamed of herself because she had been "crying at the drop of a hat." Her skin appeared puffy, and she was dismayed to find herself binging on junk food. She explained that she used to be a health-food nut and couldn't understand what had come over her. Her sleep was fitful, and she was having the most bizarre frustration nightmares in which she could never get to where she was going; something or someone always blocked her way.

The words "should" and "that's just not right!" popped up again and again as she spilled out her tale of woe amid tears of frustration. As she repeatedly reached for the tissue box on my coffee table, Rebecca apologized again and again. "You're not seeing me at my best," she said.

Rebecca's workaholic habits began early. As a student with an obsessive drive to excel, she maintained an A average throughout her school career. Married life was her next big test. Rebecca's current goal was to be the best wife, the best mother, and the best hostess she could possible be. Her house had been featured in an issue of *House and Garden* the previous year. She liked to dress the three kids in the latest yuppie clothes. And, since she had a flare for fashion, she designed all her new clothes. In fact, her friends were urging her to give up her secretarial job and open a boutique. She was running herself ragged, driving the kids to judo, synchronized swimming, and music classes. She was also active in the Home and School association and chaired the local Cancer Society fund-raising committee.

Entertaining was always done on a grand scale. Rebecca kept a card file in her kitchen, listing in minute detail what food she served to each guest, the seating plan for each occasion, who liked what dishes, what food allergies people had, what linens and flowers she had used on the table, and what she had worn. She even kept cards for the snacks she served at the coffee parties she planned for the other neighbourhood wives. "I can never offer the same thing twice," she explained. "Originality is very important to me." Lately, though, Rebecca hadn't felt like seeing her friends. Her kids were sullen and refused to clean up their mess. The youngest was spilling stuff on her new kitchen rug, and it had "terrible stains" on it. She was beginning to question whether she really was a good hostess any longer because she was too agitated to do anything properly.

As I empathized with her concerns and real distress, Rebecca slowly opened up to reveal the other side of the coin. Her husband was furious with her; he had told her she was a "real bitch" because she constantly complained and nagged him. Rebecca had never before been spoken to like that. She admitted she had been yelling at the kids a lot, and she even called her own fits "temper tantrums." "I just know Martin is going to have an affair, and he'll leave me with these dreadful kids. I just can't cope with life any more," she sobbed. Then, she took a deep breath and revealed her secret: "You know, the other day I actually stood frozen in front of the medicine cabinet and fought an overwhelming compulsion to end it all." She paused for a long time, and then grinned sheepishly. "I won though, and I feel safe here."

Rebecca had fallen short of her ideal self and, not being used to failure, had panicked and slid into despair. She felt hopeless and very angry with herself — the key elements for depression. She was no longer a "good girl" because she was behaving badly. Others expected Rebecca to be perfect too, and no one thought to give her the sympathetic support she so desperately needed.

It's important to feel competent, but dangerous to be a perfectionist. Rebecca needed to take pride in doing things well. Instead, she worried about petty details and lost sight of the real reason to entertain people. Competence falls in the realm of reality; perfectionism is idealistic.

COMPETENCE   PERFECTIONISM

1   2   3   4   5   6   7   8   9   10

Where do you fall along the perfectionism continuum? Understanding the negative effects of perfectionism may help you avoid it. Since perfectionism leads to obsessive and compulsive behaviours, we will now explore this aspect of workaholism.

OBSESSION–COMPULSION —
FRET, WORRY, AND STEW

Obsessive–compulsive people live with an ever-present anxiety that has its roots in childhood, but is reinforced by each successive trauma. Perfectionistic workaholics are unlikely to have experienced many failures early in life because they drive themselves so mercilessly and tend to play the "good boy" or "good girl" role in the family. When life events or situations backfire, or when these people make mistakes and fail at something, they are often traumatized. To distract their anxious minds, they often perform superstitious rituals. Workaholics can be seen doodling on a piece of paper, making elaborate drawings or patterns, during a telephone conversation because they feel better doing two things at once. They don't really need to listen to what is being said since they already know what they plan to do. Others follow rigid procedures when they first come into work to ensure that they will have a good day. They rarely risk testing the consequences of not following these routines to see what will happen. The more disturbed do not even recognize anxiety, since insight is blocked by repression and denial of reality. They refuse to take any personal responsibility and are experts at projecting blame onto others. Even those who recognize their anxiety and bizarre behaviour often choose to remain emotionally naive and childlike. They refuse to acknowledge that their actions or inaction may be the real reason for their distress. Vindictive revenge in the form of punishing behaviour may be used to restore their own feelings of dominance when the power and control they so desire lie outside their grasp.

An *obsession* occurs when people experience persistent and disturbing thoughts that swirl round and round in their heads. "I just know I'm going to screw up this job, like I did the last one! I just can't get words like 'failure' and 'loser' out of my system. Logically I know there was nothing anybody could have done to save the shop, but I still question this constantly." Sleep is often shallow, and crazy thoughts lead to insomnia. The obsession becomes neurotic when such spells occur more frequently and persist, and when anxiety is fuelled by increasing negativity. Obsessive thoughts are typically negative. Workaholics can ruminate obsessively over a problem because they are immobilized by fear and have become incapable of making even the most mundane of life decisions. The inner chatter repeats like a broken record. Their families and colleagues sometimes fill in the gaps and cover for them, lest everything fall apart. It is a vicious circle as these people, too, then have to overwork to compensate, and their worries and fears escalate into obsessive thoughts as well. Anger and resentment build as feelings of helplessness and depression drag everyone down.

A *compulsion* is an act a person feels compelled to engage in repeatedly, such as talking, nail biting, hair twisting, eating, shopping, or exercising. The more compulsive the behaviour, the more chaotic and out of control the person feels inside. A ritual, such as counting, checking, or cleaning, is often involved and usually recognized as irrational by the person performing it. However, recognition does not mean that the behaviour can be stopped. More disturbed individuals may develop a chronic obsessive–compulsive personality disorder, because they lack the insight to recognize their own dysfunctions.

Mild compulsiveness is common, and even useful to a point. It helps keep us productive and motivates us to get out of bed in the morning and out the door to attend to our daily activities. Most people have little rituals they perform as part of their daily life. They set their alarm to hear the 6:00 a.m. news, then make a bee-line to the front door to get the morning newspaper, then put the kettle on for coffee. If anything unexpected happens to change this ritual, it can be quite upsetting. Even compulsive ritualistic behaviours can be adaptive up to a point, since they get the job done, often in a meticulous and perfectionistic way. Making lists, sticking to a preplanned schedule, always doing household chores in a particular ordered way, conforming to well-defined rules and keeping a minutely detailed daily diary can make one more productive. Workaholics often carry their routines to extremes. Excessive neatness and orderliness seem to ease their high anxiety, as does lining up papers, pens and paper-clips on the desk. Compulsive workaholics insist that their desks be kept perfectly clean, and that the "in" basket must be cleared before they can go home. Superstition underlies much of this behaviour. "I'm okay if I don't step on the cracks," a game played in childhood, resembles this philosophy of prevention.

Emotionally drained workaholics can become debilitated by their compulsive daily rituals. When anxiety is extreme, some go back ten times to see if a door has been locked or the stove turned off. Others wring their hands or wash them repeatedly until the skin becomes raw. Compulsions can become so severe that they are crippling, rendering the person totally unable to function effectively.

Workaholics often have deep-seated, irrational fears of being "let go" from their jobs. They dread rejection in any form and avoid it at all costs. One client developed a superstitious habit of never allowing herself to leave the office until her boss had gone for the day. Never mind that the last few hours were spent mechanically going over and over reports that were, in reality, finished. She explained that she would make great long lists of jobs she would do tomorrow because she was just too exhausted to start anything new. Her habit caused her to relinquish personal control, and it left her vulnerable to the boss's whims and uncertain schedule.

The Obsessional Triangle — Guilt, Fear, and Negativity

Obsessive–compulsive behaviour is a sign of low self-esteem, persistent self-doubt, and inner chaos. Negativity becomes a very powerful force. If you tell a workaholic several positive things and one negative thing, he or she will hone in on the negative thought and totally ignore the rest. One wife, wishing to encourage her depressed husband, commented on the way home from a dinner party, "I noticed you hardly said a thing all night, honey. You can be so fascinating and entertaining, I'm sure everyone would be really interested in what you have to say." Her husband felt criticized for not saying anything, got furious, and screamed at her, saying that she was always after him and to "just leave me in peace."

Truly obsessional workaholics are caught in a dilemma where guilt, fear, and negativity can immobilize them. Conflict develops between their rational, but ambivalent thinking, which struggles between idealism and realism, and the ever-present aggressive impulses lurking in the unconscious. When a situation becomes threatening, workaholics become overly sensitive and emotional and are predisposed to rage and the fear of assault. They can develop harsh and rigid views on duty and morality. Such inner conflict gets played out externally in interpersonal relationships and in fantasies. Dominance becomes all important. In the progressive breakdown stages of workaholism, workaholics desperately need to exert control over some part of their lives. They throw their weight around, striving to maintain power and be in charge whenever or wherever this is possible.

If you win, I lose: dominance and submission trouble the obsessive person and produce both guilt and fear. When the workaholic feels dominant and omnipotent, and the ego is inflated with self-importance, the unconscious becomes more powerful to compensate, producing nagging feelings of guilt. Because domination is associated with sadism and damage to others, guilt pricks the puffed-up balloon and challenges the powerful arrogance and feelings of superiority. Take the example of Peter, a chief executive officer at a prominent law firm. Anxious about the security of his power base in the firm, he has just made a major unilateral decision, which restores his confidence temporarily and gives him a heady feeling of power. Later in the afternoon, though, his anxiety soars. He begins to anticipate some possible antagonistic reactions from one of the more ambitious men, whom he secretly fears wants his job. Nagging self-doubt about his own judgment, which hasn't been too reliable lately, robs him of peace of mind. He has a sinking feeling deep in the pit of his stomach, and feelings of dominance give way to fear.

By contrast, submission suggests weakness and vulnerability. In any submissive role or situation, the workaholic no longer feels in charge, and this feeling creates the fear of assault or reprisals. Patrick, a corporate lawyer, is never comfortable unless he is in complete control of a situation. Lately, though, obsessive worries about his ability to cope eat away at him. Nothing seems to be working for him, and more and more he suffers fits of rage or else completely withdraws and feels sorry for himself. Ellen, his wife, used to help him through such periods, but lately, as Patrick acknowledges, Ellen seems to have run out of patience and has told him she is at the end of her rope.

Monday morning, we find Patrick sitting in his office, slumped over his desk, totally unable to function. His anxiety is sky high because the fight he and Ellen had last night terminated suddenly when Ellen, badly shaken and hysterical, fled to their best friends' home for shelter. Patrick's pride was badly bruised, and he fears that now everyone will find out about his "cruel, vicious attacks," as Ellen calls them. So far she had remained loyal, but "I guess everyone has limits," he muses.

That night, Patrick goes home, determined to make amends and, for the first time, apologizes to Ellen. On similar occasions in the past, Patrick would concede only that he had acted badly. He invites Ellen out to *his* favourite restaurant.

For a while, Patrick does try to be more sensitive and less impulsive. He tries to think before he speaks, but this added stress tests his patience even more, to the point that he becomes increasingly jumpy. At times, he feels he is turning into a wimp, and besides, Ellen is remaining aloof and is just soaking up his attention.

Patrick becomes more bitter and resentful about Ellen's cool attitude, and one day a powerful urge for revenge overwhelms him. He decides to humiliate and punish Ellen. He calls their ticket agent and orders a single ticket for a meeting in Spain. He has decided that Ellen will not be allowed to go with him. The temporary satisfaction he derives from this petty act soon gives way to fear of rejection and possible retaliation from Ellen. The vicious cycle begins all over again, with Patrick bouncing between fear and anger as his desperate need to regain control drives him on to destructive acts.

Sadly, domination and submission escalate anxiety, and both extremes create further stress. So, to avoid the threats to well-being attached to dominance and submission, the obsessive workaholic often swings between the two, thus maintaining a false sense of control. Remaining in a state of flux forestalls the need to take responsibility, to make any firm decisions. The "right" decision is often reached on impulse or out of desperation to end anxiety or nagging self-doubt. Often other people cannot tolerate the waffling back and forth, and insist on a decision. The drive to re-establish dominance eventually prevails, and other people are victimized as the workaholic strives to stay "one up" by putting others down or ignoring them. For this reason, power struggles are severe for couples in which one partner is a workaholic. I often see instances in which workaholism has distorted the entire relationship between two people.

When the workaholic's dominance is threatened or challenged, the individual often experiences rages or temper tantrums. The psyche, stressed by the constant pressure of exercising dominance, becomes drained of energy. As fear of submission takes over, low-grade panic sets in and tips the balance. Some workaholics turn the rage inwards and suffer severe mood swings or anxiety attacks, although usually the build-up of pent-up feelings eventually explodes into outbursts of anger directed at family members. There is safety in numbers at work, and no one would tolerate such rages for long in the working world. If denial is strong, these rages may be unconscious or quickly forgotten by the workaholic.

A number of situations tend to threaten the workaholic: a formerly submissive wife might return to school or to the work-force, or might suddenly start to ask questions that challenge her husband's ideas; teenaged children who question rigid rules and fixed ideas can set off an explosion of rage. Often the workaholic boss is threatened by younger, very bright people climbing up the corporate ladder. Any number of things can set off one of these vindictive rages.

I'll Get Back Up

Punishing, or "vindictive triumph," a term used by Dr. Karen Horney in *Neurosis and Human Growth*, is a key concept in understanding the workaholics' need to triumph over others. It drives workaholics to be extremely competitive and to abhor anyone who knows or achieves more than they do, who wields more power, or who questions their own superiority in any way. To win an argument or advance their career, workaholics may forsake all loyalty to others. People in the grips of the compulsion can be treacherous and dangerous to others, as they will be driven to show no loyalty or regard, even to a spouse or children. These schemes to prove superiority, however, often end up being counter-productive and self-defeating. Vindictive wrath can jeopardize lives, security, jobs, and social position.

Clark, a meek-mannered research scientist, was furious with his wife, Anne, because she had started to challenge his biting criticisms and overwhelming negativity towards others. Nothing seemed important to him but his endless projects. Anne quickly became "the enemy," someone who was making him look bad. Never mind that her criticism was about his own negative behaviour. To get back up to dominance, Clark retaliated by turning a deaf ear to Anne's pleas for counselling and avoided all responsibility at home. Staying late at his lab on a regular basis began as a way to get back at his wife. Shortly after this, Clark began an affair with one of his assistants. When she sought a commitment from Clark, things got ugly. The rejected lover phoned at all hours, harassing both Anne and the teenaged children with foul language and temper tantrums. The heart-broken assistant lost her job, Clark lost the respect of his colleagues, and Anne was totally devastated by Clark's revenge. Separation and divorce broke up a once-happy family. Being unfaithful was Clark's ultimate punishment of Anne.

When the need to triumph is blatant, the workaholic punishes those who threaten his control and power. Sexual partners are exploited with no regard for their feelings or welfare. Others are used as stepping-stones in the workaholic's career plans. Still others are conquered or subdued, and stepped over on the way up the corporate ladder. Depending on how out of touch the workaholic is with his or her feelings, the behaviour can be anything from mean-spirited to ruthless. Michael Lewis in the *New York Times Book Review* (September 2, 1990) relates an episode described in Donald Trump's *Trump: Surviving at the Top*: When Trump arrived with a fashion model at one of Leona Helmsley's parties, Helmsley flew into what appeared to be a jealous rage. " 'How dare you bring that tramp to one of my parties?' she screams, in the presence of the other woman. 'At first I was shocked,' Mr. Trump says, 'but then all the things people had been telling me about Leona and her Jekyll-and-Hyde personality started coming back to me.' From then on Mrs. Helmsley, with her 'crazed personality,' heaps all manner of abuse on Mr. Trump." Lewis concludes: "This rare passage in which Mr. Trump seems at the mercy of forces beyond his control ends quickly. The roles reverse when Mr. Trump steamrollers over Mrs. Helmsley in a deal, then fires off a few gratuitous insults of his own. Mr. Trump, once again, is the Conqueror."

Civil politeness can be a sophisticated, less obvious way of being vindictive. One husband regularly thanked his wife for sharing information about workaholism, and then later discredited it by saying that "she only read things that she agreed with!" Smart-alec show-offishness or a patronizing manner often covers an underlying offensive attitude towards others. This attitude makes people feel superior when others have suffered a setback, or envious when others "hit the jackpot" and come into some luck. It makes a person secretly wish anyone who has gained a temporary advantage would stumble and fall. Dominic, a bright young entrepreneur, sheepishly confided that, when one of his friends won a lottery, he found himself feeling intensely resentful of the man's luck. Even worse, he found himself feeling "superior" and exhilarated when his competitor developed cancer. Only recently was he even aware that this was not a normal, healthy response.

The workaholic is a past master at frustrating others' simple hopes or complex dreams, their normal needs for attention and reassurance, their honest requests for more time together and need for company, and their wish for more times of enjoyment and fun. In actual fact, no spouse should have to ask to have these basic needs met. When these victims protest against a denial of their normal needs and requests, the workaholic will make excuses, saying the problem lies with the victim — he or she is too bitchy, selfish or greedy, or too sensitive, touchy, or weak. Often the victims have become so demoralized and feel so uncared-for and unloved that they learn not to expect anything, and the abuse continues unchecked.

Erotica

Workaholics often thrive on the admiration and respect shown them for the jobs that they do. Doctors and ministers experience a sense of being loved by grateful patients and parishioners. It is a safe love in that nothing is expected from them but their prescribed services. A pleasurable feeling of intense satisfaction in delivering such services substitutes for the excitement of sexual loving, which requires a more complex reciprocal exchange between the lovers.

When there is a passionate obsession with work, erotic feelings can be expressed towards the accomplishments or products of work. The senses are aroused and alive when a coveted contract is signed, a record becomes a hit, or a sought-after degree is conferred. Jacques, an accomplished but obsessive pianist, played his own compositions over and over because they aroused and excited a passion within him. He described an orgasmic response where he merged with his own creation. Music for Jacques was a substitute for the intimacy he could not sustain with real people.

Similarly, American photographer Paul Strand's third wife, Hazel Kingsbury, a photographer herself, learned to hate photography. In reviewing a film about Strand in the *Globe and Mail*, Jay Scott quotes Hazel: "I'd go up there and find him petting the photographs like you'd pet a cat or a child. They were his women; they were his children; they were his everything . . . the love of his life." Scott feels the film "confronts us with a human being difficult to forget, a dark figure who spent his life both photographing and running from the light."

Erotic feelings and voyeuristic fantasies can also be directed away from marital intimacy towards a fellow worker. Such workplace fantasies and flirtations rarely survive to become truly intimate. Limits are set by the restrictions of the setting, and when intimacy becomes too threatening, everyone can leave to go home. True intimacy means that the partners make a commitment to be emotionally there for each other at all times.

Obsession Without Guilt

In contrast to the neurotically obsessive–compulsive person, whose behaviour is affected by guilt, fear, and negative thoughts, is the more seriously disturbed obsessive–compulsive personality. These workaholics have a more permanent structure of neurotic traits and defences, and their inner conflict is denied and repressed. Defences are kept strong, personal insight is usually lacking, and anxiety is therefore low. Only when a life crisis strikes will their defence systems break down; then, they too adopt obsessive and compulsive behaviour to cover their unacceptable impulses.

Workaholics of this type tend to be uptight, intense, unemotional, cold, and moralistic. They have difficulty compromising and seeing others' points of view. Rather than say no, they tend to say "Yes, but," and then do their own thing. Secretly they want approval but, in the more severe cases, narcissism dominates and they can become ruthless and totally self-serving. These hard-core workaholics blindly pursue power and success at any cost, and run over anyone or anything in their way. Tightly defended against facing anxiety or pain, they keep their protective walls high by exercising their skepticism, judgmentalism, and generalized distrust. Things can be ordered and controlled, whereas people protest such control. Personal relationships are strained and tested constantly when workaholics seek to reassure themselves of their dominance by controlling others.

Joshua

Joshua, a surgeon, boasts proudly that he hasn't taken a holiday for more than four years. He quickly explains that the conventions he goes to are "a change of pace, and just as good as a rest." He used to go off sightseeing with his wife on a couple of afternoons during these trips, but not any more. Now he resents anything that stands in the way of work and gets sulky if Sally suggests any diversions. Even though he often dozes through some of the meetings, especially the afternoon ones, attending them makes him feel better. Joshua never gives himself too much time to think. He does, however, give himself permission to take time off to have supper with his wife. After supper, though, he turns down Sally's suggestion to go dancing because he wants to "prepare" for the next day's meetings, even when he is not presenting a paper. It is irrelevant to him that Sally loves dancing.

Sally used to like to go along on these trips; attending them made her feel a part of her husband's work, and she liked to meet his colleagues. Lately, a great deal of secrecy surrounds what her husband is doing at work, and Sally's resentment of Joshua's obsession with work is growing steadily. Sally feels like a fifth wheel on the trips now, and notices that they don't socialize as much with the other couples. In fact, others seem to avoid her husband. She has gradually lost interest in going along.

Sally would like a holiday that did not involve Joshua's work, but the one time they tried it, only three days had passed before Josh had to rush back to the city for a "prearranged" meeting. When he rejoined Sally he brought a briefcase full of what he said were important papers needing his attention. When Sally complained, Joshua said that the books she brought along were the same as his work. "I read for fun," she countered, but Joshua insisted, "My work is my hobby, and it's my kind of fun!"

Sally doesn't think Josh looks like he is having much fun. He is always intense and grey-looking, and constantly fidgets and snaps his fingers. Relaxing is impossible, and she notices he is drinking too much coffee. His ritual martini before dinner has become two, and sometimes three, as he attempts to wind down. He is spending more and more time alone in the den, and she rarely sees him smile. He forgets what she has just said, and keeps repeating things he has already told her until she wonders if he is going senile or losing his hearing. His answers to her questions are strange sometimes, and she can't figure out how what he is saying relates to what she has just asked. Although Josh is working all the time, it doesn't seem to Sally that he gets much done. Work seems to expand, but never to be finished. Any time she points out any of her concerns about his behaviour, Joshua becomes incredibly irritable and sarcastic, and then withdraws farther from her.

Sally has to organize all their social life, and it isn't any fun. She is often a nervous wreck by the time the guests arrive. Josh used to look after the drinks and tend the bar, and she prepared the food. Not any more! Now Josh snipes at her and complains about the most minuscule things. He has become very fussy and super-controlling. He badgers Sally, wanting to know how she is going to prepare this and cook that. It is like having a drill-sergeant in her kitchen. The few times he does "help," everything in the kitchen has to be cleaned up as soon as each part of the meal has been prepared. A messy counter is painful for Joshua, and he is overly meticulous about each and every detail of the preparation.

One memorable dinner party, Sally was close to tears and fighting for control so that her guests wouldn't see a red, swollen face.

Consequently, she ruined the sauce and got so flustered she lost her usually well-organized skills. Nothing she did any more was "right" in Joshua's view. When the guests did arrive, you could cut the tension with a knife. The guests were well aware of the strained atmosphere, and it was a very uncomfortable evening for all concerned.

The couple has gradually stopped entertaining since Sally has lost her confidence, and Joshua has withdrawn more into himself. The thought of entertaining and being sociable becomes increasingly stressful as Joshua's breakdown progresses. His fatigue level is so high that any extra demands thoroughly exhaust him and drive up his anxiety. No wonder entertaining produces such controlling, obsessive–compulsive behaviour. Joshua, more emotionally crippled by workaholism than was Patrick, is barely functioning socially.

In *Timebends*, Arthur Miller fondly remembers the final lecture of his sophomore psychology class in which Professor Walter Bowers Pillsbury looked out over the faces of the undergraduates, his gaze going deep, and said: "I do not presume to give you advice about your mental health, but there is one truth I hope you will always try to keep before you: never think about any one thing for too long." Miller was fascinated because the professor had been institutionalized for some years himself. At the time, this advice seemed silly to Miller, who was concentrating on his new craft and on the problems of the country during the McCarthy era. Some fifteen years later, though, Miller adds, "the old man's voice kept returning to me as I realized that there was something obsessional in my thoughts about my marriage and my work." This revelation spurred Miller on to seek help to straighten himself out.

A more relaxed approach to life includes humour, humility, and the wisdom to see yourself from a wider perspective, as one member of your family, a team player at work, and a responsible citizen in your community. The obsession with work narrows your focus and intensifies your need to control and dominate everything to achieve personal recognition and success.

RELAXED								OBSESSIVE	
1	2	3	4	5	6	7	8	9	10

Where do you fall on the continuum line for obsessive–compulsive behaviour? Are you increasingly obsessed with work? Do you engage in compulsive behaviours? Are your guilt, fear, and negativity strong? Even if *you* feel no guilt or anxiety, are others around you extremely unhappy because of your obsession with work? If so, your "everything is fine" philosophy may be covering severe workaholism. Self-awareness is essential for any recovery program.

NARCISSISM — ME, MYSELF AND I

Narcissism is alive and well and living in the "Me First" generation. Our society encourages us to put our own needs first. Many of our current social problems stem from this glorification of self. Narcissistic people have an inflated, idealized view of themselves as unique, superior, and self-confident, yet have an anxious concern for their well-being and a tendency to withdraw from others when questioned or confronted. They can be very charming, appear youthful, and tend to be takers although they see themselves as generous. Dr. Karen Horney, in *Neurosis and Human Growth*, points out that they tend to overlook flaws and turn them into virtues. "[The narcissist] does not seem to mind breaking promises, being unfaithful, incurring debts, defrauding. He is not, however, a scheming exploiter. He feels rather that his needs or his tasks are so important that they entitle him to every privilege." These people expect others to love them unconditionally and fail to see how they trespass on others' rights. At work, their plans are often too expansive or diversified, and they overestimate their capacities, unaware of their limitations. Dr. Horney adds that narcissists have the capacity to be resilient and to bounce back, but too many personal rejections or business failures may bring their self-hate and self-contempt to consciousness. Depression or psychotic episodes may crush them, or they may precipitate an accident or succumb to an illness through self-destructive urges.

The more self-centred and preoccupied with fears and anxiety workaholics become, the more narcissism threatens. Faced with failure, disappointment, or any form of rejection, their self-esteem fluctuates wildly with their mood. Manic behaviour or hyperactivity, with its frenetic pace and impulsivity, frequently occurs at such times. Faulty judgment results from the impulsive behaviour, but the narcissist will excuse or deny her own faults and exaggerate her potential worth instead. Poor impulse control is a chronic problem with workaholics in general, but narcissistic people can be especially dangerous. Combined with a one-track, egotistical mind, impulsiveness can lead to devastating actions that show total disregard for others' feelings and well-being.

The roots of narcissism lie within childhood. In moderation, narcissism is normal and is basic to the development of our self-respect, self-love, and self-pride. Drs. Heinz Kohut and Ernest Wolf, in "The Disorders of the Self and Their Treatment: An Outline," suggest that there are, in our ego development, two types of "self-objects." The first are objects that the child identifies with and experiences as part of his or her own self. The core of the personality is the self. We develop a self by identifying with an accepting and confirming parent who affirms our "innate sense of vigour, greatness and perfection." As children we see ourselves in the mirror of our parents' eyes. When our parents smile because we do a certain thing, the approval is associated and linked with positive reinforcement for that deed or act. Conversely, if we receive negative looks and feedback, we will associate that activity with unhappy feelings and disapproval. If the child lives in a dysfunctional family, where the parents are obsessed with alcohol or work or perfectionism and are emotionally unavailable, the messages the child receives are often confused or unpredictable. Living in such chaos, the child struggles to develop a firm self, but is thwarted by circumstances beyond his or her control.

The second type of "self-object," according to these authors, is the "idealized parent imago." Here the parents act as a source of idealized strength, calmness, infallibility, and omnipotence, thus providing a tranquil base from which the child may seek his or her own stability and firm sense of self. If the parents are at ease and at peace with themselves and their own strivings, they can be supportive when the child's self-confidence and inner security are tested as each new challenge is met and conquered. Calm voices, relaxed bodies, and the closeness of physical expressions of affection transfer this inner strength to the child. When children first go to nursery school or join Cubs or change schools, they typically need to regress back into the family to recover their threatened confidence. If the family is a safe, secure place where the child is accepted for who he or she is, then once again confidence is restored for another assault on the new mountain. Dysfunctional families do not provide this inner strength, and the child is left to seek some substitute, such as work, to provide the stability that is missing.

Faulty interaction between the child and his self-objects results in a damaged self. A strong self can tolerate quite wide swings in self-esteem in response to victory or defeat, success or failure. These experiences may be accompanied by triumph and joy or by despair and rage, but all are accepted and incorporated into the person's self-concept. The narcissistic workaholic, however, cannot tolerate such swings. Panic and anxiety overwhelm the fragile ego. The narcissistic workaholic bounces between two extremes. At the one end, unrealistically high self-expectations produce hyperactivity, and high levels of adrenalin are pumped into the system. At the other extreme, self-rejection and blame produce guilt and a depressive state. To avoid this state, the workaholic inflates the ego even farther.

Narcissists are usually unable to love other people unless they can control them, and loved ones are seen as extensions of themselves. The narcissistic form of love is self-serving. Narcissists control and manipulate the sources of their gratification. They take without giving, lack personal insight, and avoid responsibility by procrastinating or denying that things happened. They operate on a child-like level emotionally. Love, empathy, and giving of the self are too threatening. Instead, narcissists prefer to remain aloof, to make few demands on others, and to keep emotionally distant. As a result, they suffer from loneliness and a lost sense of identity and individuality.

Mature love relinquishes control. The well-defined self shows respect for the other person's autonomy and independence. A person capable of mature love generously gives affection and seeks harmony through compromise, so that both individuals can be happy. Both people's independent needs are respected and responded to with empathy and concern.

Narcissistic people rarely seek help of their own volition. Their persona is so well defended that they are "perfectly happy with their life, if only other people would not cause them all these problems." Professor Higgins in Shaw's *Pygmalion* expresses the ultimate: "Why can't everyone be like me?" Eliza Doolittle and Colonel Pickering were there to serve the professor's needs and to actualize his ambitions. Eliza's feelings and future fate were of no concern to Higgins, despite Pickering's protestations.

Tony

Tony, an affable and carefully polite stockbroker, arrived in my office because his partners suggested he talk to me about workaholism. He appeared very youthful for his years, and was meticulously dressed. His body was stiffly erect and rigid and, like many workaholics, he had obvious back problems. He commented on the fact that I was sitting behind my desk, and then asked if he could change his place and sit in the arm chair. That done, he settled in, prepared to answer questions, but told me he was, quite frankly, mystified about why he was there.

Tony's work was his passion, and his mind raced as he excitedly told me about how all the partners had worked twelve- to eighteen-hour days to make their dream fly. Now, Tony confided, things were going to pot, and he was the only one left to straighten things out as the other partners had gone "soft."

Tony, in his youth, had been left to fend for himself emotionally because both parents were caught up in their own ambitious pursuits. He became independent very early and showed great entrepreneurial promise. At eleven, he had his first paper route, and throughout his teenaged years he held down a variety of jobs and participated in many school projects. Even while completing the last two years of university, he held down a responsible job.

Tony's wife, Irene, organized their social schedule and made friends easily. Although Tony had lots of acquaintances, his only real friend, he admitted, was an old high-school buddy. Their paths crossed occasionally but only because they ended up in the same field. They played squash every once in a while, but Tony assured me their talk was strictly business. He didn't like other people knowing about his personal life. He knew his buddy was having some family problems, but Tony preferred "not to interfere," so he wasn't sure what it was all about. Privacy and secrecy seemed very important to him, and he told me only the briefest details of his life.

Tony mentioned that his wife had recently had surgery, and he seemed quite impatient that she hurry up and get better. No empathy was conveyed concerning Irene's condition, but he obviously resented the extra work he was left with. Several times he stressed what a busy man he was and how important his job was. It appeared that anything at home that interfered with his plans was not tolerated well.

Narcissists feel distress if others are unhappy or unavailable to give to them. They try to "fix" the other person by doing something to speed their recovery. This is done, not out of empathy and love, but because narcissists want everything to look all right. Keeping up appearances is very important. I found out later, when Irene came in to see me, that, true to form, Tony pretty much ignored his wife when she was healthy and happy and perking along. It would never occur to Tony just to sit and be with Irene in the evening, to keep her company while she was recuperating from her operation.

Tony, basically a loner, told me he preferred going into the office very early in the morning before anyone else was there, and when there was less traffic to hold him up. Traffic problems were especially abhorrent to Tony. "I work through lunch hour most days as I find small talk boring," he conceded. His routine at home included isolation, too, because he spent a great deal of time at his desk. Irene complained that he never seemed to remember where the kids were going or what her schedule was. That was her department, and he chided her if anything went wrong. In fact, if there were any problems at all, they were always Irene's fault. Tony rarely apologized or took the blame for anything. Why would he, since he was always "right"? It wasn't worth it to confront Tony because he would either explode or withdraw and sulk. As a consequence, problems rarely were resolved.

Although Tony rejected others easily if they displeased him, he himself feared rejection and couldn't tolerate anything that threatened his control. So he built up high walls and dismissed others before they rejected him. Intimacy, empathy, and sharing or any give-and-take situation threatened his identity, as they do for other narcissists. Tony's work, his needs, and his interests dominated his consciousness.

Tony let me know that he liked their house because it was unpretentious and looked small from the street. Apparently, he also kept his cars until they were ready for the junk heap. In fact, he took great pride in not keeping up with the Joneses. Narcissists secretly like people to feel sorry for them as it leads to nurturing behaviour from others. He prided himself on being very independent, and never wished to be in anyone's debt. Although he was very secretive about his finances, he could be generous at times. Irene mentioned that his gifts were typically things he liked, rather than what the other person might like. Money gave Tony power, and he wanted to keep control in his family. If others were indebted to him, he held the power to manipulate them.

Ironically, narcissists are very dependent people who take from others, although they would vehemently argue the opposite. They see themselves as very giving and generous people, and any criticism is met with a vindictive rebuttal or a withdrawal into sullenness. By avoiding insight, they shirk responsibility for seeking solutions to the problems they create for others. Fear prevents any search for a mature self.

As we spoke, it was clear Tony felt he was just fine and resented being in my office. At the end of the hour, he insisted on knowing how many sessions I was talking about — " Three, six or eight?" When I shrugged and suggested it would depend on him and what he wanted to find out about himself, he got very angry. He demanded sharply that I name a number. Because it is very threatening for the narcissist to even seek help, I was pleased that he had agreed to come. Unfortunately for Tony, it will take more life crises to challenge his strong denial, but he made the first step.

The Eternal Child

Tony's youthful appearance is significant because it is a reflection of his emotional immaturity. The eternal child — the *puer aeternus* in males and the *puer animus* in females — describes an older person whose emotional life remains at the adolescent level. Mid-life crises signal an unconscious push to grow beyond this stunted level to maturity. Daryl Sharp, in *The Survival Papers: Anatomy of a Midlife Crisis*, stresses that these people are at the mercy of their powerful unconscious, and are therefore not held responsible for their actions. Alienated from their true feelings, they are vulnerable to their instinctive drives and do what "feels right," although "what feels right one minute often feels wrong the next." Ambivalent and shifting feelings leave them vulnerable to the temptations of erotic situations or addictions such as work or alcohol.

Commitment is shunned in favour of keeping options open rather than being tied down to responsibility. Sharp points out that the ultimate fear is of being caught in a situation from which it might not be possible to escape. "His lot is seldom what he really wants, he is always 'about to' do something about it, to change his lifestyle; one day he will do what is necessary — but not just yet. Plans for the future come to nothing, life slips away in fantasies of what will be, what could be, while no decisive action is ever taken to change the here and now."

A certain amount of narcissism is adaptive. It is what makes us take pride in our appearance and keep ourselves clean and comfortable. Our own health and welfare must be a major concern if we are to have something to give to others. A good balance between giving and receiving, caring for others and ourselves, keeps our narcissism in check.

HEALTHILY SELFISH								NARCISSISTIC	
1	2	3	4	5	6	7	8	9	10

Where do you fall along the continuum line for narcissism? In this case, it is best to ask your spouse or children for feedback. The sad truth is that true narcissists do not welcome negative responses. Instead, they argue that it was the other person's problem of perception. "You just don't appreciate all the things that I have provided for you" is the common stance. Taking responsibility and making commitments is, after all, just "not my bag."

LET'S SUM UP

The progression, I hope, has become apparent to you. In the pursuit of perfection lie the seeds of the obsession to work. Most workaholics tend to be perfectionists. They want everything to be done properly. When perfectionism is out of reach, anxiety develops into obsessive–

compulsive behaviour to offset the self-imposed escalating pressures to perform, or be seen to perform, at a desired level of competence. Anxiety heightens when stress is prolonged. The single-minded nature of obsession leads to a narrowing of focus and a lop-sided, incomplete self. The individual becomes increasingly task-oriented, and more self-absorbed and preoccupied. Many chronic workaholics never really grew up. They have remained narcissistic. The narcissistic workaholic spins a web that entangles and snares whoever or whatever he or she attaches to for self-aggrandizement and security. Whereas insight is the beginning of wisdom, denial avoids reality and allows the workaholic to keep spinning the web.

Now that we have explored the basic personality traits that feed into workaholism, let us look at the way workaholics exercise these traits, and learn why denial, control and power are so essential to the survival of workaholism.

3.
Workaholism's Big Three:
Denial, Control, Power

Workaholism, hidden in the cloak of denial, becomes visible to others through the workaholic's exercise of control and power. Denial allows workaholism to grow unchecked in the individual, while society enthusiastically cheers on excellence in performance. Competition is fostered, while consumerism promotes greed and the accumulation of worldly goods as status symbols. At the same time, the personality traits of perfectionism and narcissism, which underlie the obsession with work, remain hidden from the outsider, who sees only the trappings of success.

Banff Centre director, Colin Graham, no longer under the spell of denial, describes his insights in an article by Pearl Gefen in the *Globe and Mail*: "Until recently, alas, my career had made me selfish and single-minded. You strive to become a big name and that's the only thing you think about, so you prejudice any kind of relationship. I was self-centred, rather promiscuous, and career and money were the only things that mattered in my life."

All this changed when Graham went through a spiritual awakening eight years ago at Banff. "I've always believed in God, but I paid no attention to Him. Then, one winter afternoon . . . I was looking up at the mountains, wondering why I wasn't as happy working anywhere else, and I asked myself what the point of all this struggle for fame and money was if I didn't enjoy it . . . and I decided that whatever I did in the future had to be for the sake of other people rather than myself."

Graham abandoned opera to go into a seminary and was ordained as a minister in 1987. "I thought at first I should go into the church full-time, but after four months of doing that, I realized I was turning my back on my whole life and on the talents I'd been given to use.

"Luckily, the St. Louis Opera hadn't replaced me yet — I think they were waiting me out — so now I'm still their artistic director, and work part-time and unpaid in the church, counselling and teaching embryo pastors how to use their voices."

DENIAL — THE EMPEROR'S NEW CLOTHES

"I know you call me a workaholic, but it makes me cringe." Stephen winced. "I don't honestly think I am, and you're going to have to convince me because I'm fighting that label all the way." I grew very concerned when Stephen, a forty-one-year-old financial analyst, came into my office three weeks in a row, looking progressively more grey and very pale. In a heroic attempt to close a deal for his company, Stephen had been pumping adrenalin at an alarming rate, working fourteen-hour days, six times a week. I asked Stephen if there was any history of heart problems in his family, and he reported that his father had his first heart attack at forty-one. I got permission from Stephen to put a call in to his doctor, and an appointment was arranged for the next day.

This incident acted like a catalyst, and Stephen began to develop some surprising insights into his problems. Two months later, after yet another scare, Stephen admitted I had been right to take a firm stand with him, and he gradually started to acknowledge some negative behaviour. "I didn't like the direction we were going in, but some part of me cried out for honesty. I'm so used to manipulating people! I went out of here every week for a month hopping mad."

Denial is a form of dishonesty. People like Stephen use it regularly to avoid recognizing what is really happening in their lives. It is the keystone of an addiction, since dishonesty is essential to the survival of all addictions. Remove the dishonesty stone from an arch, and the remaining structure of addiction will crumble. The absence of truth is a passive form of dishonesty, which makes it very difficult to detect and confront. Denial is the first target in the war on workaholism. True honesty and self-confrontation are essential weapons against denial. The Stephens of this world cannot expect to recover fully until the walls of deceit they have built around themselves tumble down. As one client put it: "My denial collapsed at work one day when I saw the behaviour of one of my colleagues. He was just obsessed with everything and everyone. He would scream, get anxious, nasty and out-of-control. I really did not like what I saw. But I understood him so well."

If you challenge the rigid opinion of a typical workaholic and suggest that she is wrong, or say that her behaviour has made someone else very unhappy, she will often retort: "I'm just fine, thank you very much. What's your problem?" By ignoring what she does to others, the addict can pretend there is no problem, and avoid personal responsibility by playing ostrich.

A Protective Shield

Dishonesty is commonly used to avoid confrontations. Henry, a very bright entrepreneur, had built up a chain of highly successful women's clothing shops by the time he was thirty-eight. However, he had almost no insight into his marital problems. Any time Mary Beth got up the nerve to mention a specific hurt she suffered, Henry would dismiss her feelings in a patronizing way. He also neglected to tell her about some very serious financial set-backs his company was beginning to experience as their credit ran out. Although bits and pieces of gossip hinted at trouble, he told her nothing about his imminent bankruptcy. As far as Mary Beth knew, her husband was a successful entrepreneur.

Instead of confiding in Mary Beth, Henry would castigate her for selfishness when she wanted to buy something, such as furniture for their den. In front of others, though, Henry was amazingly generous and always picked up the tab for the elaborate dinners he arranged for business associates.

At one particularly frustrating session, Henry summed it all up for himself: "My working too much is a minor problem in our marriage. Besides, it's only a temporary situation. As soon as I get this new store

on its feet, I'll be home every night to help Mary Beth with the kids."
Not to worry, Henry reassured us, everything will clear itself up then.
In reality, Henry was soon to have not only his nights free, but also his
days and weekends. Henry's judgment finally failed, and his business
went bankrupt.

Mary Beth was devastated all right, but not by the bankruptcy.
What she couldn't forgive was Henry's dishonesty and his patronizing attitude towards her. She didn't need to be looked after; she
needed a husband who shared his doubts, fears, and triumphs. Mary
Beth just couldn't relate any more to "high-handed Henry," as she
called him.

To maintain the illusion of perfection, the workaholic keeps negative information secret. Henry's "perfect" persona, that part of him
he wished others to see, had to be protected at all costs, especially as
insecurities mounted. To make matters worse, Mary Beth's push for a
"perfect" relationship placed unrealistic demands on her spouse,
which, in turn, no doubt discouraged honesty. Both parties share the
blame if the workaholic's spouse is unwilling to ask probing questions
or to challenge the workaholic's passive withdrawal. Support and a
gentle honesty must accompany such confrontations at all times.
Mary Beth never asked Henry about the rumours she was hearing
because she, too, wanted desperately to believe that everything was
okay and that their marriage was intact.

Myths can be a form of denial. The husband and wife may create
family myths, but children also get caught up in the web of denial.
They, too, protect the collective myth that broadcasts: "We are a
healthy, happy, successful family." Moms and dads in such families
discourage any talk of problems. Children, aware that all is not well,
often face others with fear: "If you really knew me, you wouldn't care
about me." This fear forces them to disown their own negative
qualities and to act like a perfect person who has his or her life in order
and is problem-free. Otherwise, they will be found out or, worse still,
abandoned — the ultimate fear of children. If parents use rejection as a
punishment, or withhold affection and approval to control the child's
behaviour, they make the problem worse. If children feel "bad" and
responsible for their parents' rejection, they will be perpetually on the
alert and anxious to please. These overly responsible children set out
to prove to one and all that they are okay. But they are not. Instead,

they are in a position to become the next generation of workaholics who must perform and succeed to feel worthwhile.

The Shadow

There used to be a radio program called "The Shadow." It was introduced with a hideously maniacal laugh and the line "What evil lurks in the hearts of men? Only the Shadow knows." My father finally forbade us to listen to the program. The Shadow is not a popular figure with anyone.

The Shadow is also a psychological concept that is intrinsically linked to denial. The Shadow, according to Dr. James Hall, a noted psychiatrist, is "that which you hope you are not, but if you are you hope nobody notices." The thoughts and actions you do not wish to recognize as belonging to you are repressed and reside in your unconscious. When you are very angry, for example, strong negative feelings from the past flood up from the unconscious to add to your present feelings. At such times, you overreact and become highly emotional. Depending on your personality, you will either lash out at others or go into dark moods and withdraw. The Shadow is now in control. You cannot think or feel. You are possessed and lack any judgment or objectivity. Very upsetting and strange things get said that are out of character for you; in fact, they are often the reverse of what you would say in a rational frame of mind. Or your thoughts are confused and jumbled and make no sense to the listener. Ironically, this often happens when someone else has done something you don't wish to identify as something you do. I may think I'm a very polite person because I rarely say rude things. My rudeness may take the form of impatience. When I'm rushed myself, I may refuse to let other drivers into the lane of traffic or neglect to take the time to be gracious and ask how others are before I begin a business talk. Instead, I'm curt, blunt, and sometimes sharp. If someone pointed out that I was being rude, I would be surprised.

People try to deal with their Shadow by denying its existence. As Dr. John Sanford, in *Evil: The Shadow Side of Reality*, points out: "Awareness of one's Shadow brings guilt and tension and forces upon us a different psychological and spiritual task." The Shadow corrupts by playing with truth and justice, and it feeds on envy, greed, and power.

As long as something is secret or unknown, it becomes very powerful. The workaholic's Shadow becomes more and more potent as more truths are repressed. The workaholic, who always wishes to present an ideal persona to the world, must repress the mercurial part that blows up in anger, that is vindictive and has uncontrolled sexual urges. Instead, the unconscious dark side is recognized in other people, but is disowned or appears foreign to the workaholic's self-image. Other people are perceived as having the projected problem, and the workaholic disapproves of *their* behaviour, or fears them lest they retaliate for his rejection. Without a realistic understanding of oneself, problems are not confronted, and healing will not take place.

My clients tell me that their biggest challenge is to learn to tell the truth. One afternoon, Louisa, an overweight woman in her fifties, admitted that she had completely lost perspective around honesty. Louisa had not only become ineffectual at work, but she was battling alcoholism. A nervous tic was making her feel even more self-conscious and uncomfortable with the people at work. "You know, I really don't know the difference between truth and dishonesty any more. Distortion has become an everyday habit with me. Some days, the truth would have been easy, but I just didn't know how to say something different from my usual response. I even rationalized that I was being 'nice' and 'protective.' " She chuckled to herself at this point. "I don't know of whom though!" Louisa was slowly conquering her Shadow of denial.

Ironically, the Shadow also contains the parts of our personality that have never been developed. If we are introverted, much of our ability to be outgoing remains buried and unavailable to us. We can become very envious of people who mingle easily at social functions, yet later criticize a spouse for paying attention to others and attracting their attention. Or cool, rational people may be openly critical and mistrustful of vulnerable, warm people who wear their hearts on their sleeves, and yet, at some level, they envy them their sensitivity and openness. Unfortunately, such harsh criticism is especially destructive to those people who value harmony above all. In the act of being critical and skeptical, the rational person is hiding his or her own tender and gentle side from awareness.

Yet, these same vital and poorly developed opposite attributes can make us whole and complete, if we can only challenge ourselves to grow and use these inner strengths to our advantage. So much wasted energy is used each day to repress unwanted thoughts. Instead we should be intrigued by and welcome our Shadow. Only when we understand our weaknesses and shortcomings can we make a conscious decision to censor and control them. Developing our opposite positive traits can help us open up new and exciting aspects of our personality. Donald, a very private and introverted man, had freed himself by developing his feelings and extroversion. An excited Donald told me: "I'm having more fun running around sharing my ideas and arguing with the guys at work. I even challenged my boss the other day, and told him his idea was crazy. You know," Donald said with a grin, "the world didn't stop, and I think he respected what I had to say. He even called me into his office this week and asked me to develop my ideas into a new project for the company."

The Birth of Denial

The seeds of the workaholic's strong denial are sown in childhood. Children who grow up with conditional love learn to lie to others as a way to gain approval. From there, it's an easy step to learn to lie to yourself. Children learn early which actions draw the approval they so desire from their parents. If praise is scarce, children lie to see if they can get these rewards at less cost. After all, everyone loves a bargain! Children are very concrete in their thinking. They find out early on that they can get away with X but not Y in this family.

The confusion and chaos in a dysfunctional family breed denial because secrecy is a very potent weapon to use against others. If parents and children keep the truth from each other to protect themselves, then reality is difficult to discern. Also, what works at their home doesn't necessarily work elsewhere, and the child knocks against many doors, trying to figure out where it is safe to lie, and with whom, and when it is necessary to be honest, or when honesty pays better dividends. If conditional love is the norm, then it just isn't safe or smart to talk about failures or weak spots. "What my parents don't know won't hurt them" echoes through the playground. The defence of rationalization is born, and most workaholics are past masters at sliding in and out of truth.

Mr. Nice Guy

Mr. Nice Guys and their female counterparts are potentially dangerous because their denial works so well. It is an alarming paradox that workaholics "honestly" see themselves as "nice people" — self-sacrificing, noble, conscientious, dutiful, hard-working, and even religious. They have developed powerful denial defences that allow them to recognize only their positive qualities. The shades of denial progress gradually as the workaholic begins to have to repress more and more negative information about himself, his effectiveness, and his effect on others. Hard-core workaholics become quite blind psychologically and are unaware of the deep personality transformations that take place when people deny reality. They must form their own reality, so develop a rich fantasy life. Unfortunately, this false reality crumbles when life events and other people challenge the workaholic, and episodes of rage become more frequent.

Percy

A typical "Mr. Nice Guy" was Percy, a forty-five-year-old distinguished-looking gentleman who had left his native England when he was in his twenties and now acted as a fire-fighting financial consultant. He would come into a company, put out existing blazes, and turn the company around to register a profit. In my office, Percy was the epitome of the overcontrolled Mr. Cool, although I did notice he was patronizing with his young wife, Stephanie. He often one-upped her stories or added his own, more articulate version. Stephanie was badly depressed and was having trouble getting out of her depression. She was always upset about something Percy had done. In my office, Percy was the perfect example of charm, patience, tact, and was extremely sympathetic to his wife's rage about his brief affair and her anxiety when he was away on business. He seemed genuinely sorry and was trying to make amends. At home, however, he was still flying into rages. Whenever Stephanie expressed her views, he was sarcastic and blunt as he argued about who was "right." He openly criticized the way she handled the children, even in their presence.

Insights into his past work patterns helped Percy realize that avoidance and denial motivated him to go to work at 7:00 a.m. even though he had become so efficient that there wasn't much to do. His top-management job had to do with communication, and it was too early to call a meeting. With no one else at the office yet, Percy used to read the paper and drink endless cups of black coffee, psyching himself up with an adrenalin fix. "I could have done that at home, but I never allowed myself to be relaxed and casual about anything, let alone breakfast. My rigid schedule was important to keep me from confronting my behaviour at home. My family reminded me that all was not well, and I wanted to stay away from anything that made me feel guilty. God, I hate feeling guilty!" At home, Percy's bad temper was creating anxiety in everyone, and his "perfect" family was falling apart. Percy was full of energy at work, but he left nothing for his family. Mr. Nice Guy checked his charm at the door and emotionally withdrew.

For the workaholic, the self-image of Mr. Nice Guy dies hard. It was after a trip home that Percy's wall of denial collapsed. He saw his family with new eyes and was forced to confront old memories. "You know, if we had remained in England, my family and my old cronies would have found me suffocatingly arrogant and cruel. My father would have been shocked at how I put down Stephanie in public. A stern rebuke was what I needed, but I was always on my best behaviour the few times we did make it back home.

"Come to think of it, we never used to go home that often. I felt that family ties were just another burden to be suffered through, and I used to think I didn't need anybody, let alone my parents and brothers." He began to understand that, in his lust for power, he mapped out a career path in which the most opportune business strategies determined where the family would live. Percy never considered what the packing up, leaving friends and journeying on had done to his wife and children. The family's survival depended on his financial support, he rationalized, and besides, "they all enjoyed the upwardly mobile lifestyle that my promotions brought me."

Percy knew his old ideal image didn't fit any more. He also realized that his fatigue level was very high, and it was taking him longer to rebound from periods of high productivity. Some inside wisdom told him that slowing down might not be that bad. In fact, Percy had started a garden, and his thoughts now turned to his mother's rose garden back home. He had blocked his memories of that magic place for years.

Feedback from Others

Other people's opinions can make a difference. In fact, reality-testing is a necessary prerequisite for recovery. I encourage people to ask friends, family members, and colleagues whom they trust for comments on their behaviour. Through this process, they can open themselves to the hurt and anger their Shadow has caused others. They also open themselves to the support and caring they have missed. Julie, a very creative young woman working her way up in the advertising world, was starting to ask questions as a way of confronting her Shadow. At work, she was told, it was not so much what she was saying to her co-workers as how she addressed them. Julie had become so intense that she underlined everything she said with great emphasis, used a strong, sharp, blunt approach, and swore like a trooper — something new for her. "I think I was trying to shock people, to provoke them," she mused. "On the other hand, from what I know now, it maybe was my cry for help!"

Julie found herself complaining a lot about her work, something she found disloyal and off-putting in others. So, one day, she took aside a fellow employee whom she trusted and asked her how she was coming across. "It's not that you do it so often, Julie, but I gotta tell you that when you do it, it's dynamite. You look incredibly intense, your face gets sort of contorted, and your whole jaw locks tight in determination." Then the colleague added in support, "But I know how important it is for you to do things just right. Maybe you could relax a bit and tone down your message so the rest of us don't get so devastated." Julie was really pleased with the added support she got as she tried to change her behaviour.

Hard-core narcissistic workaholics treasure their privacy and would not dream of letting down their tall walls to let others in. Instead, they remain happy with themselves and their lifestyles long after others have become aware of severe relationship problems. Even when other family members are in obvious distress and "act out" for attention and affection, or "act in" with depression, physical illness, and anxiety or phobias, they remain aloof and dissociated from their feelings, or lash out, projecting their negative feelings onto others. A frequent response might be: "Problems? Not me. I'm doing my job and a lot more. You should be grateful for all the material goods I provide you. You're never satisfied. I'm sick of hearing about your needs. Get hold of yourself, for crying out loud. You're acting like a snivelling child." It's the old story of the pot calling the kettle black.

The Professional Mask

The mask created by workaholics in the professions protects a carefully defended persona these people have taken years to perfect. As long as you wear a mask, however, you will be performing. Your real character, after a time, will get lost in the performance.

Professions that involve health or spiritual care, such as medicine, dentistry, and the ministry, often produce workaholics who are respected and revered by their clientele. There is a certain nobility in the self-sacrificing image of medical doctors going on rounds both Saturday and Sunday mornings. Always craving approval and attention, workaholics relish situations in which others feel sorry for them. The praise and adulation received from grateful patients, parishioners, or students are the nourishment they use to drive their bodies and souls to perform heroic feats.

The other side of the coin is their home lives. Often spouses and children go without adequate personal attention and affection, and certainly never have the "quantity time" so essential for intimacy. Positive signals that family members are appreciated and valued above all else are missing. In order to survive at all, family members are forced to become more independent and to seek affirmation and appreciation from other sources. Some kids plug into other families where there is warmth and a substitute father or mother figure. Some spouses, desperate for attention and self-affirmation, seek reassurance and comfort in extramarital affairs. Many go to church or join groups, seeking some solace from belonging to a fellowship of friendly people who accept them as they are. They plan outings with other supportive friends who will listen to their accounts of their plight and offer love, while the ambitious spouse works for adoration and the financial rewards of "success." For the workaholic, friends take up too much precious time.

The spouse often becomes depressed, and is in danger of becoming the martyr who faithfully tends to the hearth, becomes resigned to what is, and asks for nothing. Healthier spouses wonder what is wrong with their judgment when other people keep telling them what a "great person" their spouse is. Sooner or later, the wife or husband no longer agrees and, in fact, feels abandoned, hurt, and totally rejected. As a consequence, a wife no longer welcomes home her "conquering hero," having just resigned her membership in his fan club. Her own anger bounces off his inflated ego and his underlying guilt and fears. One such physician was a past master at turning the tables around so that everything his wife complained about became her fault, especially the fact that he worked all the time. Gaylord's world was cracking; everything he touched turned sour. One night he flew into a rage and screamed: "I'm not appreciated in my own house. It's incredible justice that after all I've done and the wonderful lifestyle I provide for you and the kids, all I get in return is constant bitching." Gaylord has absolutely no awareness that his work is done for his own self-aggrandizement. And the dreaded dance goes on, as each undermines the other's security and self-esteem. This is the tragedy of the workaholic family.

As long as denial remains strong, families are helpless to help, and no rescue operation will be effective. Workaholics, after all, will argue and defend their own views vehemently because they are always "right." They resent any criticism and feel ganged-up on if their children tend to support or defend the other parent's point of view. This is where family triangles form and cause havoc to the intact family system, a dynamic that will be explored later, in Chapter 6.

Mr. or Ms. Real

Denial and reality are poor bedfellows.

"What a relief to finally let go of my phony mask!" Nancy grinned as she spoke. "I feel more balanced and even somewhat peaceful these days. Best of all, I'm finally just accepting myself — warts and all." Nancy's relief is a common experience in psychotherapy, but it comes about only through painful self-confrontation. These brave individuals learn to re-establish their feelings and to love themselves unconditionally, thereby bringing compassion to both themselves and others.

Try rating yourself on this checklist from 1 to 10, using 5 as the mid-point.

1   2   3   4   5   6   7   8   9   10

Mr. Nice Guy or Gal	Mr. or Ms. Real
____ Arrogant	____ Humble
____ Self-centred, self-absorbed	____ Self-and other-centred
____ Perfectionist	____ Realistic — able to understand limits
____ Obsessive	____ Thorough
____ Competitive	____ Values harmony
____ Performance, goal-oriented	____ Self-directed
____ Ambitious, hard-driving	____ Competent
____ Impatient	____ Patient
____ Critical, skeptical	____ Accepting
____ Judgmental	____ Tolerant
____ Rigid, uptight	____ Flexible, open
____ Overly responsible at work	____ Responsible at work
____ Avoids personal responsibility	____ Responsible personally
____ Lacking objectivity, one-tracked	____ Objective, aware
____ Restless, seeking	____ Peaceful, calm
____ Too busy to take stock	____ Contemplative
____ Intense	____ Easy-going
____ Blows things out of proportion	____ Keeps things in perspective
____ Secretive, private	____ Open, available
____ Sarcastic, superiority-based humour	____ Gentle sense of humour
____ I must, I should	____ I want, I will

"In Japan, there's a saying that the higher the rice grows, it gets closer to the ground, because, you know, the head gets heavy. In Western terms, you might say the more you develop the humbler you are. For me, to say I'm the best at anything is to stop learning." This wise thought by Takeo Yamashiro, a Japanese-Canadian musician quoted by Liam Lacey in the *Globe and Mail*, sums up the best reason for being "Real." To keep growing and searching for the self requires the utmost humility.

HIDDEN CONTROL — THE "TERRIBLE TWIST"

Workaholics use a quiet, manipulative type of control to maintain dominance over others. The "Terrible Twist" goes as follows.

Step 1 The workaholic feels inner discontent and projects anxiety or anger outwards by lashing out or undermining the other person.

Step 2 The other person feels hurt, rejected, or unfairly criticized by what has been said. The other person then reacts or withdraws.

Step 3 The workaholic becomes annoyed or angry at the other person for his or her response. The precipitating outburst is totally ignored, as if it didn't happen. "It's all your fault!" is the message to the spouse, child or co-worker who is blamed for the whole incident.

This type of exchange leaves the recipient of the "Terrible Twist" feeling devastated, or in disbelief, with no way of knowing what brought on the original angry or anxious projection. Even the workaholic often does not understand what has happened since he or she has repressed or denied so many feelings. Often the spouse or child's psychological and financial security may be so wrapped up with the workaholic that escape from such abuse is not a simple matter.

Here's what happened one Sunday morning to one of my clients. Larry, an ambitious young lawyer, arrived home unexpectedly a day early from Europe. His wife, Cindy, had been scheduled to give a talk at the church that morning. When Cindy came home, she and her daughter were discussing how well the talk had gone. Feeling left out and irritable, Larry suddenly announced he was going to the fruit market to get tomatoes. Cindy asked him to please get some lettuce and crusty bread too.

A little while later, Larry arrived home empty-handed. Cindy asked where the parcels were. The check-out line was too long, he said. Larry avoided line-ups on principle. She apologized for not having lunch ready, but added, "I thought I might as well wait till you got home so we could eat the fresh stuff." As Cindy prepared some soup, Larry muttered something under his breath. When asked what was the matter, Larry lashed out: "The reason I had to go to the market in the first place was that you didn't go shopping yesterday!" (Step 1)

Cindy snapped angrily that she was busy working on her talk and, besides, she hadn't expected him home anyway. (Step 2)

Larry then exploded and said that what he *really* was angry about was what Cindy had said. He accused her of saying: "I had my heart set on eating what you brought home from the market."

Close to tears by now, Cindy denied that she had said that at all. She repeated what she had, in fact, said and demanded that Larry apologize. Larry accused her of lying and distorting things. (Step 3)

"I would never even think to say those words!" screamed Cindy. "I can't live with someone who repeatedly lies to me about what I've said." She ran out of the room, sobbing.

In actual fact, Larry was annoyed and hurt that no one seemed glad he had come home early. But he was unable to express his disappointment. His wife and daughter had planned the weekend around their own individual needs. Larry was used to the family focusing on *his* plans and catering to *his* needs.

Workaholics commonly blame other people when they feel out of control. It takes a strong, healthy ego on the part of the other person to break free from this cycle of emotional abuse. Spouses who value harmony above all will sacrifice everything, even themselves, to ensure that peace prevails. Sometimes spouses have no choice but to leave. Children unfortunately have no such option when they are small. Living with someone who is emotionally unavailable or abusive leads to hopelessness and despair, and eventually to chronic anxiety or depression.

The "Terrible Twist" is dangerous because it is so devious, and frequent exposure to it often causes other people to question their own sanity. Being constantly blamed for things makes you lose your confidence, and you feel hopeless or helpless to change the situation. Some practical advice came from Mary, a down-to-earth social worker, who discovered a way to survive the Twist. Mary began a diary in which she wrote down what her husband said to her when he was in a rage. Since Alan typically denied having said "any such thing" the next day, the diary was a way of "reality-testing" for them both. Mary simply mentioned that he was welcome to read what she reported at the time of the incident, but he never took her up on it, and the conversation ended there. At least Mary felt better, as she was able to keep some objectivity and not be dragged into defending her version of what happened, after the fact. Post-mortem discussions typically end up with two people arguing about what was said and who was right.

"Looking Good"

The Nice Guys and Gals are masters at disguising their attempts to control. Ever so subtly, these workaholics learn to get their own way, at any cost, especially when their insecurity is high. At such times, there is hell to pay for those who live and work with them if this control is challenged. By projecting blame onto others, workaholics are left "looking good." They avoid personal responsibility, yet leave the impression that they are cool, reserved, and removed from the chaos they create. It is the others who are seen as angry and hysterical because they have risen to the bait of the projected blame.

Let's look at some of the different styles of hidden control that workaholics use. Each different style uses a different means of controlling others — among them, dishonesty, phoniness, secrecy, thoughtlessness, arrogance.

The Benevolent Dictator

This workaholic has a charming way of saying yes, but meaning no. A dictator appears to listen and agree with everything you say while you are in her office. Everything, from motherhood issues to complaints about other staff members, is handled in an agreeable way. The staff member is placated reassuringly: "Not to worry, everything will change for the best." Nothing, however, is done. This boss will rationalize that her philosophy is: "Don't fix what ain't broken!" Denying that there is a problem and thereby refusing to accept someone else's reality means that she keeps control of what reality is.

Neither is prevention of problems a high priority for her. Employees, overwhelmed by this snow-job, feel guilty for rocking the boat, then wonder if they were overreacting after all. The boss, meanwhile, drives ahead full-steam, following her own set agenda, disregarding any ground swells of discontent.

The Absent-Minded Professor

"I've got my mind made up. Don't confuse me with the facts!" These workaholics can best be described as other-worldly and off on another orbit. The Professor's lab technicians have learned not to bother the "great mind," as they call him, unless something is earth-shattering or about to blow up in their faces. He is often moody and depressed, and his antennae are attuned to his own subjective world of complex abstract theories. He manages not to answer the probing questions of his Ph.D. students, and he tunes out their clever insights into why something is not working, even when they quote the latest scientific journals. His methodologies are the same ones he has always used, and the state-of-the-art technology is beyond his scope. Tenure keeps him on the job. He controls through a stubborn determination to do his own thing, in his own way. Those technicians who enjoy the lax atmosphere of the status quo remain. The bright inquiring minds, attracted to the job by the professor's early reputation, depart disillusioned.

The Secret Agent

This workaholic usually resides behind a closed door, or, if the office door is ajar, the chairs inside are uncomfortably stiff and the office is drab and sparsely furnished in a utilitarian manner. The owner's personality is also top secret. Business is business, and she doesn't mix business with pleasure — or spend money on luxuries. She is clever about the way she delays picking up the luncheon bill until the other person offers to pay. Business strategies are kept secret to make sure the competition doesn't "scoop" an idea. The problem is that she keeps her colleagues in the dark too. No brain-storming ever generates "better mousetraps," and tasks are replicated throughout the system because of the secrecy surrounding "who does what." She is not a good team player, and appears to be joyless and unenthusiastic about what she does. Others have to pick up the slack, and nobody has much fun working in this gloomy atmosphere. She refuses to share control lest anyone find out whether she really is effective.

Super-person

"I'd really like to delegate more, but my experience is that it's easier and better to do it myself." This stance is typical of the workaholic in the breakdown stages. "I can't be replaced, but my partners could," responded an arrogant chief executive. "We're unlikely to cut back the technical side of the company because marketing, sales, and accounting are the bare bones of our industry." Then, in all seriousness, he added, "Those who are good managers of the people side of the business are a dime a dozen. That's where we get serious with the scalpel." With no social skills of his own, this executive showed no appreciation for others who kept employees motivated and enthusiastic.

The Super-person accepts all the high-profile committee jobs and shoves the routine chores into the "in" basket. Like a squirrel collecting nuts for the winter, he hordes the plum jobs to protect his empire. Power comes from being indispensable and keeping control close to the vest. Self-aggrandizement is the name of this game.

OVERT CONTROL —
THE FLASHING-NEON VARIETY

If you are always right, then it makes perfect sense for you to tell other folks what they should do, say, think, or feel — doesn't it? This rationalization permits workaholics to control blatantly because they often lack the insight to see what their actions do to others. Instead, they perceive their behaviour as helpful.

Kevin

Kevin found it almost impossible to say no, and more often than not added, "And this is what I can do for you!" Kevin was a cocky car salesman and, at thirty-two, had won the salesman-of-the-year award for five consecutive years. The skills he used for selling "iceboxes to the Eskimos," he used on all occasions. Kevin's young wife had recently left him, and with her went "their" friends. He was so agitated that he pushed his chair aside and began to pace my office, spilling out his incredible story. Kevin had alienated almost everyone in his world and was completely baffled about what had gone wrong.

Kevin's ego boundaries were vague. Where his responsibilities stopped and others' began was not clear to him at all. He was the ultimate do-gooder who desperately wanted to please and gain approval. He ran himself ragged, "helping" others, lecturing or giving advice at the drop of a hat. After all, why should others be left to make mistakes when Kevin knew what was best. He showed me a long list of errands and tasks for his customers. His chief complaint was that most of these people he helped ended up being unappreciative. "I gave my shirt away, and they took it" was his summation.

Jeannie had tried to have some say in the way things were done around the house, but Kevin always knew a better way. He rarely listened since he was a jump ahead, anticipating what he should say and do next. Kevin rationalized that he could second-guess what other people wanted or thought. In reality, his attempts to control his own environment meant that situations were altered to fit his own needs.

Kevin's acquaintances, as it turned out, were either younger or older than himself. He chummed with the secretaries and the mechanics at work rather than with his fellow salespeople. He even ended up doing errands for the mother of one of the secretaries, and arranged for some legal help for a distant aunt in that family. Peer relationships are threatening to people like Kevin because peers resent being controlled in a friendship, whereas young or older people tend to look up to them. Dependent people who don't challenge offers of help were perfect targets for Kevin. Gifts of help are rarely free of strings, however, and when Kevin asked for favours in return, he met resentment.

Kevin's control was illusory. His desperate need for approval left him dependent on others. He drove himself crazy by obsessively rehearsing what he would say and what the other person would say back. Being clever and witty became an obsession. Kevin would emerge exhausted from such encounters. His scripts weren't working, and his anxiety was sky high. He had done it all wrong. He would catch his reflection in the mirror at work, and adjust his tie or slick his hair back so that he looked "self-confident and mature." His self-confidence had reached an all-time low.

The peculiar thing to me about Kevin's story was that he barely mentioned Jeannie. She was gone, and he had erased her from his memory — or so it seemed. "These things happen sometimes!" he answered in a sing-song voice to anyone who asked about their separation. Kevin was avoiding dealing with the legal side of things since he refused to let reality tarnish his image.

Under Kevin's controlled world lay rage and bitterness. When things didn't go his way, or certain people resented him instead of being grateful, Kevin would become extremely agitated. Underneath the bluster and rage, however, was a frightened child facing the terror of abandonment. Once Kevin learned to love this vulnerable part of himself, and to nurture himself any time his fears escalated, he needed to control others less and less. However, it was too late to salvage Kevin's marriage: Jeannie had found a man who genuinely cared for her, and they were happily sharing their lives. Kevin eventually stopped manipulating and "helping" others, and let others be responsible for their choice to make mistakes or fail and to learn by trial-and-error. He became calmer and genuinely relaxed as our sessions became a refuge in the storm of his life.

Letting Go of Control

Since workaholics feel safest when work and life are predictable and consistent, they overcontrol, overplan, and overorganize everyone and everything around them. Letting go of control is frightening, but without it there can be no flexibility, spontaneity, or risk.

Recovering workaholics need to become much more realistic about the scope of their job, and to give up some of their idealistic perfectionism. They need to learn to delegate and to reconsider their priorities.

It is not easy to give up controlling behaviour, but by taking it a step at a time, it can be done. Start at work. Consider some of the questions to ask yourself when you begin to let go.

1. How can I cut back my responsibilities and reduce my hours of work, and still be able to direct policy and influence others?

2. If we down-size the company, will my prestige, even my job, be left intact?

3. Are my colleagues going to cut back my earning power and salary if I work more normal hours? What will happen to my financial security?

4. Self-preservation is a factor for fellow staff members. If I quit now, what will happen to them? What is my corporate responsibility?

5. Instead of being the responsible person who gives out favours and helps others, can I accept support and genuine concern shown by my fellow workers and my boss?

6. Can I give up being a company man and focus on my health and my family's welfare?

7. Will people think I'm lazy, irresponsible, and selfish? Can I find the courage to change?

8. Can I give up trying to be "the best" and settle for "good" or "better" instead?

9. If I work fewer hours, what will I do with myself? Can I find some hobbies or sports to enjoy in my free time?

10. What interesting things can my spouse and I do together, and how can I be of more help at home?

POWER — "THE KING OF THE CASTLE"

Power can be used for good or evil. Power eventually corrupts if it is combined with a growing arrogance, but power coupled with love has infinite possibilities for good.

Power arises from two opposite sources: greed and love. Greed is fed by ambition, perfectionism, competition, anger, and guilt. Love encourages empathy, compassion, generosity, goodwill, and compromise. Power based on greed causes the individual to seek not only personal control, but control over other people, objects, organizations, and even whole industries. Strategies, tactics, manipulations, gamesmanship, and exploitation are used to exercise that power. This power arises out of the aggressive instinct, while the power of love comes from the nurturing and sexual instinct.

Recovery comes to the workaholic when the power of love replaces the power of greed. The capacity to love encourages the sensory and emotional experience of union with people, places, and things. According to Dr. Jay Rohrlich, in *Work and Love: The Crucial Balance*, love is "impaired by the imposition of intellect, of words, symbols, and definitions. It is expansive rather than reductive, and is oriented to present, immediate experience, apprehended by the senses of sight, hearing, taste, smell, and touch. Love is the opposite of work in all respects."

The workplace is one arena where power is sought. Power becomes the temptress, the powerful mistress who lures the insecure workaholic away from his or her family. When attempts at intimacy sour or indifference sets in at home, the workaholic seeks power in the more impersonal corporate world, where intimacy is discouraged. The obsession with work soon sucks up all available energy, the person becomes one-dimensional, and feelings grow flat and restricted. The ability to love others deadens as, self-absorbed and otherwise preoccupied, the workaholic relentlessly pursues power and dominance to prove once again that he or she can perform and thereby be a success. To be accepted and admired by his or her peers, the workaholic will sacrifice others' happiness and personal integrity. Power is the elusive phantom, always demanding more and more.

Work, whether it is job- or leisure-related, is the outcome of the aggressive instinct that underlies power. Even words such as "compete," "drive," "master," "manipulate," and "dominate" suggest a battle to organize and control our environment and its materials, to use them to our best advantage. It is sometimes difficult to determine when power corrupts, because aggressive pursuits are typically rationalized as being necessary to support the family, or to enhance the welfare of the community or society at large. Our own security, stability, and lifestyles are often the justification for working harder and longer hours. The danger is that work can become a state of mind, an obsession to achieve increasing levels of competence, excellence, or greatness. High achievement and performance bring responsibility, along with the perks and trappings of power.

If aggressive instincts lead to a satisfactory mastery of the work environment, then power is gained. If competitive efforts fail, frustration and blocked aggression often turn to fear, hostility, and destructive rage. Vindictive acts are the exercise of that rage. By putting others down, the workaholic seeks to regain the dominant position, at least temporarily. Someone else is left in the submissive, one-down position. Someone wins, and someone loses!

Unfortunately, an aggressive drive for power usually means that others are pushed aside in the climb up the ladder. Without compassion and empathy, competition can lead workers to sacrifice their integrity and honesty to get ahead. Enough is never enough when a person becomes addicted to power and control, and personal responsibility to others gets lost in one's own narcissistic goals.

Competition

Power brings workaholics prestige, money and possessions. These, temporarily at least, produce pride and raise self-esteem to appease strong needs for approval and success. As we will learn, however, fear escalates as arrogance and self-delusion lure the workaholic into a false sense of power and an obsessive need to remain dominant and retain control. Under a jaunty, genial surface often lie envy and greed. Excelling or winning eases the hostility and helplessness these emotions create, and dominating others makes workaholics feel less vulnerable and less afraid. Unfortunately, each step up the corporate ladder means fellow workers are bypassed. Each contract signed means other competitors lose. Each ruthlessly independent decision oversteps group consensus. When the workaholic's own need for power is fulfilled at the expense of others, fears of retribution and resentment soon threaten any new-found success and security.

The more prestige workaholics acquire, the more likely they are to be protected from the humiliation and shame attached to failure. An expensive address or even publicized good works sets a person above the ordinary. Success and displays of wealth often distance a person from others, resulting in loneliness and isolation. Eventually, attempts to remain dominant will fail as competition continues, especially as arrogance brings self-delusions and increasing fears of toppling from power. Self-punishing and masochistic behaviour often hastens this decline as unconscious paranoia and guilt undermine the person's self-confidence.

"Impression management" is a term used in the literature on co-dependence. Workaholics tend to use others as a mirror because they are out of tune with their own feelings and have no internal referent to tell them how they are doing. Workaholics believe they can control the way others see them, and it is essential that others see them as "good" people. They are adept at figuring out what other people like and want, and then they try to deliver the goods. Unfortunately, if they fail to please, workaholics often believe they are personal failures. They try to hide their mistakes and refuse to admit they cannot meet expectations and quotas. Dishonesty leads to loss of integrity and trust when errors eventually are discovered.

Michael Lewis, in his review of *Trump: Surviving at the Top*, gives a good example of impression management. "Mr. Trump's relentless accumulation leads people often to mistake his motive for greed, when what drives the man seems to me to be more a pathological need for control. But control of what? Perhaps there was a time when he wanted to control his business; now he seems merely to want to control the opinion others hold of him. Mr. Trump has come to believe that if he nurtures his fame his business will follow. 'Success,' he writes, 'so often, is just a matter of perception.' That may explain why he goes berserk when a journalist tries to tinker with his image. ... The man whose first impulse after he buys a building is to change the facade has become nothing but a facade."

Competition and Compassion

Competition and compassion are like oil and water; they do not mix. Competition can become unhealthy if one constantly needs to measure oneself against others and to come out ahead, or if competition itself is motivated by destructive rather than constructive and creative tendencies. Dr. Karen Horney, in her essay "Neurotic Competitiveness," points out that, in all neurotic competitiveness, one "fights against feeling any gratitude" because giving someone else credit for anything is humbling. Workaholics, it is noted, rarely apologize when they realize they have been wrong, and someone else right. Saying "I'm sorry" is difficult, because it is an admission that one is wrong. Humility comes hard, and agreeing to disagree, or considering that both people might be right, is foreign to a workaholic's thinking.

Compassion, by contrasts, does not deal in winners and losers. It does not isolate, separate or estrange. Dr. Matthew Fox, in *A Spir-*

ituality Named Compassion and the Healing of the Global Village, stresses that compassion seeks out our common likenesses rather than differences. It unites us, makes us one, and moves us towards celebrating thankfulness. The art of love-making is often defeated by the competitive need to "defeat, subdue and humiliate" the partner. Because workaholics lack compassion, they often carry their competitive natures home and develop power struggles in their marriages.

Competition can take a much more subtle form. It can become a passive denial of the partner's wishes or an avoidance of sexuality altogether. A number of my clients make it a habit to go to bed later than their spouses, rationalizing that they want to get their work done when no one is around to bother them. In fact, they admit to a real fear of intimacy because it requires one to be submissive, vulnerable, and compassionate. When they do make love, they cannot sustain intimacy, so they use punishing behaviour to restore their compulsive need to dominate. One man ruthlessly criticized his wife after love-making, reminding her that nothing she did was right. This is particularly devastating to the mate at such a moment of vulnerability. Just when she is finally receiving some attention, touching and caressing, all the things that are missing from the marriage, she is belittled once again. The play *Who's Afraid of Virginia Woolf?* portrayed the devastation of this style of competitive and destructive sparring.

In the workplace, personally humiliating another individual would be frowned upon, to say the least. To put down and criticize your opponent after winning a match or closing an important deal would be considered bad form. Many workaholics would never treat the people at work like they do their spouse at home. Occasionally, they slip up in a public situation, and their true colours are revealed. One man told me that he and his colleagues observed one executive putting down his wife at a company dinner. Those who witnessed this behaviour exchanged knowing glances: If he does that in public, then he must certainly do it at home. That man remained at his level and was not advanced in the company. In the corporate world, on the other hand, competition is the name of the game. There, it is perfectly acceptable for companies and corporations to celebrate and advertise their Brand X as being better than their Brand Y. In a personal relationship, such comparisons create serious disharmony.

Compulsion and Compassion

Compulsive behaviour, acts a person feels compelled to engage in repeatedly, correlates negatively with compassion. The more compulsion drives the workaholic to control, dominate, and perform, the more narcissism fosters an ignorance of others' needs and feelings. Compulsion encourages a single-mindedness where one's faults and shortcomings are disowned and repressed into the unconscious. As a result, criticism is projected outwards, and others are judged and found wanting.

Compassion, however, involves being fully conscious of both the self's and others' frailties and strengths. The freedom to have one's own ideas is respected, and equality is a treasured value between individuals. Dr. Matthew Fox sums it up well: "Power in a compulsive setting implies control, dominance and ruling of others and thus reinforces any basic inequalities already existing. Power in the compassionate context implies an equal distribution of power to all the people. This kind of power, namely an equally distributed one, will not corrupt."

Creativity, celebration, laughter and joy come with mature compassion, while the compulsive drive for more power, prestige, and possessions leaves one spiritually empty and emotionally crippled.

Gordon

Gordon, a very ambitious financial analyst, was totally obsessed with power and control when we first met. The brightest boy on the block had his star plummet as workaholism gradually eroded his judgment and efficiency. Gordon was a prime example of the dualistic thinker, and his rigid either-or ideas limited the way he saw everything. There were no greys, only black-and-white judgments. He consequently made several costly errors that undermined his early reputation with his company, and he had been passed over for two major promotions. Devastated because failure was foreign to his life experience, Gordon had been carrying his rage home.

Gordon's temper tantrums had the whole family traumatized. He relentlessly criticized his wife, Carolyn. Whenever she expressed an opinion that differed from his, either a blow-up or the silent treatment would follow from Gordon. Carolyn had suffered a great deal and had been ill for months.

Then Carolyn heard me speak on radio and recognized the symptoms of the workaholic breakdown. Gordon was still healthy enough to recognize that he needed help, but it was six months before his strong denial system broke down. He began to experience genuine guilt and shame for what he had done to his family. The couple were just beginning to share power and re-establish respect and trust in their relationship when Gordon's first temptation came.

Management had recognized signs of Gordon's recovery and was again ready to promote him. The lure was to a top-management job in the United States, a move that would restore his prestige and credibility in the company. It would also make him part of a well-acknowledged workaholic team. I told Gordon frankly that I felt he was in no shape to start pumping adrenalin and working crazy hours again. He was still too arrogant, and his children were not yet free from anxiety symptoms. Only the week before, Gordon had lashed out at one of the little girls in a fit of temper over a senseless thing. His wife still didn't trust his judgment, and she was reluctant to risk the small gains they had made towards intimacy.

Gordon did turn down the offer, supposedly out of concern for his family and his own health, but the career move had enough negatives of its own to make him cautious. The family settled in, prepared to consolidate the gains they were all making. Less than a month later, Gord sailed into my office, high on the news that there had been a better offer that would help fulfil dreams he had of doing international work. Power was again luring Gordon to tempt fate. The soul-searching and balancing act began all over again. "Ten years from now, will I regret it if I don't take this job now?" Carolyn, torn between wanting her husband to be happy and fulfilled and fearing for the survival of her family, battled with guilt and anger. "After all, isn't it time we came first in his life?"

In effect, Gordon's decision would steer the course his family would travel. Consensus, however, was necessary if this couple's marriage was to last. Previous unilateral decisions made by Gordon, such as buying a house without Carolyn's having seen it, had left his wife with no sense of power over her own destiny. If they could work through this challenge together and reach a shared decision, then their marriage would be able to survive any traumas that came their way. The temptations of power had come too soon, and Gordon's narcissism and control needs were still very strong. Humility was not yet one of Gordon's strengths.

Power, as we have seen, can be used for good or evil. Only if humility and compassion are maintained as well will the workaholic be in a position to control the direction that power takes him or her in. If feelings are continually dominated by ambitious thinking, then the ability to feel empathy and compassion for others will atrophy.

Next, we will explore how the loss of feelings takes place as the workaholic gradually ceases to function effectively. By understanding this breakdown syndrome, and recognizing where one is in the process, the workaholic can take steps to restore the healthy balance between feeling and thinking, and, like Carolyn and Gordon, be able to establish his or her family's welfare as first priority.

4.
The Breakdown Syndrome:
The Emotional Turmoil

"It's a sad, pathetic waste of lives — like watching someone die slowly of cancer! Emotionally, the kids and I are just exhausted by the trauma." Justine, a forty-year-old mother of three teenagers, sat across from me for almost an hour, grimly recounting how her husband's workaholism had led to the breakdown of her marriage. All her hopes for a happy, peaceful life with her family were dashed. "I've tried so hard to be cheerful and keep my sense of humour," she said with a weak smile. "It's just not funny, though." And, with that, the tears of frustration and hurt began to trickle down her cheeks.

Suddenly I wished that all those people who glibly laugh about being a workaholic could witness her pain. They would see that there's nothing laughable about a lonely marriage that ends in a bitter divorce.

For Justine, it was too late. Her husband still denied that he had a problem. For other families, there is still hope, but only if the work-aholic can recognize early enough that work has become an addiction that threatens the family as well as the self.

When does a hard worker become an addict? Why does work-aholism creep up on us by surprise, and why don't people recognize their own addiction? How do these intelligent "nice" people become emotionally crippled? Why are they so moody and irritable, and why do they say they are "confused"? What is their emotional turmoil all about? Why do they become so fearful and guilt-ridden, and suffer from chronic fatigue? And, finally, why is working less not a solution?

To answer these questions, we need to explore the psyche of the workaholic. Then, perhaps, we can learn to recognize the warning signs and symptoms of this addiction before it becomes too destructive. As the saying goes: "an ounce of prevention is worth a pound of cure."

TIMING OF THE BREAKDOWN

When does a hard worker become a workaholic? Changes in the workaholic's psyche take place gradually and almost imperceptibly over many years. The breakdown is internal, so is not readily observed. Once she recognized her own addiction, one usually over-controlled middle-aged executive became very excited and burst out: "You know, I've suddenly recognized that this has been going on for at least twenty years!" Later, she explained: "It's insidious — it creeps up on you ever so slowly. You wake up one day, and you look around you. Your life is a total disaster! I'm firmly convinced it's just like alcoholism!"

Many people — mostly men — in their forties and fifties say the gradual disintegration took place over a twenty-year period. Their families tended to be traditional. Their wives generally stayed home with the children and ran the household, providing the family with stability and giving the children a strong, consistent central figure to relate to. Unlike young women today, these wives accepted their role. Family activities revolved around the husband's work schedule, and no one thought to question priorities. Many male clients have admitted to me that their wives placed as low as fifth in importance on their list of priorities. No wonder so many of their wives felt unappreciated and became so anxious and depressed.

In these traditional families, the workaholic father can take out his frustrations at home because the family colludes with him to maintain an increasingly unhealthy system. The wife, by making excuses for her husband, protects him from the full consequences of his moods, his broken promises, his forgetfulness, and often his prolonged absences. It is a sad commentary on human nature, but the family does not question its normalcy and health until something goes wrong. You just assume, after all, that other families are not much different from your own.

Today, younger workaholics — male and female — describe a more rapid breakdown period of only five to ten years. It always surprises me, but almost inevitably the breakdown takes place over either a twenty-year period, or a five- or six-year period. Many younger workaholics are married to other workaholics and children are not in the picture yet. A typical "yuppie" couple will work full tilt all day at their respective jobs, but spend their evenings either in front of the TV in a state of exhaustion or driven by anxiety, rushing compulsively from cooking class to conversational French class, to investment group — always honing and perfecting their skills. Increasingly, time is spent apart, and their sexual life becomes almost non-existent. No wonder modern marriages are breaking down at such an alarming rate.

Carol Orsborn, in her book about her own battle with workaholism, *Enough Is Enough: Exploding the Myth of Having It All*, suggests that "cope, balance and juggle" are the three Rs of superwomanism. Orsborn points out that two paycheques allowed members of the largest, most educated work-force in history, the Baby Boomers, to establish easy lines of credit; buy big homes, cottages or condos; travel to Europe; compulsively consume the latest gadgets; and frequent the most "in" restaurants. With biological clocks ticking at the same time as careers are peaking, the modern "Super Mom" gets caught up in advancing her career, while still trying to accomplish all the tasks her mom did as a full-time homemaker. Fathers are now changing diapers and picking up children at day care. These same men are straining to compete in an impersonal world of corporate takeovers, attempting to meet demands for increased productivity and "bottom-line" financing. Plagued by anxiety, and always driving themselves to perform better, these workaholics compete and clash with fellow ego-building colleagues. Such clashes create only more tension in an already chaotic environment.

When I ask clients if they can pin-point the point at which the breakdown began, the older men especially remember prior feelings of being on top of the world. They had reached some sought-after goal, family life seemed on an even keel, and they were living in a lovely home. Self-congratulations and peer recognition bolstered these feelings of success. Claude, a forty-five-year-old corporate lawyer in a well-known law firm, recalls the day he felt he had reached the zenith of his career. His self-doubts and worries of ever being made a partner could now be set to rest. "I was on my way home on a busy Friday afternoon. I kept telling myself I should be feeling ecstatic, but an uneasy feeling rose from the pit of my stomach. The closer I got to home, the more nauseated I felt. From that day on, things started to go wrong at home." Then Claude added as an afterthought, "Or maybe it was only then that I took some time to notice!" The younger workaholics, I feel, are less able to be objective about themselves. They are still living upwardly mobile lives and are so engrossed in pursuing their goals that no time is taken to be reflective.

Although timing of the breakdown varies, the process itself follows a predictable path. The hard worker is proud of her fast rise in the academic or corporate world, and receives attention and accolades for her success. As the ego assumes an overriding importance in the psyche and builds unchecked, it becomes inflated with self-importance and "puffs up" to arrogance. The person becomes more ego-centred, self-focused, and self-absorbed. If this process continues unchecked for a long period of time, the individual may lose touch with reality, and may suffer some psychotic breaks. One poignant story told to me was of a young man who flipped out totally. He had been sent home because of severe depression. However, one day he suddenly appeared at the office with a teddy bear under one arm and a megaphone in his hand. The startled secretaries watched as he set himself up in the boardroom and started to broadcast that everyone must work harder. This case was extreme. Most workaholics manage to function with only periodic fits of anxiety or periods of depression, but frequently they can relate to no one intimately.

HOW DO WORKAHOLICS BECOME EMOTIONALLY CRIPPLED?

Someone who is a hard worker, but obsessive in his actions or driven to excel, is not necessarily a work addict. A workaholic cannot *not* work for any extended period of time without growing anxious. The long hours spent at work are only a sign that the person is not being effective. It may now take twelve hours to do what used to be done in eight. Working less is not a solution because it is what is happening in the inner psyche that produces the profound personality changes that cripple the workaholic. To illustrate this process, I will describe one personality type that is particularly prone to workaholism: the introverted thinker. These people process information by taking it in and forming their own subjective way of viewing the world. Because these people are introverted, and tend not to check with others, it is easy for them to get lost in a fantasy world where their ideas are tied to inner images rather than to reality. Such people are often indifferent to the opinions of other people and are prone to view their own ideas as "right," meaning for them, logical, rational, and fair. Humility is rarely one of their attributes. In *Personality Types: Jung's Model of Typology*, Daryl Sharp explains that introverted thinkers can be charming, but become less so the more they grow attached to their own ideas or inner images. "Then their convictions become rigid and unbending, their judgment cold, inflexible, arbitrary. In the extreme case, they may lose all connection with objective reality and so become isolated from friends, family and colleagues."

Maureen, a scientist and researcher working in a drug company, became so obsessed with following some obscure "pet" theory that she lost track of the overall picture and got bogged down in obsessive detail. Her colleagues could not understand the relevance of her findings to other research being done in the lab. She consequently became paranoid and secretive about her results, hoping to protect her work from peer review and criticism. Maureen became more unhappy and started to withdraw and isolate herself at home too. Stubborn and proud, she didn't want her husband to know her research was not going well and grant money for her lab was scarce. She needed a great deal of support, but instead made it impossible for people to understand what was going on. No one could get close enough to her to give her the support she needed.

Introverted thinkers are naturally stubborn and intense, and their concentration is narrowly focused. A narrow focus, of course, can allow a person to concentrate on one thing at a time to the exclusion of all else. The danger comes when solving the problem becomes the *only* focus of a person's life. Then the addiction to work gradually pushes him or her to work harder and longer to achieve power and control in the form of success. When the highly developed "superior" thinking function is overused, and obsessive thinking wears the person out, a crisis usually occurs causing the person's best function to stop working effectively. At this point, the psyche will compensate by seeking a correction. This correction may take the form of anxiety attacks or depression, both of which force feelings up to awareness in the form of emotionality. If people can take advantage of the crisis and learn to develop their "inferior" feelings into a positive, healthy function that can also be used to make wise decisions, then a whole new potential in themselves will be rediscovered. Feeling and thinking functions should support each other, thus creating a more balanced psyche.

Thinking, unfortunately, can overrun and flatten feeling. A person can feel as if he or she has been "run over by a bus" when logical, rational thought squashes sensitive, considerate opinions. This situation is easier to see when two personalities are interacting, for example, in a dialogue. However, thinking can dominate feeling within the individual too. Our society has honoured and revered thinking and rational thought and devalued feeling decisions based on what one appreciates and values. Fortunately, there is much evidence of a shift towards recognizing the importance of feeling values. In the past, men have depended on women to carry the feeling values for the couple, but women today want a sharing of intimacy, where both take responsibility for feelings.

The following diagram illustrates what happens in the psyche of the workaholic when thinking is worn out, and the breakdown symptoms become more severe.

As feeling is suppressed and ceases to function healthily on a conscious level in the workaholic, intuition, which is based on a sixth sense or "gut" feeling, also sinks into the unconscious and becomes ineffectual. Intuition sees things more globally and holistically — the forest and not the trees, the whole picture. It is future-oriented and goal-directed and loves ideas, theories, and symbolism. The ability to use intuition for brainstorming, problem-solving, and planning for the future is thus curtailed. The sensation function relates to all our senses. The positive side of sensation uses all the senses — sees each

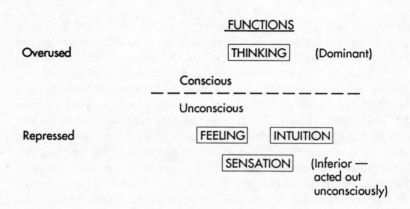

FUNCTIONS

Overused   THINKING   (Dominant)

Conscious
— — — — — — — — — — — — —
Unconscious

Repressed   FEELING   INTUITION

SENSATION   (Inferior —
acted out
unconsciously)

tree, is fascinated by details, facts, figures — and is past- and present-oriented. The negative side of sensation gets obsessive and picky about details, facts, and figures, and loses sight of the whole situation. Thus, the workaholic chooses one alternative and stubbornly argues to prove the point that he or she is certain is "right."

Ironically, many workaholics have become successful because of their original ideas and strong intuitive skills. However, when depression and anxiety overwhelm them, they act out of their less developed "inferior" sensation function. Workaholics then use all their senses, but not in the healthy way of being aware of sights, sounds, smells, taste, and touch. Instead, they become obsessed with small details.

Laughing in embarrassed recognition after hearing this explanation, one of my clients told me he remembered totally dominating conversations with endless tales of the intricacies of his latest schemes. "I used to bore people to death, telling them about every wrinkle of these hare-brained tactics I would plan out. I had lists a mile long of people to see and strategies that would work for each person. I can't believe I took everything to such extremes."

Neatness and order, in contrast, became Audrey's obsession. She was drying the dishes, she recalled, and stopped in mid-sentence to flick some cobwebs out of the pot lights in the kitchen with a tea towel. Ordinarily, intuitives would not notice such small detail as they look at things more globally. The movie *Diary of a Mad Housewife* portrayed the dramatic decline of a workaholic who took obsessiveness to an extreme.

The workaholic, as the breakdown progresses, sees only limited possibilities and rigidly adheres to what is known and safe. Addicts are prone to use dualistic thinking because it reduces the very complex into two simplistic choices. One must be right; the other wrong. There are very few greys in the world of the workaholic. At this stage, unlimited options are too confusing and upsetting. However, the answer often lies beyond the two options. Anne Wilson Schaef and Diane Fassel, in *The Addictive Organization*, point out that "in the addictive system, the continual moving back and forth between two choices serves to keep one stuck. Inevitably, neither of the two choices in a dualism looks desirable." I've seen it happen again and again in my office. One partner will argue, for example, that things would get better if only the spouse would be on time. This is presented as a concrete answer to their problem. "If you wouldn't be so rigid and uptight all the time, then I wouldn't be so nervous! I can't rush when I'm upset!" counters the other. They go back and forth between the two positions. No other compromises or solutions are sought.

When one's thinking becomes rigid and dogmatic, the unconscious, overloaded with repressed contrary information, will become increasingly powerful. The underdeveloped feeling function, dormant in the unconscious, also now begins to rumble. At such times, the workaholic becomes moody and irritable or withdraws and sulks. Because unconscious inferior functions in general tend to be negative, primitive, and childlike, the feelings that flood into awareness feel foreign and are experienced as disruptive, unpleasant, and quite unsettling. One client felt a keen envy when a competitor came up with a smart advertising gimmick, becoming totally irrational and furious about not thinking of it first. He went into a dark mood and became irritable and despondent. "I must be losing it," he said with a groan. It is important to note that this process may be quite unconscious, and the person may not know what he or she has said. If questioned later about his or her feelings, the person may be quite threatened.

When unconscious anxiety increases, there is a tendency to disown unwanted negative feelings and project them onto others, especially spouses and children. The workaholic wants to remain the Nice Guy or Gal, but explosive tempers and general irritability over trivial matters threaten this persona. The workaholic, not wanting to see her own moodiness and sarcasm, gets annoyed and blames her husband for his brusque, sharp response, which she, in fact, triggered in him. Later, fellow workers will bear the brunt of these unwelcome projections as the ego becomes more fragile, and the carefully built persona cracks.

THREE TYPES OF WORKAHOLICS

Although workaholics have certain characteristics in common, I have differentiated three types — the Controller, the Narcissistic Controller, and the Pleaser.

The Controller and the Narcissistic Controller

Controller workaholics are very independent, ambitious, driven, and intense. These people are energetic, need little sleep, enjoy keeping busy, and rarely relax. They can be charming and witty, and appear to be sociable, but they have few close friends. Secrecy and privacy are important to them, and sharing is not natural. They are impatient and impulsive. Many controllers are thinking types. Because they value independence so highly, they are often found in top-management positions or working for themselves.

When increasing anxiety heightens their insecurity, these hard-driving people become even more active and pump adrenalin all the time to keep up this high energy level. They go flat out until exhaustion sets in. Then they become immobilized and cease to function properly until the body is able to restore its energy. Stressed out, controllers begin to devalue things and put down other people, and become short-tempered, sharp, and blunt. They lash out, bully, become argumentative, or complain and lecture with quasi-logical thinking that does not quite make sense. As insecurity surfaces into consciousness, controllers become very critical and defensively project blame out onto others. Things are always the other person's fault. Controllers create an atmosphere that ranges from sullen, dark, and oppressive to hostile and destructive, as anger turns to rage and the workaholic devastates family members or fellow workers. The controller's chief defences are denial, rationalization, avoidance, and procrastination.

Controllers, normally independent and aloof people, become more dependent in the later stages of the breakdown, as they cease to function normally. Seeking approval becomes more important as insecurity and confusion threaten. Unfortunately, helpless feelings cause them to lash out and dump on the very people who are trying to be patient with them.

Sam, the vice-president of marketing for a big advertising firm, is having a great deal of trouble concentrating these days because Virginia, his wife, has threatened to leave if he won't go to counselling. She can't stand his lashing out at her in "these awful rages," as she calls them, and he can't remember saying what she tells him he has said. The kids are being obnoxious and doing crazy things to get his attention. Sam has no patience for any of this.

Lately, he has had to rely more and more on his assistant to cover for his growing inefficiency. Grace doesn't do things *his* way though. He has blown his cool too often, and criticized and barked at her until she has dissolved in tears. This just makes him more uncomfortable and his anxiety soars higher — if she quits, he is a goner!

This morning, Sam feels as if his head is sizzling, but he forces himself to keep going. Underneath, an acute panic reaction is building. It is taking all his energy just to keep functioning at work. He is having panic attacks more often and is beginning to realize he is out of control — an intolerable thought for him. Suddenly, unable to cope at all, he makes up some quick white lie and escapes to his car. His shirt is soaked through, and his legs feel like jelly. Sam has told no one about these attacks, and he forces himself to muster some energy to drive himself home. He lets himself in and lies on the bed, motionless but unable to relax. His heart continues to pound until he finally falls asleep in exhaustion. If Virginia only knew how frightened Sam is, she could be more supportive.

A second type, the more disturbed Narcissistic Controller, has similar reactions, but tends to resort to dissociation when stress climbs too high. Dissociation occurs when a person splits off and represses negative feelings about things, other people, and him or herself. Unwanted things cease to exist; people are ignored. The person does not remember that things have happened. These work-aholics are narcissistic and have not developed the capacity to truly love others unconditionally. They are the takers who manipulate others to serve their own ends. Stubborn and proud, they view image as everything.

Kathleen, a typical example of this type, appears arrogant and aloof, but still has managed to build up a very successful medical practice. Her patients all admire her and think she is an accomplished, competent clinician. However, they hate being kept waiting for hours in her small, dingy waiting room, where there is nothing to read but a battered old *Time* magazine. She secretly likes people to feel sorry for her, so shuns any display of wealth. Kathleen can be very charming, though, so all is usually forgiven. Ordinarily, she likes to impress the junior interns and tries to be "buddy-buddy" with them.

Lately, Kathleen has become more preoccupied and aloof, but is unaware of how she affects her staff and junior interns. She is consulting with people less and less often, and her lectures are real ego trips, full of "I, I, I." She's making rather odd, arbitrary decisions, too. If one of the interns challenges her opinion, Kathleen shuts herself off with a blank stare and acts like an automaton. Her body has become rigid, and she suffers ongoing back pain. Yesterday, she had a weird feeling that her body didn't belong to her. She put her hands to her face to make sure she was still there. Kathleen was frightened, but would never seek help as it might destroy her carefully developed persona. Instead, she spends more and more time closeted in her office, compulsively taking on more committee jobs. Committees make her feel important, but lately her angry outbursts have alienated other members. Above all else, she desires peer approval, but colleagues sense her protective reserve and respond with superficial politeness.

Kathleen's defences are extremely high, and if some major threat to her independence occurs, she may have a psychotic break. She will withdraw even farther, rationalize what has happened by distorting reality and then pull herself together again.

People like Kathleen live provisional lives, as their psyches are very fragile. Unfortunately, they rarely come for help as they get quite paranoid when upset. They don't trust others, because deep down they are living in an illusionary world where they are fine and others are the problem.

The Pleaser

Pleaser workaholics tend to be less ambitious, more sociable people who are keenly aware of other people and other people's needs. They enjoy being with others, but can be too dependent on them. They take middle-management jobs because feedback from others and the boss's seal of approval are important to them. They tend to avoid making waves and will act out passively rather than risk rejection and disapproval with overt anger. When things start to go wrong, emotions build up inside. Sometimes anger gets misdirected to someone or something else. Fear and resentment make them overly sensitive to criticism, and some become paranoid. Instead of verbalizing their hurt and confusion, pleasers absorb their anger and feel guilty. Since guilt is self-anger, it only adds to their distress. They become depressed, moody, and more distant and uninvolved. They may walk away to avoid their own anger or to get away from others' anger. Some unconsciously even position themselves near a door in an uncomfortable situation. Many carry grudges for long periods of time, and unresolved anger arises each time a related issue surfaces. They have elephant-memories, and become "historical" in listing their complaints. Like a slow volcanic eruption, passive–aggressive anger, both conscious and unconscious, bubbles away as the workaholic senses the increasing insecurity and hidden rage building up inside.

This lack of inner control and the underlying inferiority feelings increase as more and more problems are avoided, and more effort is needed to cover the growing inner anxiety. Clients have told me of explosive rages in which they frightened themselves and their families by smashing objects, throwing furniture, or hitting a wife or child. Repression, projection of blame, obsessive thinking, as well as denial, rationalization, and procrastination, are common defence mechanisms for the pleasers.

When Pleaser workaholics do communicate their negative feelings and thoughts, it is usually through passive–aggressive anger. This type of anger is expressed in the following unhealthy ways: (1) they physically or emotionally withdraw; they tune out of a conversation, listen selectively, change the subject, distract themselves; they become bored, or boring, or yawn; (2) they use subtle put-downs and sarcasm; they lecture, preach, or make generalizations to avoid taking responsibility for stating their own feelings; (3) they procrastinate; they use fatigue as an excuse; they become indifferent and write people off; they refuse to take responsibility for the relationship; (4) they patronize; they are overly friendly or polite or phony and insincere; (5) they forget; they lie or avoid honesty; they promise and then renege; they are unreliable; they avoid, rationalize, and deny; (6) they are shy and refuse to give any part of themselves; they are jealous and possessive, claiming ownership of and seeing others as extensions of themselves.

George, our Pleaser, is a supervisor in the claims department of a well-known insurance company. He tries to be everybody's friend, and tends to be overly helpful, putting his nose into everyone else's business. It's getting harder and harder for George to stay cheerful. Work is becoming overwhelming because it seems endless. Everyone keeps coming to him for help. There are so many interruptions, George forgets what he is supposed to be doing. His own work is in disarray. Every night he goes home exhausted and collapses on the chesterfield in front of the TV. He hardly notices what he is watching, but when his wife and kids nag him to do things, he gets furious. They are giving up hope, and find it easier just to leave him out of things altogether. He doesn't even know where his kids are half the time. He forgets what his wife told him two minutes ago, and he is beginning to worry that he has Alzheimer's. His eyes fill up with tears at the oddest times, and he feels sorry for himself most of the time.

People like George really do believe they are "nice" people because they work so hard to please others. It is difficult for them to identify their passive and hidden anger until it erupts in rages. They resist believing that their behaviour is often manipulative and self-serving rather than truly generous.

Workaholic families suffer greatly during the breakdown stage. Whether or not the workaholic's anger is overt, passive–aggressive or totally buried through repression, it will be painfully obvious when anger does surface. The wives and children, unable to address this subtle or sometimes blatant abuse, become "victims" of the workaholic system. They too suffer severe anxiety, insecurity, and low self-esteem. Many do not even recognize these destructive patterns as abusive because they have grown up believing this is normal behaviour and have come to expect it and feel helpless. This is their reality, their world.

THE MAJOR SIGNS OF WORKAHOLIC BREAKDOWN

Prevention is an important concept to keep in mind as we look at the process the breakdown follows. If you recognize the major warning signs early enough, negative effects can be reversed before the addiction causes further emotional damage. As Lyle Longelaws, a First Nations elder, says, "Before the healing can take place, the poison must be exposed."

Awareness is essential to recovery. Let's look at some of the signs of breakdown. If you recognize any of these warning signs in yourself, your spouse, or a friend, understanding them now can lead to recovery later.

- Are you aware of increasing obsessive or compulsive behaviours?
- Are you becoming cross-addicted to other addictive substances or behaviours?
- Are fears eroding your self-confidence and increasing your anxiety?
- Are you suffering from periodic spells of extreme fatigue?
- Is guilt damaging your self-esteem?

Workaholic breakdown is what these problems are all about! Let's look at them individually.

Obsessive and Compulsive Symptoms

Other people usually recognize when you become anxious. Ask for feedback from those close to you. As they become increasingly aware of their feelings, clients report the following behaviour: repetitious acts of nervousness, such as drumming of fingers on a desk or table or finger snapping; nervous tics; twitching of the mouth; grimacing; clenched jaws; gritting of teeth in sleep; and frequent sighing. Others become aware that they make clicking sounds, or cough nervously at the end of a statement, as John Turner was prone to do in public speeches. Some mannerisms become chronic and can cause physical damage. One client's grinding of his teeth in his sleep led to massive dental work to correct a faulty bite, while another chronically uptight physician suffered neurological pain from locking and tensing her jaw.

Many overcontrolled workaholics become compulsively neat and straighten things they would not notice ordinarily. Pens and pencils are lined up, piles of papers must be stacked just so, and some obsessively insist that everything be kept out of sight. Other workaholics develop superstitious habits to counteract their anxiety. They must add up columns three times for good luck! Reports must be rewritten at least twice. They cannot go home without their briefcases, even after working late at the office. The briefcase becomes like a child's security blanket; they feel more at ease if it is there. A Nice Gal, Charlene, stressed out because she couldn't say no, threw up her arms in mock despair: "My dream each day is to just once get through my crazy list, cross off each and every item one by one, and then take off for home without my damn briefcase. But, by afternoon, the office is an absolute mad-house, I get miles behind, and it just never happens! Home it comes, and it sits in the front hall haunting me 'til I can't resist its pull. You know," added Charlene, "I'm actually afraid not to take it home. Sort of like a superstition or something."

I notice that in my waiting room workaholics often have their briefcases open if they arrive early. In my office, the briefcase is opened again, a notebook comes out, and ideas and thoughts are noted down throughout the session. Some do this because anxiety or depression hampers their ability to remember. For others, time and efficiency are enormously important, as are a sense of a need to hurry and of urgency.

A rigid body often reflects the inner dynamics of a constricted psyche. Workaholics frequently develop back problems, and their movements appear stiff and machine-like. Functioning mainly from the neck up, and ever absorbed in their thoughts and ideas, workaholics are not receptive to the feeling signals sent through nerves and muscles to the brain for processing. Oblivious to increase or decrease in adrenalin or to tightly crossed arms and legs, they cannot distinguish or identify their unconscious feelings. The facial muscles tend to be taut, and jaws are often locked and set, especially as the breakdown progresses.

Claustrophobic episodes are not uncommon during the breakdown phase because the workaholic has become so tightly overcontrolled. The heart begins to pound, adrenalin pumps, and there is a sense of urgency or of being out of control. Garth, a hard-driving electronics executive, told me about his two worst-possible scenarios. "It would be to be placed in a simulated space capsule at Disneyland, ready to be shot out into space. My hands and feet would be strapped in readiness for the take-off. Even telling you this throws me into a tail spin!" He laughed. "The other one that really freaks me out is imagining myself lying out in a coffin, all decked out in my tuxedo. Someone has just put the lid on to see if it fits!" The more anxious Garth became, the more often he thought of these nightmares. Even sleeping in a tent at a camp site with his kids became almost unbearable. He would break out in a cold sweat in elevators if he was having a bad day at work. Flying on business became impossible, so he journeyed by train instead. He wondered how long he would be able to keep his job if management found out about his flying phobia. His supervisor was helping him keep the secret from his boss, but how long could he hide his disability?

Workaholics love lists. Most well-organized people make lists, but workaholics use them compulsively. Their drive to categorize, organize, and define, combined with their perfectionism, can lead to pathological orderliness. Some workaholics must check off items on a list before a job is considered complete. In psychotherapy, Lois, a high-school teacher, described herself as an "inveterate hopeless list-maker." I asked her to draw a cartoon of herself making such a list. While drawing, Lois mused: "I'd be writing a list to keep track of my lists! — a continuous list." She was asked to work on her need to handle anxiety through busy work, and gradually started to feel less compulsive. A month later, Lois was still making lists, but they were simple, not obsessive, "not the ridiculous two-page lists with forty items." Lists were a defence against acting. "I gave myself artificial deadlines — I had to do five things by the weekend. I was a good person if I finished a certain number of things. I set myself up by breaking it down into so many tiny things. I might finish three, but there were still thirty-nine more! I do have an organizational ability, but I can see it was getting a bit nuts!" Obsessive list-making only added to Lois's escalating anxiety. Had she not got her anxiety under control, she would have eventually been immobilized by the need for longer and longer lists.

Retirement often causes panic attacks in the workaholic. What will he do with himself? He has no hobbies and very few friends. The big question becomes "What is next?" Pierre, a sixty-four-year-old physician, handled his anxiety by drawing up an elaborately detailed list of work projects he planned to do at the cottage. From then on, weekends at the cottage saw him up and out by 6:00 a.m. Pierre worked incessantly the whole day, hardly even stopping for lunch. "I even stopped going to the beach. I know it sounds funny, but I had to cross off the items I did get done. It gave me a lot of satisfaction to chart my progress this way. It was like giving myself a report card or a gold star!" Other clients develop weekly rituals, such as adding up bank balances every Friday night to reassure themselves they will be financially stable after retirement. It is a form of superstitious behaviour — "If I perform my rituals, everything will turn out all right. If I don't, then fears of what might happen immobilize me."

Superstition also leads workaholics to an obsessive need to rewrite letters, proposals, or grants before considering them finished. Just one last change, one more paragraph, one more draft. Nothing is ever finished for these anxious perfectionists. Anxiety interferes with both thinking and feeling functions, so judgments become irrational and of poor quality. No wonder it now takes twelve hours to do what was done in six when performance efficiency was high.

Homemakers too can be obsessive workaholics. Talk about frantic! These Super-Moms organize their children's lives according to a hectic, frantic schedule. Isaac must be driven to lessons and endless activities. Sarah's projects and homework involve the whole family and several trips to the local library. Added stimulation and expensive entertainments are considered necessities, not frills. Too much "free time" makes these families anxious. The calendar is crammed full of notations. Time out together as a couple takes second place because children's activities occupy all their free time.

Do you recognize any of these warning signs? Obsessions won't go away until the source of the anxiety is understood and healthier responses to stress are learned.

Cross-Addiction Symptoms

Some work addicts function well during the work week when tasks are defined by their jobs. Little initiative is needed when patients wait to be cured, teeth need to be fixed, and work projects must be completed by deadline. But, on weekends, the structure dictated by the job is missing. Dr. Jay Rohrlich, in *Work and Love: The Crucial Balance*, tells of one of his medical colleagues who was addicted to amphetamines on weekends and vacations. Work provided the "push" the physician needed during the week, "but he lacked sufficient self-definition or desire on weekends to take the initiative and identify what he wanted to do." In the personal sphere, this man was helpless, lost, and very dependent. He always deferred to his wife's wishes, rationalizing that he was being accommodating and kind. She, in turn, felt burdened and was resentful about carrying all the responsibility for planning and organizing their social life.

As dependency increases and becomes more apparent, workaholics will become passive–aggressive. Resentful of their own dependency, yet growing more irresponsible as efforts at decision-making fail, they soon experience irritability. They blame others for anything that goes wrong, and lash out in an obnoxious or sarcastic manner. Overly passive workaholics will go along with whatever is planned, but will then sabotage the evening. They may sleep through much of the symphony or read a business journal or mark papers while "listening." The stubborn type refuses to make any decisions at all about how the evening is spent or drinks to excess to drown growing resentment.

Miserable and unhappy as the breakdown progresses, the workaholic shuts down and no longer knows what he would like to do, where she would like to go. Sense of self is lost as the work persona becomes a fuzzy and confused image. At such times, cross-addictions to work and alcohol develop. Some keep alcohol hidden in their desks; others wait for the weekend to drink themselves into oblivion. Smoking to excess is a common distraction from growing insecurity. Even those who don't ordinarily smoke start. Substance abuse is common as well — drugs, food or caffeine are common cross-addictions. Others become addicted to sex, relationships or "getting high" on adrenalin by engaging in frantic activities or overscheduling their days.

Weekends become shorter and shorter, partly because work schedules expand with inefficiency, but also because too much free time leads to "thank God it's Monday" thinking. The weekend's tranquillity and lack of regular schedule cause anxiety and depression, and black moods and irritability fester. The easiest solution for the workaholic is to work weekends to alleviate the pressure, or to make an excuse to go back to the office to get another "fix" of adrenalin when anxiety gets high. When working overtime is discouraged in a company, workaholics must substitute other addictive behaviours to help drown out weekend anxiety.

Freeing the workaholic from cross-addictions makes the process of recovery more complicated. If alcohol or drugs are the added problem, then help from treatment centres or Alcoholics Anonymous is a must. As soon as you become aware that workaholism is a problem, confront your denial defences and honestly examine your lifestyle and habits.

Chronic Fears

Behind every obsession is some fear. The source of the workaholic's breakdown is a "chicken and egg" issue. Does he have a long history of insecurity and failure because of personal inadequacies? Or has the single-minded pursuit of personal success and society's approval led to inadequacies in other areas of life?

If you are a workaholic, or are living with someone who is, it is important to be able to recognize those life events that trigger crises. The family may have more objectivity than the overinvolved workaholic. Any situation where criticism or rejection is present has this potential. Annual employee evaluations, censorship of ideas or projects, threatened demotions, forced transfers, or the fear of being let go can set up various levels of panic reactions. Even if the intensity of work lets up because of poor markets or sales, the individual may personalize the company's failures to produce, and inner security can be threatened.

Let's look at the six fears most commonly cited by workaholics that cause anxiety.

1. *Fear of Failure*
As children, perfectionists were rewarded for "doing" and "perform-

ing." Their families' conditional love dictated that they were "good" only if their behaviour won the parents' nod of approval. Sometimes sibling rivalry also drives the future workaholic to strive to outshine a brother or sister. Sometimes parents see the children as extensions of themselves and create unrealistic expectations for performance that the child cannot satisfy. They may wish the child to do things they never did. The unwritten message is that the child must be a credit to them.

The perfectionist's life tends to be relatively free of failures since these people strive hard to excel. They have not learned, as others have, that failing is not the end of the world. When life throws them a curve and they finally do fail at something, the experience can be totally devastating.

University can be a trying time for perfectionists. High-school students in the top 5 percent of their class embark on higher education full of confidence, ready to take on the world. University, however, pits them against the brightest and the best, and they face the possibility of failure for the first time in their lives. Rather than fail, these students drive themselves relentlessly. Enormous energy is spent obsessively studying, staying in libraries late into the night in a frantic effort to "catch up." I suspect many student suicides may reflect a failure to recover former glory.

Some don't face failure until later. Mark was financially strapped after the bankruptcy of his family business, a popular chain of hardware stores. Celebrated as a yuppie success story, Mark had become so arrogant that he overestimated the potential market. Expansion become his obsession, and branch after branch opened to great fanfare. His strong fear of future failure caused Mark to become severely depressed. He was still unclear about what had gone wrong and what he would do now. "I'm trying to get to a state where I can *exist* again," he said. "Right now, I'm trying to survive and protect myself, period!" Mark needed to recognize that the failure of his business would not make him a "bad" person.

Even promotions can lead to failure situations. Hard-working, ambitious workaholics often get pushed up the ladder to a level beyond their competency. More senior jobs often require excellent "people skills" — communication techniques, diplomacy, tact, sensitivity, empathy, and an understanding of what is needed in mediation. Many workaholics lack these skills, especially the emotionally crippled who are unable to respond to others' needs.

Peggy, a radio broadcaster, was under stress in her new challenging position and was terrified about the added responsibility. She had spent the weekend riveted by the televised coverage of the Calgary Olympics. She identified with every one of the Canadian athletes. "I'm glad those people wanted to win so badly," she said admiringly. "The Olympics are held only once in four years, though!" She hesitated, and her voice broke: "The difference is, I have to do it every day!" Facing the possibility of failure on a daily basis would be stressful to anyone. For a workaholic like Peggy, however, it can become incapacitating.

Declining decision-making capabilities feed into self-doubts, which hinder the workaholic's need to increase productivity, expand markets, introduce new products, take over competitors, or discover new avenues of research. If the workaholic "rests his oars" for a moment, he will sink into failure. "Hooked" on work, obsessively worrying even when not at work, the workaholic becomes immersed in the moment, and loses touch with objectivity and long-term goals. Fears of failure haunt her as she loses power and the competitive edge that gave her her former feelings of power and omnipotence.

To get past the fear of failure, the workaholic needs to become more realistic about setting goals. Idealism and perfectionism need to be tempered with more realistic views of what constitutes a job well done. Values will change when feelings are functioning fully and people become more important than the trappings of success.

2. *Fear of Boredom*

The constant need to be "doing" and "performing" covers up the workaholic's growing anxiety. To avoid confronting what is going on inside psychologically, and outside in his environment, he gets into what I call the "gerbil-wheel syndrome." Once on the wheel, the workaholic cannot get off and must constantly go faster and faster. This process is similar to the alcoholic's need for an ever greater quantity of stimulant to cover increasing anxiety.

Also, the denial system works best with lots of distractions. "Doing" or "making" something implies goal-directedness and gives one a sense of purpose and accomplishment. Any enforced rest, such as an illness, a long vacation or future retirement, is feared because it would deny the workaholic his "fix" or drug. Workaholics will not allow themselves long periods of total relaxation. Instead, they plan brief weekend jaunts or a week's holiday crammed so full of activities there is no time to contemplate or to evaluate the purpose of life.

Listening to Elsie talking about the three months she was planning to take off to "find herself" and recover from the severe fatigue her workaholism had caused in her, I thought of a new book title — *The Fear of NOT Flying*! "I am so scared of the time I won't have this job. I'm terrified of being bored. The contrast in my life then and now will be so dramatic, the different levels of energy so extreme!" We talked about whether she could ever give herself permission to be bored, to break through the threshold of anxiety, to go over this hurdle to discover another underdeveloped part of herself. She needed time to truly relax, and to begin the search for a calm, centred self. Narrowly focused workaholics ironically become what they fear: boring people.

Workaholics rarely stay home from work when they are sick. Even broken bones do not keep them down for long. If forced to stay home, either they become irritable, demanding attention and sympathy, or they withdraw into themselves and suffer their anxiety and discomfort silently. After a radio interview I did, the staff decided to book a self-confessed "happy workaholic" for the next day's show. (One wonders whether, had I been talking about heroin addiction, they would have been so eager to feature a happy addict? There are many workaholics in radio; perhaps the subject hit a nerve.) This man admitted that he got very restless after holidays lasting four or five days. "By the end of the week, I was really antsy and had to leave early." He had probably never allowed himself to get bored, and his holidays got shorter as the breakdown symptoms became more severe. He then cheerfully suggested that workaholism had improved his health. "I don't get colds. I don't eat vegetables, not much meat, and I don't eat fruit. I should be dead! I had the flu last year, but it was because the dentist did a root canal and he weakened me." True to form, it is always the other guy's fault!

Mid-life often represents the "tailing off of achievement" for the workaholic, according to Dr. Jay Rohrlich, in *Work and Love: The Crucial Balance*. It is a time when incomes and promotions hit a plateau. The workaholic has moved up from the base of the corporate hierarchy. With fewer top jobs available the higher he goes in the hierarchy, the workaholic's sense of self grows tenuous without the reinforcement of future advancement and the external symbols of prestige and power that go with it. "Time keeps passing, is lost, and we need more and more signs of accomplishment to master its loss," says Dr. Rohrlich. Retirement presents a more extreme identity crisis. With no solid works to preserve the past, no concrete signs of self-definition, no external structure, no specific goals, and no ulterior purpose, Dr. Rohrlich says, many people experience retirement as a stage in the death of the self.

To overcome the fear of boredom, the workaholic needs to put energy into a wider variety of interests. Hobbies and sports, for example, often expose one to a new group of people. They, in turn, expose the workaholic to fresh ideas and interests.

3. *Fear of Laziness*
Fear of boredom is closely tied in with the fear of laziness. The workaholic does not allow himself to get bored long enough to find out if he is lazy! Marilyn Machlowitz, in *Workaholics: Living with Them, Working with Them*, suggests that workaholics suspect that "deep down inside they are actually lazy. They keep driving themselves because they think that if they let up, natural laziness will do them in." In fact, this fear of laziness may be compensating for their overly developed sense of responsibility. Fears of being thought lazy drive the workaholic away from relaxation or from time to just let go and "veg," or be silly and frivolous, or simply just have fun. Life must remain serious and goal-directed, lest temptation prove distracting. They *must* succeed at all costs!

To counteract their fear of laziness, many workaholics take on physical exercise. They even do two things at once while keeping fit to distract themselves from their worries. Gary Lautens in his *Toronto Star* column "Do You Suffer From This Dreaded Disease?" describes a training room at the downtown Y. Sweaty men pedal away on exercise bikes and read the business section of the newspaper instead of pretending they are on the last leg of the Tour de France. Everyone is doing more than one thing at a time. He uses the examples of drivers using car-phones; walkers listening to Walkmans; commuters catching up on paper work on the Go train. Even his wife, he jokingly adds, at the same time as she is throwing her back out reorganizing furniture is learning a second language from a tape playing in the background.

An article in *Vanity Fair* (October 1988) by Tony Schwartz shows a picture of *USA Today* publisher Cathy Black dashing to board a waiting helicopter. The caption reads: "Cathy Black commutes between D.C. (office, husband, son) and all fifty states, pumping up advertisers. Her mail is Federal Expressed to her. Her home is hooked up to the office computer. Her computerized schedule booked through 1990."

Recognizing the fear of laziness is difficult because the workaholic often also suffers from chronic fatigue, and looks like a "couch potato." Depression also causes some workaholics to oversleep, and is misinterpreted as laziness.

4. *Fear of Discovery*
"There are two kinds of people: those who have dreams about being discovered and those who have nightmares about it" — so says the "Morning Smile" in the *Globe and Mail* (April 25, 1989). As the workaholic becomes more inefficient and confused, she worries more and more about the visibility of her mistakes. She knows it is taking longer and longer to do her reports. She just can't concentrate. Her boss's phone suddenly sounds louder, and the typewriter outside her office must be on the blink too. She keeps looking out the window as claustrophobic feelings increase. Her own secretary, a co-dependent in the workaholic system, must cover for her poor memory and inability to concentrate. Even the simplest decisions seem monumental at times. Her persona of professional competence is cracking.

"I feel like a phony, not real sometimes," Terry, an agitated career woman, had told me weeks ago. She constantly worried about whether people would see behind her mask of self-assurance. One afternoon, she phoned, in a complete state of alarm: "I'm having the most bizarre feelings. It's as if I don't exist. I can't feel my body! I'm looking down at my legs, but it's as if they belong to someone else. I feel hollow and empty. You've got to help me! Can I come to see you right now?" This depersonalization and the loss of personal identity occur when the persona assumed by a person is breaking down. Dr. Carl Jung explains the process this way: "Through his more or less complete identification with the attitude of the moment, he at least deceives others, and also himself, as to his real character. He puts on a mask, which he knows corresponds with his conscious intentions, while it also meets with the requirements and opinions of his environment, so that first one motive then the other is in the ascendant. This mask, viz. the ad hoc adopted attitude, I have called the persona, which was the designation given to the mask worn by the actors of antiquity" (from Dr. Robert Campbell, *Psychiatric Dictionary*).

Overcontrolling becomes even more important when the workaholic fears being discovered. No one must find out, and to delegate would be to hand over power and leave one more vulnerable to discovery. One way to keep control in one's hands is to keep everyone else off balance. Organizational psychologist Dr. Peter Stephenson, in "Management by Mayhem," an article in *Report on Business* (May 1989), refers to one executive who preferred "to keep his subordinates off balance, uncertain of their authority." Memos he sent were vague as to lines of authority, and everyone was preoccupied for six months, wondering who was in charge, where their authority stopped and started. This situation allowed this addict to change the rules at the last moment. Since he retained the power to veto any decision, he kept his power intact.

In contrast, some workaholics love to delegate. They take on ever-increasing responsibility to feel more powerful and to prop up their sagging egos. They can't risk saying no and letting others know they are stressed out. So, they take on more, and then delegate large parts of the jobs to others. These workaholics end up stretched incredibly thin, but amazingly still search for more projects and more power. The game goes on until they crash.

Workaholics worry constantly that they do not measure up to their peers, that they will be found out or found wanting. Some dare not be away from work for any period of time lest the other staff find them dispensable. So, they take only short holidays, often cancel at the last minute if their work is not caught up, or refuse to take holidays at all. Wives tell me that their husbands phone in every day they are away to check with secretaries and colleagues. They do not want to discover that the company may be able to get along without them. The reality, however, is that fellow workers welcome such reprieves. The pressure-cooker atmosphere workaholics create eases in their absence.

Secretaries relax and celebrate some freedom. It is often a time to let off steam and to complain openly about the boss.

Workaholics are often secretive and will withhold essential information from others to maintain the myth that they are irreplaceable and indispensable. Guarding privacy is one way of staying in control. They fear others will take over their work and will do it better, or the work itself will be found to be obsolete. They even balk at interference from people with a perfect right to intervene, or resist writing out job descriptions that might limit or restrict their power.

Robert, a distinguished-looking entrepreneur, pointed out that, in his industry, "fast track" information is available in a continual stream. Letting information out to the "lesser gods" in the organization, such as junior executives, enhances his own status and reputation as Mr. Nice Guy. However, he cautions that people must be secretive with information when potential organizational rivals are concerned in the transactions. The workaholic must be aware of who is receiving what information at all times if he is to maintain his power base. All that detail adds more pressure and could cause paranoia in some at later stages of the breakdown.

If other people see through the workaholic's mask of efficiency, the fragile ego may be bombarded by questions that expose the workaholic's mistakes and avoidance of responsibility. But if the workaholic recognizes this fear early enough, then he can seek help before dissociation and paranoia overwhelm.

5. *Fear of Self-Discovery*

Self-discovery is even scarier for workaholics. One morning in my office, Penny, a mother of three and an ambitious personnel manager, realized that the fear of discovery she was experiencing at the time of a major promotion was, in fact, really a deep-seated fear of self-discovery. Penny didn't want to "rock the boat" and disturb the "Good Gal" image she held of herself. Her frantic work schedule kept her from facing who she was, separate from what she did. Finally Penny's unhappiness became unbearable, and she got up the courage to confront her weaknesses and realized just how fragile her mask was. "I can't keep this front up any longer. I'm really play-acting that I feel good about myself. It puts an incredible pressure on me to always stay up."

She went on to tell me how she felt when she was down. "Yester-day, I wanted to slink into my office, close the door, and just stay there. But I know others are out there talking and watching, and somehow they are going to find out. People notice me more now that I'm manager." Later Penny's new-found confidence allowed her to feel comfortable with peers and management alike, and she stopped worrying about her image.

Addicts typically form their definition of self by guessing how others see them. Workaholics, too, judge their success by how other people perceive them. This external frame of reference leaves them very vulnerable, especially as confidence erodes and negativity in-creases. The workaholic, progressively more out-of-touch with his own feelings, does not know what he wants and is unable to validate his own feelings about himself. Ego boundaries are blurred as to where he stops and others begin. Self-centred, but without a clear sense of self, the workaholic finds it difficult to distinguish and affirm the separateness of significant others. Ironically, the lack of insight does not stop the workaholic from problem-solving and telling other members of the family what is best for them! Tragically, children pick up on the faulty judgment and confused thinking. One frustrated young high-school student, Michael, lashed out furiously at his father: "My old man thinks he knows it all! 'When I was your age,' he says. What a bunch of garbage! He went on and on the other day, and I didn't have the slightest clue whether he was talking about me or him. What he was telling me was so garbled it made no sense at all!" Michael was probably quite right. His father had probably lost his ability to differentiate himself from others.

Dr. Scott Peck, in *The Road Less Traveled*, points out that if people do not begin the "search for self " at times of crises in their lives, they will continue to ego build. Because the workaholic is so centred on ego-building through "doing" and "performing," when fears and self-doubt escalate, this journey of exploration seems a very arduous one. Narcissistic workaholics can rarely sustain this search because their denial system is so strong, and their sense of self so tenuous.

I drew this diagram to help my clients understand Dr. Peck's concept of the curve of entropy. In medical terms, explains Dr. Peck, the physical curve of entropy begins at birth, hits a high at optimum

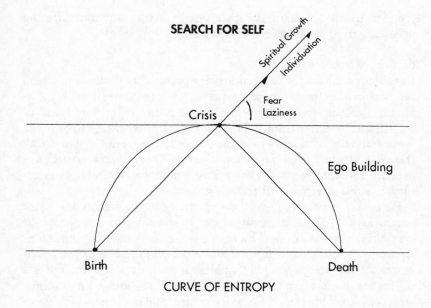

physical growth, and then curves down in an arc as the body deterio-
rates and loses its strength, and death occurs.

A similar psychic downward curve occurs, I believe, when the ego-
building person becomes more self-centred, self-absorbed, and out of
touch with others and with reality. At this point, the workaholic is in
danger of suffering a psychological death. The alternative path is to
use the crisis — which may take the form of a depression or physical
illness — to discover the self, and eventually the centre of self, the
soul. This is the process of individuation, which is a lifetime task and
has no upward limit. You can never learn enough about yourself or
others. Self-discipline, not laziness, is essential for this painful journey of self-confrontation.

Dr. Peck believes that laziness is original sin, and laziness and fear
of pain prevent people from growing and discovering their true self,
separate from what they do. I would add that, unless you gain insight
into what is wrong with you psychologically, then true change is not
possible. The workaholic, overwhelmed by fears and high anxiety, is

tempted to opt for laziness rather than risk the pain and suffering necessary to journey towards wholeness.

6. *Fear of Persecution*

Paranoia, or the fear of persecution, is a personality disorder in which the person affected is "hypersensitive, rigid and unwarrantably suspicious, jealous, and envious. He often has an exaggerated sense of self-importance, must always be right and/or prove others to be in the wrong, and has a tendency to blame others and to ascribe evil to them" (Dr. R. Campbell, *Psychiatric Dictionary*). These characteristics understandably interfere with the person's ability to maintain satisfactory, healthy interpersonal relations.

Paranoia can be very powerful and can make you feel, as one client put it, as if "part of an army is out to get you, to disapprove of everything you have done." Increased self-doubts and extreme defensiveness often lead to such persecution phobias in advanced stages of workaholism. Jerry, a highly ambitious corporate lawyer, felt his colleagues did not like him and were trying to sabotage his committee's decisions. However, his wife, Laurie, told me she had felt there was genuine respect and affection being shown him at functions she attended with him. A year later, however, Laurie began to notice the same people were leaving them alone. She overheard talk of parties they had not been invited to, and she began to wonder what was wrong. Paranoia is almost a self-fulfilling prophecy in that what the addict fears does eventually come to pass. The persona cracks, and the depressed or anxious workaholic "acts in" or "acts out" and alienates or offends the very people he or she so wants to impress!

Unfortunately, when the spouse attempts to confront the workaholic's secretive avoidance of truth or asks why something outrageous was said, the workaholic feels deceived, betrayed, or persecuted. Workaholics resent criticism at the best of times, but when paranoia is high, such confrontations are met with hostility and suspicion. Often the spouse is simply trying to hold onto his own reality, and confirm his own experiences. This search for truth is intended to be caring and supportive, but the overly sensitive workaholic feels only criticism. This dynamic becomes horrific for all concerned, as home is no longer a safe sanctuary. The concerned spouse now becomes the "enemy," someone else to mistrust, who threatens the workaholic's need for independence and her own unique reality. Secrecy and privacy become necessary to protect this nebulous inner sense of false reality. True intimacy is not possible in this environment. Isolated and confused, the workaholic tends to magnify minor slights and distorts everyday happenings. No reality checks are sought from those who could offer objectivity and restrain the growing suspicions and fantasies. The spouse often feels helpless and grows depressed as caring is misinterpreted and twisted around to mean something negative.

If paranoid feelings persist over time, a full-blown paranoid condition will develop in which psychotic breaks will occur more frequently. Chronic delusions are a central feature. When something upsetting happens, the paranoid goes inside and depends on herself for both stimulation *and* reinforcement. She alone confirms her own idiosyncratic view of the situation. Feeling powerful and superior once again, she presents her "correct" beliefs in a rational and systematic way. She is "right," and others are disturbed. Her ego is intact again, and for a while she can function "normally" because order has been restored in her own mind.

While all the fears are unsettling, it is obvious that paranoia is the most disturbing. People who are paranoid are difficult to help because they grow to distrust people and to attribute negative motivation to them. Therapists are no exception. At the first sign of persistent paranoid thoughts, the workaholic should seek psychological help immediately. This condition makes recovery very difficult, if not impossible. If paranoia becomes severe, improvements in functioning will be limited to trying to help the paranoid share fears and to test reality with others. One hopes that psychotic breaks will be less frequent, but these people may live a provisional life at best. Prevention is all-important here.

Chronic Fatigue

Throughout the breakdown, workaholics suffer from periodic bouts of fatigue, which eventually can become chronic and totally debilitating. Fatigue can take the form of physical and emotional exhaustion or can be covered up by hyperactivity.

The introvert is especially prone to psychasthenia, a term Dr. Carl Jung defines as "a malady characterized on the one hand by extreme sensitivity and on the other by great proneness to exhaustion and chronic fatigue" (in C. Jung, *Psychological Types*). Claudette is a perfect example. "On weekends I completely collapse and literally do nothing. Last Saturday, I lay on the sofa for twelve hours, too tired to even get up to eat. I was too exhausted even to sleep. I feel like a zombie, and frankly, it is very frightening!"

Tension and chronic fatigue are a sign that conflict within the workaholic's psyche has heightened. When one is constantly fearful, the body, the mind, and the soul all become progressively rigid. Often muscles in the neck, shoulders, back, and face are chronically tensed up. This physical stress, along with emotional turmoil, leave the workaholic drained and exhausted. He begins to fall asleep anywhere, any time, and has trouble keeping his eyes open. Some become "couch potatoes," staring at the TV for hours. Many isolate themselves in dens or bedrooms because no "performance" is necessary when no one else is around. As Super-Mom Kathy remarked, the only time she felt she did not have to wear one of her many masks was in the long bath she promised herself every night. The kids were all in bed, her husband was watching TV or was in bed ahead of her, and she could close her eyes and escape. The rest of the time she was hyper-alert, forced into the lion's share of responsibility for both home and job. Her very dependent and passive–aggressive husband had opted out.

In this fast-paced society in which we find ourselves, the process of coming down after the adrenalin has been pumping all day at work has become a job in itself. Judith Sprankle and Dr. Henry Ebel, in *The Workaholic Syndrome*, quote the reflections of the head of a communications group: "The most striking thing about my workday is that when it's over, I don't even know what it has done to me! Phase one of my evening is the drive home, which is brief and neither taxing nor relaxing. Then comes a lie-down with some taped classical music, which usually leads to an hour or so of sleep. Then I begin to realize how tired I am, but also how cramped-up and tense." He then takes his son with him to the gym. He goes swimming to work out the cramps, while the son works out in the weights room. "I get home just in time to hit the sack. No TV, no puttering about, no extended conversations.

Just sleep." This pattern is familiar to many workaholics who confess to the need to "wind down" almost every night.

Chronic fatigue and anxiety are often masked by hyperactivity or restlessness. Many workaholics cannot settle on any one activity for long, and jump from one task to another. Such scattered attention leads to inefficiency and to long hours spent doing what used to take far less time. They have no time for co-workers and friends, if there are any outside of work, and isolation and alienation result. Family support is usually lessening because the workaholic's "acting out" or "acting in" has alienated the spouse and children.

Other workaholics become more selective about what they do as their energy decreases during the breakdown stage. They tend to leave undone boring, routine work in favour of the more stimulating and praise-worthy "visible" work. Adrenalin acts as a drug to cover the fatigue. This selectivity makes the workaholic more selfish about just doing "his thing," often completely ignoring the wishes and needs of co-workers or the spouse. Many serious family problems arise out of this selectivity of jobs, and the self-centred avoidance of responsibility to others. They relinquish control, but only at home. They offer token "help," using the excuse that they "don't have time" or are "too tired." The more dependent workaholics wait for the spouse to delegate chores.

Guilt

"Make sure you talk about guilt in your book. God, do I hate feeling guilty!" said Eugene. Running from the pain of guilt, Eugene drove himself until he lost all perspective. He pondered his own mixed-up sense of priorities. "It felt tremendously important that I be at work. I'd race in traffic to get back to work just to get there. I might get back and find there was not much activity going on. It was so important to me that I set the right example because I was convinced my staff depended on me to do just that. My arrogance drove me to feel responsible out of all proportion to my real job. I was always looking for more brass on my uniform." Work, with its titles and promotions, distracted Eugene from dealing with his guilt for staying away from home and not being emotionally available to his family.

There are two kinds of guilt. One can be adaptive and serves to alert us to behaviour that goes against our sense of what is morally and ethically right. The other can be destructive. It is self-anger, which is directed inward to punish the self or projected outward to punish others through cruel or vindictive behaviour. Both kinds of guilt drive the workaholic.

Workaholics suffer tremendous guilt as their breakdown leads to increasingly ugly behaviour. Rages, vindictive put-downs, and sarcasm can leave others devastated. Feelings of frustration, shame, and failure flood up. Quentin Hyder, in *The Christian Handbook of Psychiatry*, describes the complexity of guilt: "Guilt is an uncomfortable feeling. It is a mixture of many emotions and thoughts which destroy inner peace. It is partly the unpleasant knowledge that something wrong has been done. It is a fear of punishment. It is shame, regret, or remorse. It is resentment and hostility toward the authority figure against whom the wrong has been done. It is a feeling of low self-worth or inferiority. It leads to alienation, not only from others but also from oneself because of the discrepancy between what one really is and what one would like to be. This leads to loneliness and isolation. Guilt, therefore, is partly depression and partly anxiety. It is partly true and partly false."

Guilt, I believe, is really self-anger. Unfortunately, the anger gets projected out onto other people and things. Guilt causes people to lecture or preach or try to "fix" others, instead of listening or trying to understand. Not wishing to face rejection or feelings of inadequacy, they reject others first so that they can feel superior again. Often the inability to forgive, or to experience forgiveness, which was felt in childhood, surfaces from the unconscious in the form of anxiety. It is this anxiety, fed by fear and guilt, that underlies many of the workaholic's psychosomatic illnesses, depressions, feelings of worthlessness, and anxiety attacks. It also activates the defences of repression and projection of blame so commonly used by workaholics.

If the workaholic can learn to identify when he or she is projecting and recognize guilt as self-anger, then internal feelings can be dealt with. This is a very important step in the recovery process, and identifying projections of guilt onto others is a crucial task in psychotherapy.

The emotional turmoil described in this chapter will be recognized by the workaholic who has some self-awareness and insight. The workaholic's family can often recognize these signs more easily, but because they occur over long periods of time, it is difficult to understand what is happening. Unfortunately, narcissistic types may be quite unaware of many of their own fears and repressed guilt. Self-correction is therefore unlikely without therapeutic intervention.

If you recognize these fears, if you suffer from guilt and chronic fatigue, I hope you will realize that your psychological health will only deteriorate as the breakdown progresses. There is a good chance for recovery if insight is gained in time to prevent the severe changes in personality that occur when the Dr. Jekyll "nice" person becomes a Mr. Hyde.

5.
The Breakdown Syndrome:
Personality Changes

Workaholics are Dr. Jekyll one day, and Mr. Hyde the next. Their personalities change as the breakdown progresses because of a series of losses. "Something awful is going on in our family," Muriel told me. "The funny thing is I've known this intuitively for a long time, but my own crazy optimism always drowned it out!"

Every day in my office, I listen to the cries of frustration and pain as spouses and sometimes children express their confusion and despair. Help me understand what is going on, and tell me how to get through to this person! In the more chronic stages of the breakdown, the Mr. Hyde personality becomes more dominant. Many spouses tell me they feel like they are living with a split personality. Annie, a slightly dishevelled and depressed housewife, tells me that she looks at her husband sometimes in disbelief: "I hardly know him, he's changed so much. Last night, I finally exploded!" she confessed. "I literally screamed at him 'You're always so jumpy! You're driving me absolutely nuts! It's like living with a ticking time bomb when you're home. I just get relaxed, feel comfortable, and feel close again, and then pow!' "

As the workaholic breakdown progresses, profound personality changes occur. Many of these changes remain unconscious, and workaholics are unaware of them. The repressed feelings and negative qualities are instead projected onto and seen in others. Poor judgment and serious flaws in character result as the Shadow side becomes more powerful. Eventually, the workaholic's denial system can no longer repress the growing fears, anxieties, and obsessions being forced into awareness. It is a struggle even to maintain the status quo. Totally self-absorbed, increasingly anxious, and closed off by denial, many workaholics remain unaware of the effect their behaviour has on other people. They become irresponsible, cold, and uncaring. The workaholic's family sees the changes and the obsessive need to work. What the family does not recognize or understand is that the workaholic is fighting for survival.

Many spouses, battling their own depression, must consider whether they can remain in the workaholic family without suffering their own breakdown. One morning, Cynthia told me that she had been listening to the radio on her way to work and heard some radio announcers joking around about the fate of the local baseball team. Out of the blue, something hit a chord in her. She suddenly realized that other people really do laugh and joke around; they're cheerful and nice to each other! Cynthia pondered the question this raised: How long had it been since she and Frank laughed together? The change had been so gradual that she couldn't put her finger on the moment when things started to go wrong. Later, at home that night, amid tears of frustration, Cynthia tried to tell Frank how she was feeling: "We don't laugh any more. You hardly ever smile. Your face is stone-like. Your eyes have no expression." Many months later, Cynthia could stand it no longer: "There's no joy or enthusiasm in you. You're such a wet blanket, a kill-joy! I just can't live this way any more!" Their many discussions of her needs and feelings had fallen on deaf ears, and Frank was unable to meet her halfway. He knew things weren't great, but he didn't know how bad they were. "My wife is always exaggerating things," he rationalized.

The flip-flop in personality leaves co-workers mystified and resentful, too. Jay, a young ambitious salesman, had become agitated and was suffering severe anxiety attacks. After a difficult week, Jay was pacing my office. "My boss is like a chameleon. She's driving me crazy! One day she's the tough guy. Like yesterday morning, she put me down in front of everybody at the staff meeting, then bullied and shouted at her secretary, and was unbelievably blunt and caustic with one of our best customers. It's hard to believe, but after lunch, this same woman comes back all smiles, turns on the old charm and wit, and then wows the board with one of her brilliant speeches!" Then Jay adds, "I've either got to quit this job or get tough as nails!" Such unpredictable behaviour keeps everyone off balance and tense. It is also a great way of controlling others. This insight helped Jay understand how to begin to distance himself and be more objective so that his boss's behaviour was no longer Jay's problem. He also learned how to deal with other controlling people in a firm but diplomatic way. His boss, however, might have almost no awareness of what she has done to her staff. If she has become narcissistic, then she will expect unconditional loyalty from them.

Until workaholics themselves become fully conscious of the fears underlying their work obsession and confront chronic fatigue and guilt feelings, denial will prevent any chance of recovery. Even after months of psychotherapy, many workaholics will say: "I know you still think I'm a workaholic, but I'm not totally convinced." "I only believe half of what you say," a skeptical young workaholic told me one day. I laughed, and said that didn't surprise me because he is naturally skeptical and questioning. Personalities don't change overnight, but workaholism gradually curtails the ability to function as a whole and balanced person.

LOSSES

As feelings are repressed to avoid pain and unwanted personal responsibility, eight major losses occur. These must be addressed if health is to be restored. The breakdown leads to these losses, and the personality changes accordingly. Awareness of each of these losses is the first important step in the recovery process. The second is to understand what is healthy so that one can set informed goals.

Loss of Communication Skills
Communication breaks down in tandem with the loss of a healthy balance between "doing" and "being," between "thinking" and "feeling." As we learned earlier, in the workaholic the "being" and "feel-

ing" side is repressed and shrinks, just as a muscle that is not used eventually atrophies. There is no time for this "being" side of the personality since Saturdays, Sundays, evenings, holidays, vacations, and any free time get edged out by work-related pressures.

Workaholics themselves describe the feeling as "stale," "dried up," or "burned-out." Their eyes become blood-shot, bones feel weary, backs seize up with tension, and stress causes them to experience a sizzling sensation in the head, like a live wire humming a high-pitched sound. Overloaded, they start to run away from problems to avoid any more responsibility. Some die-hards rush frantically flat out and then, emptied, collapse for a few days unable to move. Rose, a young and relentlessly ambitious securities trader, said she would sit at her desk in a fog for days until finally some energy would creep back into her system. After she had thawed out, she would gradually begin to function again. At such times, if any extra demands are made by a spouse or children cry for attention, the workaholic just cannot cope. She lashes out, or withdraws and hides somewhere out-of-sight. Co-workers who want decisions made at such times encounter similar resistance and delay tactics.

Confused thinking and feeling become a chronic problem at this stage. Alcoholics Anonymous literature uses the term "stinkin' thinkin' " to describe thinking that appears logical, but makes no sense. This thinking is often circular, goes nowhere. People obsessively go over the same issues again and again, but never resolve problems or get results. There are often tangential distortions: thoughts get added or retracted, and messages change. Or communication can be too cryptic and not enough information is provided to enable the other person to understand. Abstract concepts, such as "I'm keeping all the balls in the air," mean something to workaholics, but are unclear to the person who has asked how they are feeling.

There is often a hidden agenda as well. Workaholics may wish to hide what they have or have not done, to conceal their fears, or to avoid taking responsibility for the turmoil going on inside. That is why workaholic couples often cannot solve their problems and become hopelessly stuck.

Quasi-logical messages place other people in a "double-bind" situation in which they are damned if they do, and damned if they don't. A naive narcissistic controller who had considerable expertise in the

"Terrible Twist," but little insight, told his wife that there was nothing wrong with either of them — each was intelligent, well-adjusted, and mature. "We're just fine! The problem is the relationship!" he announced in all seriousness. No matter that he was married to his work, refused to take his wife on holidays or business trips, had to be "right" or felt criticized and sulked. He manipulated his wife through his withdrawal. And his passive–aggressive anger, he rationalized, was just him being "easy to get along with." Since the next day he denied his occasional volcanic eruptions of anger, they didn't count in his appraisal of the situation.

Conrad, equally naive, was firmly convinced that he and his wife, Elizabeth, did not need to come to my office every week to solve their problems. Thoroughly distraught by his wife's outburst of anger in the session, Conrad blurted out: "The only time we talk about anything serious is in this room! Why doesn't she just tell me these things quietly in the privacy of our home?" He shouted, "If she just learns to follow a few simple rules, and keeps herself and the house neat and tidy, I'll be able to communicate. It's really very simple!" When I pointed out that his wife was obviously still afraid of his rages and didn't trust him yet, he dismissed the idea. He went right on telling me what his wife and the kids had to do to make their home the peaceful place *he* deserved.

Similarly, Abe, an enterprising entrepreneur, told me that he wasn't going to tell his wife about his new job offer. "Not yet, anyway. No point in worrying Liz about anything until I've accepted and we've signed on the dotted line. She tends to be fragile these days, you know," he cautioned, thinking he was being thoughtful. No matter that the job involved a move to an industrial town halfway across the country. He assured me that the kids, aged nine, eleven, and fourteen, didn't care where they lived. "They're old enough to enjoy new people. It will be a great challenge. Besides, I'll buy them some nice new furniture." Then he added tentatively, "Life's got pretty boring here because I hardly ever see my kids any more. They're always off with their friends!" Abe, jealous and hurt, was prepared to move his kids at an age when friends are all important. Abe feared that if he shared power and decision-making with his family, the chaos would be more than he could cope with. Nothing was going too well in his life any more, so why ask for trouble? He just couldn't afford to give up his control right now.

"You never apologize for the things you don't know you're doing," retorted a workaholic when her husband said that she rarely apologized to him because she always thought she was "right." Confusion and anxiety spread throughout the family as listeners strain to follow this pseudo-logical thinking. Even in her own home, the workaholic feels misunderstood, grows even more anxious, and finally blows up in frustration. Again, it is the spouse's fault for not understanding. Workaholics rarely question whether they have been sending clear messages. To make things even worse, the distortion in a statement forces others to make assumptions about what was meant, and they in turn act on their interpretation. "Can't you do anything right?" screams the angry addict who thinks she is being perfectly clear and is mystified by the other's actions. No one listens to me any more, she believes.

The spouse or co-worker who genuinely tries to understand what is going on often becomes confused, too, about what reality really is and sinks deeper into the co-dependent role. Someone who is confused has no power, is easily controlled and manipulated, and is very vulnerable. By remaining in a state of confusion, the co-dependent also avoids responsibility. The chain reaction is insidious, and it is no wonder workaholic families become so dysfunctional, and office politics damage people's lives.

The distortion of reality occurs when you deny your own or others' experience and dismiss feedback. Innuendo, veiled references to others, gossip, and straight lies are forms of distortions. Unless the workaholic checks to see whether his or her message has been received as it was intended and makes the effort to try again to get the message across, abnormal thinking processes can slip into paranoia and the misunderstood individual can feel: "No one cares about me! My wife doesn't understand me! Everyone hates me!" and then give up in frustration and withdraw. It does not occur to workaholics that they may not be "right" or able to communicate clearly.

Brad, predictably concrete in his thinking, got very angry after three attempts to explain his interpretation of a stormy scene he and his wife had had the previous evening over his wife's blasé approach to house cleaning. He lashed out and accused me of not listening, of colluding with his wife to "gang up on him." Neither she nor I had been able to follow his logic, and I was really struggling to comprehend what it was that he was trying to get me to see. In the next session, I persevered and finally understood that, until his surroundings were orderly and the house was meticulously clean, he couldn't even entertain thoughts of intimacy. He needed control of his environment before he could even think about letting go to show his positive feelings.

Chronic confusion and distortion lead to a loss of control and to panic. Dr. A. Schaef, in *When Society Becomes an Addict*, believes that the division between left brain, as logical, rational, and linear, and right brain, as emotional, intuitive, and non-linear or lateral, is an oversimplification. Dr. Schaef suggests that the emotion of panic belongs to the left hemisphere. Whenever the logical, rational mind is "threatened with the loss of its illusion of control, it panics. This panic is a primitive, undifferentiated sort of panic, not nearly as sophisticated or evolved as the emotions produced when the brain is utilized as a whole." New research shows that the most functional, clear, and powerful thinking occurs in the interaction between both hemispheres of the brain and the brain stem. This thinking allows you to check for distortions, confusion, and dishonesty.

Such low-grade panic may explain the fuzzy, confused thinking reported by workaholics. They are often in a constant state of confused anxiety, but are puzzled about its source. I was fascinated as one of my clients eloquently described her panic. Elsa was in a frenzy to wrap up her production-manager job with an opera company. She described what had been happening to her: "My brain moves so fast when I'm working, I have trouble keeping up with all the ideas and plans jumping around in my mind. No one person can do all that, and I almost need three people to carry out everything that keeps swirling around in my head. I can't focus, and there's never enough time to work anything through. I start to lose track, and my famous things-to-do list gets completely out of control. I forget to write things down, to cross them off. I lose sight of my goals. Anxiety-fatigue-confusion — it's a spiral! I don't know how to get off, so I panic! The only solution is to keep working because I'm so far behind. I've taken on way too much. When I feel like superwoman, I start to feel scared. I want so much to be seen to be good at what I do, to be valued. I want to feel needed by the industry and the friends I work with." Elsa was upset about what people would say about her disorganization. She kept everything in her head and rarely took time to record anything. "I feel that if I walk out, the company will collapse. I have built a pack of cards. They will blame all the things that go wrong on me!"

Outwardly, people like Elsa are calm and controlled. The person has a poker-face. The repressed feelings that lie within the unconscious are not experienced, unless strong emotion, such as anger, rage, or fear, forces them up to consciousness. Then these negative feelings usually get projected out onto other people or onto things or situations. Awareness and insight faculties are blunted by repression, and the range of feelings is narrow and constricted. The person becomes rigid and lacks the ability to be spontaneous and open with others. Panic brings impulsive untypical behaviour, which demonstrates just how bad the workaholic's judgment has become. Overcontrol has given way to "acting out" behaviour.

A more global view of the need for balance is presented by Alvin Toffler in *The Third Wave*. He suggests that people in the future will come to crave balance in their lives — "balance between work and play, between production and consumption, between headwork and handwork, between the abstract and the concrete, between objectivity and subjectivity." There is a glimpse of this trend in companies that now recruit executives who have "balanced" personalities. They look for a person with intelligence and wisdom combined, someone with broad and diverse interests. Rhodes scholars are chosen for these same qualities, and perhaps the ideal could serve as a role model for the ideal personality of the future.

Wisdom comes from this balance. Workaholics are very intelligent, interesting, often witty and charming people, but they lack this inner wisdom. The crises in their lives attest to this. Good judgment comes when your logical and rational thoughts and ideas are supported by a gut reaction that the decision "feels" right, and you can live comfortably with the consequences of your action. Inner wisdom goes even farther because the decision not only feels right, but it also fits in with your values and beliefs. Something deep inside you can answer "Yes!"

Loss of Empathy

Empathy is placing yourself in another person's psychological space and trying to imagine what that person may be thinking and feeling and what his or her actions mean. A crucial step in true empathy is to ask other people how they really are feeling. Only then can you know the accuracy of your projection. Dr. Carl Rogers, a well-known and respected psychologist, built his reputation on his empathic therapeutic approach to clients. His definition of empathy (quoted in R. Campbell, *Psychiatric Dictionary*) is "the ability to accompany another to wherever the other person's feelings lead him, no matter how strong, deep, destructive, or abnormal they may seem."

People whose feelings are repressed cannot be empathic with others, since they don't know how they themselves feel. Repressed feelings work slowly, and tend to be negative, childlike, or primitively unformed. If you ask workaholics how they feel, they will tell you what they think instead, or fake a standard reaction they think might be appropriate. They are slow to decide how they do feel, and must translate thinking into feeling words. It can take a half-hour, days, or sometimes weeks to figure out feelings.

Empathy requires that you recognize another person as an individual, and know where you as a unique person stop and the other person begins. Workaholics, growing up in dysfunctional families where ego boundaries are unclear, have trouble knowing where their personal responsibility stops. They believe they can solve other people's problems for them, but they often are not in touch with their own inner wisdom or refuse to listen to it. Sadly, they will not even read or learn about how others have searched for their own understandings and insights. Controllers, especially, rarely read self-help books, using the excuse that they are too busy or do not agree with them. Their own thinking is so strong that opinions different from theirs are not considered.

People who are self-centred lack the ability to be empathic. As work overshadows everything in importance, the addict becomes focused on self-aggrandizement and getting a work "fix" in order to build up a sagging ego. Later, as survival becomes a focus, fears and anxieties drain away any excess energy. The centre of their own universe, they are unavailable to others, or even aware of others' needs. Margaret, the wife of a well-to-do lawyer, had become addicted to rescuing the foundering relationship with her unfaithful, middle-aged, workaholic husband. Jack had put his whole family through a kind of hell as he refused to terminate an affair he was having with one of his clients. Margaret was slowly losing all her confidence and self-esteem as Jack broke off and then resumed the affair. Broken promises, cover-up lies, and blatant betrayals when he would go off on a "business" holiday with the other woman became a way of life. Each week, this saga dragged on, and at times became almost unbelievable — like a bad B-movie. Margaret was addressing her own addiction to the relationship, and was slowly becoming more assertive and setting limits of acceptable behaviour. Jack, however, seemed to have absolutely no insight into what he was doing to his family. Although he often talked about his guilt and remorse, his behaviour did not change at all. Margaret exclaimed: "All we hear about at our house is me, me, me. I am so sick of hearing about *me*! Now I'm getting tough. If I hear 'poor me' creeping into the conversation, it gets terminated quick! Enough already!" She was gradually getting strong enough to have the option to leave this unhealthy marriage.

Lack of empathy eventually generalizes to thoughtless and insensitive behaviour towards others. The general population too become victims. How often have you been kept waiting for an hour or more in your doctor's or dentist's waiting room, or been kept dangling on the end of a phone, waiting for some information from a thoughtless salesperson? There is no compensation offered for your lost time and your lost money, although you hear occasionally about an irate patient who has sent his doctor a bill for time lost! The lives and feelings of the ordinary person lose importance when the workaholic is barely functioning. Unfortunately, the recipient is most often the sensitive, empathic person who tends to put up with others' foibles, and does not complain and demand better service. This passivity is equally unhealthy and needs to be confronted as it perpetuates the rude and inconsiderate behaviour. Everyone is avoiding responsibility. Failure to make waves, to confront, to risk rejection or disfavour keeps many co-dependent people caught in the power and control of the workaholic system. Others with thicker skins who protest and shout back tend to be treated with more respect.

When workaholics become paranoid, someone who disagrees with them, they assume, thinks they are "wrong." In their logic, two people can't both be right if they disagree. Even discussing a movie can provoke heated arguments. Their opinionated, often strong, blunt delivery alienates and distances them from others. Their sensitive, gentle, diplomatic feeling side is missing. The idea expressed in the song: "I want to be happy, but I can't be happy, unless I make you happy too" is alien to their way of thinking. Without realizing it, they have become blind to others' needs and happiness.

The workaholics' feelings of guilt and shame also decrease their empathy for others. By feeling sorry for themselves and constantly worrying if they have done the right thing, they become even more self-absorbed. Shame comes from their feeling that they have fallen short of perfection. Consequently, workaholics often berate themselves mercilessly with self-criticism. Underneath the "I'm all right" façade, they are insecure and worried about the next battle to prove their superiority.

Empathy is missing to different degrees in the three types of workaholics. Pleasers want to know about other people's needs and wishes so they can gain the approval that is so essential to their well-being. Controllers have to be self-absorbed to focus inwardly on their own needs and wishes in order to motivate them to seek the control and power they so ardently desire. For narcissists, self-centredness is a prime attribute. Even when they are presumably "giving" to others, it is self-serving. They want their spouse and children to have the best, but their real concern is the quality of their own performance, and the approval they will get for the things they do for their families or communities. Narcissists cannot tolerate distress in a spouse because it is a negative reflection on them. When a wife, for example, is happy, the husband ignores her. As Dr. Jay Rohrlich, in *Work and Love: The Crucial Balance*, suggests, when a wife is ill or distressed, this "means that she is paying some attention to herself and is not completely available to him. He immediately tries to 'do something about it'; he is unable to simply listen and empathize. In fact, in his effort to restore her availability to him, he turns her discomfort or sadness into a work project for himself." These people are the "takers" of the world, and their complete lack of empathy prevents them from ever truly loving another person, except for what that person can do or give to them. Genuine love comes from true empathy and respect for the other person's happiness, health, and individuality.

Loss of Intimacy

Intimacy is not possible without empathy, trust, and a well-defined sense of self. Intimacy is a "merging and fusion of the self and other — which involves the threat of losing one's own separate personality," according to Dr. Maggie Scarf, in her excellent book *Intimate Partners*. My personal view is that a commitment to intimacy involves a sharing of love and understanding with another significant person. It means that each person expresses affection and cares for the other, affirms the other, and values and respects the other emotionally, intellectually, and physically. Because workaholics need the illusion of being in control and try to control others, it is difficult for them to relinquish their control long enough to be intimate. The sense of their self separate from the work persona is not strong enough for them to risk possible self-annihilation in an intimate blending with their mate. As one woman confided: "My insecurities have left me with a deep fear of intimacy. I find it very difficult to express my innermost hopes and fears and feelings and find it embarrassing to have others express them for me."

Intimacy requires an easy give and take, to receive and not control, to give without expectations or strings attached. You can "give in" to people and let them have their way, but unless others' happiness is foremost in your thoughts, this is not unconditional giving.

True intimacy involves shared communication. A wide range of feelings, both positive and negative, needs to be expressed. The expression of negative feelings can be very intimate if positive solutions are sought and supported by positive feelings. Uncomfortable and not at ease with their own feelings, workaholics often freeze, and even hold their breath, when someone else is emotional or displays feelings, especially in public. "Get control of yourself, for heaven's sake!" is a breathless plea often heard. They use expressions like: "I feel *locked in*. It's as if I'm *caught in a vise* when she tells me her expectations." "I feel *suffocated and trapped* when he tells me he needs me to touch him." "She *dogs me* all the time, following behind like a puppy, *snapping* at my heels." "I'm going to get *swallowed up* if I give in to her!" Terrified of intimacy, commitment, and responsibility, these individuals guard their autonomy jealously. They are afraid of situations in which they will be alone with their spouse for an extended period of time. Many workaholic executives are not only unaware of their own need for a vacation, but are insensitive to the fact that their spouses are worn out too. Co-dependent spouses and employees need regular vacations. They often do not have the stamina and energy of the workaholic, yet try to keep pace. "Why should my secretary be away on vacation when I'm slaving away here, trying to get this deal signed!" sighed one frantic executive. Workaholics can get along without breaks or holidays for long periods of time. "Isn't everyone like me?" they ask.

Intimacy is a sharing of power. The workaholic is reluctant to give up any of his or her hard-won power. Accustomed to giving orders all day, workaholics often run their marriages the way they run their businesses. In my office one day, a very frustrated Sandra exploded: "I'm not one of your employees, you know, I'm *me*!" Her husband, thinking he was being funny, told her he would "make her vice-president then!" Of course, this was a perfect example of their power struggle. When I pointed out that it was not really his right to "make her" anything, he looked sheepish. A peer relationship where a couple shares power is especially difficult for the "introverted thinker" who feels safer when in charge. These people feel more comfortable in one-up positions because it helps them feel superior. It is less threatening to relate to children or older folks than to peers because people in a dependent role are more likely to value the workaholic's "helpful" problem-solving.

Sexual difficulties are very common in workaholic couples as the breakdown progresses. Infrequent sex or no sexual involvement for years are commonly heard complaints in my practice. Workaholics, afraid of intimacy, become "married" to their work. That is where their commitment and energy go. The well-known experts on sexual problems Dr. William Masters and Virginia Johnson, in *The Pleasure Bond*, blame sexual dysfunctions on increasing fatigue, distraction and worries about work, and the loss of feeling function coupled with the principle that "being productive is always more important than being pleasured, that work comes before play." A colleague of theirs, Dr. Helen Singer Kaplan, studied the reasons for the loss of libido, or sex drive, in her book, *Disorders of Sexual Desire: The New Sex Therapy*. She found that anger, stress, depression, drugs, and hormonal changes all serve to shut down the sex centres. This shutdown occurs on an unconscious level and is involuntary, meaning the message bypasses the brain and goes directly to the nerve or organ. Since one of the first signs of depression is a decrease or increase in libido, or sexual drive, it is not surprising that sexuality suffers when workaholics become depressed or suffer extreme fatigue. Dr. Kaplan points out that couples unconsciously learn to activate the "turn-off" mechanisms that shut down the sex centres. They focus on memories of the partner's unacceptable behaviour or past injustices when they have a sexual opportunity. They may find fault with their own or with the other's physical appearance or mannerisms, or distract themselves with thoughts of work, children, or money issues. They are unaware they have turned themselves off psychologically, yet lose interest sexually. The physiological mechanisms do not function properly. The woman's mucous membranes do not engorge with blood and the vagina does not lubricate, so penetration is not comfortable. The man may not be able to achieve an erection. Sexual impotence is a common complaint of workaholics. Pleasers experience the opposite reaction: their libido increases, and they seek comfort and nurturing from their spouse. The more disturbed seek out prostitutes or have affairs when the breakdown leads to loss of integrity and infidelity.

Many workaholics tend to "perform" sexually. They see love-making as another job to be done. Others compulsively try to beat what they think is the "national norm" for frequency, habitually using their spouse to relieve tension or gain nurturance. One angry wife complained that her husband insisted on intercourse every morning after a crisis threatened his work world. Others feel guilty because they are not working, so distract themselves with job worries and inhibit desire further. Others stay overly busy, and avoid going to bed until the spouse is asleep. Many habitually stay up until one in the morning, working or watching TV to avoid intimacy. Chronically fatigued, worn out from work, and often alienated from the spouse, workaholics cannot risk being vulnerable, especially as confidence erodes. Spouses who are well aware that they come in second, or even fifth, begin to lose confidence in their own desirability. This, in turn, acts as a further turn-off. The couple no longer enjoys sex for its own sake. They cannot be relaxed, spontaneous, and enjoy each other's bodies. Sex becomes serious business too.

Creative love-making and romantic times become impossible as the workaholic becomes more rigid and controlling. The spouse often complains that foreplay is unimaginative or too brief. When the workaholic is impulsive, impatient, or insensitive to the other's needs or wishes, and the focus is on self-pleasure or performance, no wonder the tenuous link holding the couple together is damaged. Sexual intimacy is not the bonding, healing magic that it should be, and the workaholic's marriage disintegrates.

It is important in understanding workaholism to distinguish between romantic love and true love. Romantic love is an idealistic projection onto another person, based on who we want that person to be to satisfy our own needs and wishes. Since it is based on an illusion, romantic love cannot last. True love is not a projection, but a sincere appreciation of the other person's strengths and values and a tolerance for their weaknesses. The other's happiness, growth, and health become a focus. True and lasting love must be mutual and reciprocal, or love becomes an obsession and fades. Dr. Robert Johnson, in his book *We: Understanding the Psychology of Romantic Love*, paraphrases Saint Paul's message on love, and highlights the differences between a self-serving ego left to its own devices and one under the influence of genuine love: "My ego is concerned only with itself; but 'love suffers long and is kind.' My ego is envious, always seeking to inflate itself with illusions of absolute power and control, but 'love does not vaunt itself, is not puffed up.' My ego, left to its ego-centeredness, will always betray, but 'love never fails.' My ego only knows how to affirm itself and its desires, but love 'seeks not her own way.' Love affirms all of life: 'bears all things, believes all things, hopes all things.'"

Many workaholics never make the transition from falling into romantic love to growing into real love. Many fall out of love, withdraw, or seek romantic love elsewhere. Dr. Johnson likens human love to "stirring the oatmeal," where the unexciting, difficult, and mundane things in life are transformed into a "joyful and fulfilling component of life. By contrast, romantic love can only last so long as the money lasts and the entertainments are exciting." The cult of romance teaches us to expect that all our projections will be borne, our desires satisfied, and our fantasies made to come true in the person we are "in love" with.

Intimacy is a goal for many of the workaholics I deal with, and the struggle is a challenging, exciting one for those who make the journey. "I used to feel yukky when Phil made love to me because he just took all my love and gave it away to others," Janice confided. "Now that he's so in touch with his feelings, he is really there for me. He's so sensitive and thoughtful now. I'm a real person to him again! We can't thank you enough." She beamed in delight. "It's truly a miracle!"

It is important to differentiate real intimacy from a pseudo intimacy where the corporation, the boss, and the team become a collective personality or family. Judith Sprankle and Dr. Henry Ebel, in *The Workaholic Syndrome*, warn: "The day you find yourself referring to the fiction that employs you as if it were a parent, spouse, lover, or child is the day you know you are in danger of making some very bad mistakes!" Sixty-hour weeks spent working in a stimulating atmosphere, surviving pressures together, leads to a strong affinity towards one's co-workers. These authors describe the bonds that a man and woman develop as they "get to know each other's minds and emotions amid daily scenes of stress and financial risk. The bonds forged through a process of this kind can make those of a marriage seem pale by comparison, especially when a dual-career couple arrives home too late to share a dinner and too tired even to think about the office." All their energy has been consumed in pumping adrenalin, seeking approval and confirmation from equally stressed peers and bosses.

Although many couples choose to stay together for financial reasons, and infidelity can be an accepted part of these marriages, the workaholic's loss of intimacy, integrity, and respect erodes family life and threatens the emotional lives of their children. The pull between work and family has never been greater.

Loss of Integrity and Respect

The loss of integrity occurs when ethics in business and personal life take a back seat to success. Gregory, a recovering workaholic, describes his views: "The top dollar and accolades at work are the driving force for most of us. Then there is the 'good-looking' wife at home, hung with diamonds like a Christmas tree, driving a pretty little Mercedes, BMW, or 4-wheel drive. All this glitter is a tribute to the 'look at me' ego. It's a curious and dangerous situation since the top man usually sets the example, and establishes the 'culture' within an organization. Insider trading is just around the corner here, and I fear that it is not the disregard for ethics that is the issue. It's whether or not you get caught! I'm afraid that 'getting away with it' is held in awe in my business!"

Respect is nurtured or destroyed by dishonesty. Dishonesty takes different forms. Pleasers, by omission, neglect to tell the truth, and get caught in the trap of saying what they think others want to hear. They avoid saying what they want to do, but then sabotage others' plans; they agree, then do their own thing; they guess what others want from subtle cues, instead of asking them. This subtle dishonesty is passively irresponsible and highly manipulative. This type of dishonesty bewilders, and leads to confusion and chaos. Reality and honesty get lost in pathological lying. As family support lessens, the Pleaser struggles for control and resorts to blatant lies, blanket denials, and secrecy. Trust breaks down completely, and spouses react with suspicion by confronting the omissions or excuses offered when the workaholic arrives home late. "Where have you been?" worried spouses ask. The workaholics lash back, accusing their spouses of "nagging" and "constantly complaining." The "Terrible Twist" saves the day for the workaholic, who must come out on top: "No wonder our marriage is such a disaster," said one self-righteous physician after such an exchange.

Controllers are more inclined to smooth-talk to keep control; they make blatant assumptions about what others want, instead of asking; they develop expertise in knowing the best tactics to get their way; and they use steam-rolling thinking to overrule others' wishes to get their way. Controllers will lie, cheat, and steal, if necessary. Integrity can go missing as these people lose all sight of how their goal is reached. Their obsession with power and control means that they do not concern themselves with how they affect others or what is best for their family.

Disillusioned and often neglected children, growing up in these dysfunctional families, typically learn not to trust adults. Small lies grow. Promises mean nothing. Johnny fights back tears of frustration, because his dad forgot about helping with his project. Mary keeps looking for Mom to appear in the audience and forgets her lines. Mom rushes in during the last act, and tells her daughter that an important meeting suddenly came up that she couldn't do anything about. Another mother is always so upset because Dad is late that meals get to be trauma-time. The children of such parents do not know that other families function differently, and do not dare confront a father whose temper is getting worse by the day. As Kent told me: "I'm afraid if I tell Daddy I cried when he didn't come to my baseball game the other day, he'll just blow up at me again." Looking frightened, he confided: "Besides, I think he might be going away forever! Since Daddy took that new job, things aren't so good at our house any more!"

Infidelity and the dishonesty surrounding affairs destroy integrity and respect. Moral superiority and values collapse when liaisons are sought to build up sagging egos. Gary, a well-respected chief of police, tragically abandoned his wife of thirty years and his university-aged children to live with his twenty-five-year-old secretary. The children were openly disgusted and refused to see their father. Often workaholics "act out" by having affairs with someone below their social level as this makes them feel superior, or act out juvenile fantasies with younger partners. It is not unusual for workaholics to justify their actions by devaluing and blaming the spouse for what is missing in the relationship. The more disturbed go farther and dissociate, acting as though the spouse does not count or even exist. They refuse to give financial support and lie about their incomes or holdings. Workaholics' drive to dominate, or craving to be loved and appreciated, unhappily ends in lost integrity and broken families.

Respectability and trust earned through hard work and devotion to the company can be lost overnight. Tales of indiscretions and of inappropriate, foolish, and amoral behaviour abound. Newspapers, tabloids, and scandal sheets document each and every detail. It is called by some the "mid-life" crisis. Narcissistic workaholics, who tend to use people, to be the "takers," are the most likely to fall victim to base instincts. They also lack insight into what is wrong, and therefore make poor judgments.

Ironically, this fall from grace can be the turning-point and can force awareness. Public knowledge of indiscretions means the workaholic can no longer see himself as a Nice Guy or Gal, and shame and guilt force a self-confrontation and create a crisis in the marriage. If this crisis causes those in these troubled marriages to seek help, then many good things can come out of bad. My office is full of couples who rediscover each other and, in doing so, find themselves. It is a very painful but rewarding process to confront and own your own negative Shadow side. Only then can the couple work through relationship problems. When the struggle brings insight, then joy and laughter and peace are the rewards for the family that stays intact.

Loss of Independence

Controllers, especially, pride themselves on their independence. They have always stayed on the periphery of a group, remaining slightly aloof and uninvolved. They are the loners who relish privacy and secrecy. As the breakdown symptoms become more severe, however, emotional dependency on others must increase if they are to cover up their growing inability to cope. Clive was barely functioning in his managerial job because he was badly depressed and always exhausted. His own feelings were flat, and he did not know how he should feel, or what was appropriate. He told me he would tell his wife about incidents at work and then watch to see how she reacted. He would then go back the next day and react as she had. More and more dependent on his wife to know how he felt, Clive was like a child who is constantly looking to see if Mom and Dad approve of what he is doing.

Pleasers, naturally more dependent personalities already, cling to the family when depression or anxiety cripples them. They are the ones who turn into couch potatoes. Often the couple stops seeing old friends and becomes isolated because they are living with uncertainty and insecurity. The spouse may have tried to keep up their social friendships, but may have lost patience and become embarrassed because of the workaholic's thoughtlessness and lack of caring. Friends get upset because they are fed up with unempathic responses, cancelled dates, and "forgotten" appointments, or they resent being put off for work commitments. Tragically, both members of the couple become isolated, cut off from the nurturing friends provide.

Personal power and influence over others decline as the workaholic becomes more and more dependent on others for "reality testing." Dr. Carl Jung, in *Psychological Types*, says: "The more ego struggles, the more it becomes enslaved to objective data." Workaholics become more concrete, and focus on things that represent independence. Financial security becomes a "bee in a bonnet." What if someone finds out what a mess they are in and fires them? Money, after all, represents power, independence, freedom, and proof of one's personhood. Saving money, storing up resources, and figuring out all the angles become obsessive projects, especially if retirement is fast approaching. Money spent on recreation often becomes an issue. Wayne Oates, in his own *Confessions of a Workaholic*, tells of one doctor who borrowed the money to go on vacation because he would punish himself with work to pay it back, like a "penance for the pleasure of not working." Self-punitive behaviour is a common result of stored guilt, and it is not unusual for narcissistic workaholics especially to live a lifestyle well below their income level. Unable to enjoy themselves with the fruit of their labours, they seem to enjoy people feeling sorry for them as they crave sympathy and approval.

Paranoid workaholics begin to worry excessively about public opinion, what other people will say and think. Unable to trust their own judgment, they seek affirmation that they are okay. Even Controllers, usually much less concerned about how others feel, begin to worry about their public image. Insecurity forces a restriction of their own freedom of action because they are too vulnerable at this point to risk failure. Paula, a well-established engineer, would not go on holidays because some of her staff might resent her going away when their jobs were in jeopardy because of cut-backs. She wanted to protect her "hard-working" persona, and any thoughts that her staff might be delighted with a break from her intensity and constant surveillance never crossed her mind. Criticism and rejection had to be avoided at all costs.

A very sad truth is that, as the workaholic grows more and more out of touch with herself, it becomes less likely that the independent initiative and bravery necessary to confront denial will be present. The sooner help is sought, the better the chance for a faster and complete recovery.

Loss of Spirituality

One has to love oneself before spirituality is possible. Growing fears, obsessions, and the many losses that occur when feeling is missing all erode self-love. Mr. Hyde is not lovable, or loving.

It is my belief that denial and dishonesty lead to spiritual decline and the loss of self — the pathway to the soul and one's connection with a higher being. As personalities change, so do values. Faith weakens when no energy is given to the spiritual side of life. People, relationships, and family get pushed aside by the drive to perform. Work becomes the "sacred cow." Wayne Oates captures their fatalistic thinking. A workaholic reading his book, *Confessions of a Workaholic*, might say: "Yes, much of what you say is true, but there is nothing anybody can do about it. It has always been this way and always will be." The workaholic, as the breakdown progresses, gradually feels powerless over decisions relating to his own life and expects the worst. If things do work out well, it is a result of luck, accident, or odds. While both positions are fatalistic, they also show a distancing, a splitting-off of self, a projection onto someone or something else of one's own responsibility for life's situations.

Religious affiliation may be very much a part of the Nice Guy or Gal public persona, and many workaholics do attend a place of worship regularly. Attendance often changes when fears and confusion lead to severe inefficiency problems and the obsession with work becomes a survival issue. The workaholic cannot find enough hours in the week to catch up. Depression or anxiety attacks may also keep the workaholic away because isolation and insecurity cause people to avoid social settings. The more dedicated still attend regularly because routine provides some stability in a chaotic world, and they recognize the need for spiritual support. Many are physically present, but lost in work-related thoughts and oblivious to the service. Those with chronic fatigue nod off and are nudged awake by family members. The real religion of the workaholic may become the performing of practical good deeds for others. Unfortunately, this "do-gooder" philosophy can end up being a way of controlling people by placing them in your debt. When there is an ulterior motive, people can sense it, and feel uncomfortable and awkward.

Since dysfunctional homes tend not to be spiritually oriented, worship has never been a part of life for many workaholics. Controllers, especially the "self-made" types, feel independently powerful and omnipotent. They have little need of spiritual support, and letting go of control to anyone, even God, is too threatening. When you are frantically busy, an important person in the community, worship may not be a priority. When depression and anxiety hit, these workaholics have no spiritual centre to ease the pain and help them find direction for a more meaningful existence.

The chronic workaholic, emotionally crippled and without empathy and love, often grows depressed, sometimes severely, and may experience an "existential crisis." Some religious existentialists like Søren Kierkegaard thought that technology and the belief in pure rationalism and logic have alienated and estranged man from society, from himself, and from God. They emphasized instead the view of man as a person of faith, someone personally and passionately involved in life, and in touch with the self, and connected with God. When such a crisis strikes, these questions arise: "Who am I?"; "Where am I going?"; "Why am I killing myself?"; "Does any one really care about me, or what I do?" Illnesses and lay-offs often trigger such a crisis. The workaholic often does not like the answers to these questions, and tragically, some commit suicide. Dr. Frank Minirth and Dr. Paul Meier in "Do 'Nice Guys' Finish Last?," report that professionals often have obsessive compulsive traits, and therefore are more likely than other types to get depressed at some time in their life. Physicians, dentists, and musicians have the highest suicide rates and, not surprisingly, medicine, dentistry, and the ministry are professions with the highest rate of workaholism.

In another book, *The Workaholic and His Family*, Dr. Frank Minirth and four other recovered workaholics suggest that "self-aggrandizement" is the real religion of the workaholic. The Nice Guy who is "self-sacrificing, overly conscientious, overdutiful, hard working, and frequently quite religious" struggles with personal selfishness. The selfishness of the perfectionist is a subtle one. "He helps mankind partially out of love and compassion, but mostly as an unconscious compensation for his insecurity, and as a means of fulfilling both his strong need for society's approval and his driving urge to be perfect. He is self-critical and deep within himself feels inferior. He feels like a nobody, and spends the bulk of his life working at a frantic pace to amass wealth, power, and prestige in order to prove to himself that he is really not (as he suspects deep within) a nobody. In his own eyes, and in the eyes of society, he is the epitome of human dedication." Yet he becomes angry when his wife and children place demands on him and call him selfish. The authors say that, in reality, he is blind to the truth. Families suffer severely from loneliness, neglect, and lack of love. Often children of pastors, missionaries, and doctors seek attention through rebellious acts, or in a desperate need for approval become workaholics, modelling the parental example. As one physician's son said in recognition, "Right on! That's why I'm in this goddamned profession!"

True spirituality requires strong feelings, empathy, and belief in the power of a higher being. Receptivity and openness are essentially feeling characteristics, which, along with humility, are necessary to worship and receive God. Arrogance, together with an inflated ego and selfishness, run counter to this, and some workaholics are atheists. Workaholics who are rigidly stuck in dualistic thinking, or focus solely on their own point of view, are not open to receiving spiritual wisdom and fail to make the inner journey towards clarity.

Genuine love implies commitment and the exercise of wisdom. Dr. Scott Peck, in *The Road Less Traveled*, defines love as "the *will* to extend oneself for the purpose of nurturing one's own or another's spiritual growth. Genuine love is volitional rather than emotional." Dr. Peck believes that people make a decision to be loving, whether or not they feel loving at the moment. The commitment to love is there, and is still exercised. "My feelings of love may be unbounded, but my capacity to be loving is limited. I therefore must choose the person on whom to focus my capacity to love, towards whom to direct my will to love. True love is not a feeling by which we are overwhelmed. It is a committed, thoughtful decision." Genuine love, intimacy, and spirituality are goals for those workaholics who seek existential answers.

Loss of Sense of Humour and the Ability to Play

As the workaholic breakdown progresses, life becomes overly serious and empty of meaning and fulfilment. The workaholic becomes intense, joyless, and pessimistic. A sense of loss overwhelms any childlike wonder. Chronically tired and self-absorbed, workaholics fail to stand back and gain the objectivity needed to see humour in situations. Since they cannot relax enough to see the funny side of life, humour becomes scarce. If any humour does rise out of the dark moods and irritability, it is black humour or sarcasm, both of which arise out of the aggressive instinct. They put down others, or make fun of others' misfortunes. The ulterior motive is to make themselves feel superior.

The ability to produce and to appreciate humour is an essential component of maturity. Humour and pleasure can be used to gain valuable perspective. The mature person is able to laugh at himself, and see her own situation in a humorous light. Humour helps us accept our weaknesses and shortcomings. It helps us to moderate intense feelings. Depression and anxiety cause people to become humourless. Listen for feedback. It may take time, but sooner or later, some member of the family is bound to tell you that you haven't laughed for ages or you don't joke around like you used to. "It's been a dog's age since our home reverberated with any joy or laughter! It's like living in the city morgue," remarked one despondent spouse.

Some workaholics use humour as a defence against getting too involved or too close. One fourteen-year-old daughter, fighting back tears, complained to her mother: "Dad never takes me seriously. I try to talk to him, and he makes everything into a joke. He tells me not to worry so much, everything will be all right. He's so patronizing I could scream. He makes me feel this high!" — she motioned with her hand — "Can't you talk to him and tell him I'm a big girl now! Besides, who is he to talk, he spends all his time up in his den, stewing about that pile of junk on his desk."

Play, for a workaholic, usually means "working" at play. Real play, on the other hand, is an important part of creativity. To be considered play, an activity must be free from any duty, obligation, or business connection. Play should free us to discover new facets of ourselves as we explore new adventures, try out new hobbies, or consider different perspectives of familiar activities. Play involves laughter and sharing, feeling light and carefree, or experiencing joy in quiet moments of contemplation. Play is a celebration of life. Extroverts are energized by being with other people, so their play usually involves others. Introverts can be drained by too much people-contact, and being alone restores their energy in more solitary play.

While work is oriented towards goals and efficiency, play is frivolous and time-wasting. Perfectionism and the aggressive instinct drive workaholics to work even as they are playing. They must master the game, accomplish some task, or reach some goal or desired score. Pleasure, for its own sake, is alien to their thinking. To compete, to win, to "shoot-to-score" — this is their language. Workaholics analyse their game, strive for continual improvement, and get angry with themselves if they have a bad day. Many ugly moods, thrown racquets or bats, and foul language colour the courts and playing fields as the workaholic "works" at his or her game.

Play is an integral part of adult life; it helps keep a person healthy and open to growth, and leads to a balanced lifestyle. The child within the adult needs to express itself. Anne Brennan and Janice Brewi, in *Mid-life Directions: Praying and Playing Sources of New Dynamism*, suggest that while the Puritan work ethic highlighted thrift, increasing toil, and the deferral of gratification, their opposites "to give and spend lavishly, to take genuine rest and leisure and to experience fully and with the deepest satisfaction" are an important balance.

One of our greatest pleasures in the second half of life can be to develop our opposite functions. For example, people with very high intuitive powers, who are quite restless and impatient by nature, will do well to develop the opposite sensation function. They can choose to use all five senses to contact the earth through gardening, sitting and watching patterns in water, stooping to smell the flowers, or stopping to touch a sculpture, or cock their ears to hear a marvellous bird call. Such activities serve to centre them in the here-and-now, rather than always being future-oriented and driven to see what is around the corner, as intuitive people are inclined to do.

Hard workers who, during the first half of life, often sacrificed play welcome the opportunity to slow down and make up for lost time. Not so, workaholics! The white rabbit in *Alice in Wonderland* typifies the workaholic's lament: "I'm late, I'm late, for a very important date. No time to say hello, goodbye, I'm late, I'm late, I'm late!" The workaholic too rushes nowhere. His work ethic says that work must be finished before he can play. In the beginning years, the functioning workaholic too enjoys his work, but as personality changes create problems, and pressures become too great, work can become onerous, overwhelming, or boring and meaningless. But anxiety drives the workaholic anyway. Many of my clients confess they have grown to hate their work, and would give anything to be able to quit.

The spending of money for leisure and pleasure can become a contentious issue for many couples as the breakdown progresses. Money represents power and control, so workaholics can become totally irrational when money is discussed. "Tell me about it," groaned one exasperated spouse. Since workaholics want to keep money management secretive and in their control, they often completely refuse to discuss money issues with their partners. The spouse seldom knows what the workaholic makes, spends, or saves, or where securities, life insurance, etc., are kept. If there is a sudden death, the spouse is left in the dark. Money represents power for power's sake. Secrecy is a way of holding on to power, and secrecy becomes more important as inner chaos increases. Love as a power itself, forgiveness as an inner power, and the celebration of life and joy are foreign values to workaholic thinking.

For recovery to take place, the workaholic needs to find the child within who likes to play. Vacations are necessary to restore balance, and give one time to watch water and to contemplate life. Family and friends are most precious, and they blossom when laughter and play encourage healthy relationships.

Loss of Physical and Psychological Health

Although most workaholics suffer occasional bouts of severe fatigue and exhaustion, they have remarkable stamina. This allows them to stubbornly persevere at their work throughout their lifetime. Some never retire, working well into their eighties. No wonder, since they have no other hobbies or interests. The eccentric, devoted old man used to be treated with tolerance, especially in the family business. Now the "bottom line" is all important, and tolerance suffers. It is devastating for older workaholics to find that their office space is needed when budgets are cut, that others want the prestige of their title or their bigger office for their own status, and that the corporate mentality of produce-or-else leaves them with no one to appreciate and value their wisdom.

Younger workaholics get caught in a vicious circle that ensures that the work obsession cannot be broken. Society, in fact, encourages and supports this cycle. A number of my clients urged me to stress the importance of recognizing this pattern. The workaholic suffers a period of extreme fatigue and confusion and, under pressure from family, colleagues, or a physician, decides to cut down the hours of work. When work then piles up, the pressure builds within, and feelings of being out of control begin to flood up to consciousness. Some report feelings of being overwhelmed and panicky, and experience claustrophobic sensations. A few experience feelings of emptiness, loss, and disorientation. The workaholic then becomes irritable, restless, and overly sensitive, and takes everything personally. Chaotic feelings build, so the solution is to stay late to finish some project. "Just this once" is the rationale. Re-establishing control feels good, and concerned friends or family heave a sigh of relief. It is better than being shouted at or ignored. Things are back to normal. To prove she is all right, she takes on yet another task or promotion to build up her fragile ego. Once again, the addict succumbs to join the rat race. There are many temptations to regain power and be seen by peers and the public to be a successful person. Since many workaholics are highly visible people in the community, they are often asked to join boards or do committee work for charities. Some are lured back to the workaholic whirl by offers of more prestigious jobs. As internal security is threatened, a strong public image becomes even more important. Achieving the goal they have worked so hard to attain, many are left with little else to pursue; or if they fail to achieve it, they are left frustrated and feel inadequate. Failure is unthinkable, so workaholics set new goals. Top is where the Controller wants to be. Second-best is not enough, so these people set higher, more stringent standards for themselves and want to climb a bigger mountain or build a better mousetrap. Soon, they are back pumping more adrenalin, straining their system to the limit.

Excessive pumping of adrenalin will eventually result in chronic fatigue. This fatigue acts as a circuit-breaker to warn of danger to the system. Fatigue also is a symptom of the hopelessness that feeds into depression. Guilt for past failures and deeds also leaves one feeling helpless and depressed. Some of the signs of depression to watch for, in addition to chronic fatigue, are: changes in eating and sleeping patterns; poor concentration when attempting to focus attention; loss of motivation to work or play; mental, physical, and emotional exhaustion; crying spells; loss of libido, or an increase in sexual drive; depersonalization — distancing yourself from a problem, and not caring any more; irrational anger or cynicism; and a tendency to isolate yourself from family and friends. Loss of memory and forgetfulness are severe problems for workaholics. Intense self-preoccupation and "poor me" and "I, I, I" talk are signals of depression. Depression is very dangerous: the worse you feel about yourself, the less you do, and the more your insecurity and low self-worth build. The spiral downwards can be very fast, or it can go on for years and become a habitual life-pattern.

Physiological responses to workaholism include excess stomach sensitivity, abnormal blood pressure, heart trouble, nervousness, lack of vitality, and total inability to relax. Anxiety reactions may include disturbed breathing, increased heart activity, vasomotor changes, and musculoskeletal disturbances such as trembling or paralysis, or increased sweating. Workaholics often report a feeling of pressure in their chest, constricted breathing, and dizziness and light-headedness.

Psychological responses to anxiety may come from external stimuli and the demands of reality, or from internal pressure pushing for discharge and gratification of drives. Dr. Robert Campbell, editor of *Psychiatric Dictionary*, explains: "As stress increases so will defenses increase until there may result distortion or even alteration of the ego." Defensive responses may vary from normal emergency reactions such as escapes into fantasy to exaggeration of normal function where the organs of the body express the mental troubles of the individual in psychosomatic complaints, or partial withdrawal where a person dissociates and pretends something didn't happen, or panic attacks when a fragile ego ruptures temporarily, or a full retreat into a psychotic state where reality and fantasy blur, or a complete disintegration of the ego or suicide.

In the early stages of the workaholic breakdown, the individual still functions normally, but has periodic anxiety. She may have alarming feelings that she is powerless to do anything about some personal matter. She has an apprehension that some real or imagined danger is impending, and this may make her chronically tense and alert. "It's as if I was facing an on-going emergency twenty-four hours a day," one woman tried to explain. Total self-absorption interferes with awareness of reality. Problem-solving skills give way, and unfinished business builds up. Worrying becomes excessive. Those who develop paranoia experience high levels of crippling doubt. They fear that bad things will happen, and can become paralysed and unable to contemplate solutions because of extreme anxiety.

Faced with guilt and heightened stress and anxiety, the workaholic eventually is forced to confront himself because he is no longer functioning, or is faced with an ultimatum by a spouse to shape up. Psychotherapy is recommended for true and lasting personality changes. Working less temporarily reduces the fatigue, but it also gives more time for fears and guilt to disturb the workaholic. Renewed anxiety causes judgment to go out the window! Remember that when you are living in a dysfunctional family, you lose sight of what is normal. An important part of psychotherapy is to learn what a healthy family and marriage is all about.

One success story concerns a strong-minded, successful lawyer who reluctantly came in to "help out" his wife. Sally was suffering extreme distress and depression because of a brief affair her husband had. He denied that it was anything but a regrettable mid-life crisis, and claimed that the woman meant nothing to him. To Sally, it meant she could no longer trust or respect her husband. The trauma and intense pain she experienced had destroyed her peaceful world and her own confidence in herself as an attractive woman. After a few sessions, Richard began to come for himself, as insight after insight gave him hope for salvaging his marriage.

One afternoon, Richard was attempting to let me know how he had progressed. "You showed me my value system was way off-base. I never saw as equals other colleagues who did not wish to excel, but now I do. I am starting to be proud of being a good father and husband."

In a telephone conversation several months after completing psychotherapy, Richard confessed: "It's a slow learning process. My wife still has to tell me when I put others down. Sometimes I just don't see it myself. Each time I am confronted with some old behaviour, I recognize how deeply anchored my ideas are to my roots, education, and early home life. It's hard to undo." In summation, he mused: "Workaholics are really not very nice people. If I had to choose a friend six months ago, it wouldn't have been me!" We shared a good laugh at this insight.

We will now explore how the workaholic's breakdown affects the members of the family. The timing of the breakdown alters the children's development greatly, and we will see why the family dynamics have such long-term effects on the children in these workaholic families.

6.
The Workaholic Family:
Dysfunctional
Patterns and
Dynamics

BETRAYAL OF VOWS

The family is the real victim of workaholism. Workaholics become married to their work, and their vows to love and honour their spouse are no longer meaningful. My client Betty and I were discussing the betrayal and helplessness she felt. "I realize I've spent five years of my life running a poor second to a lethal obsession. I should have been smarter, but, silly me, I was still in love with my husband. Absolutely no earthly mortal can be expected to cope with all this crazy-making behaviour!"

She's right. Nobody can compete with an all-consuming obsession. We were having a wrap-up session, and Betty was telling me about her more frequent moments of peace. "It's one thing to choose a path in life that leads to tragedy; it's quite another to be dragged kicking and screaming along that path because you love someone and want to help rescue them. You know" — her gaze dropped and her voice became shaky — "the absolute worst hell was watching my kids suffer along with me. I'm slowly coming to terms with my own pain at having our marriage breakdown. It's just not something I ever thought would happen to me. I know now that two people must be equally involved in reconciliation, and John's still insisting that there's no such thing as workaholism! But I'll never stop wishing the kids could have shared our battle against this wretched addiction together. I want them to know that problems can be solved if two people still love each other."

Betty, lost in thought for a moment, added: "I know that John would never treat anyone else in his world as he has me." Then she laughed. "Couldn't you please invent a cure for a 'trapped unconscious'?"

Betty's joking remark has stayed with me. Because of the veil of denial, her children were robbed of the ultimate gift every child deserves: the knowledge of how to resolve conflicts acquired by watching healthy parents solve their own problems. Only when power struggles cease and punishing behaviour stops can trust develop once again so that there can be a reciprocal give-and-take between couples.

This chapter will highlight some of the unhealthy family patterns that develop as a result of workaholism, and other patterns that contribute to its initial growth. The workaholic is a key player in these family dynamics for a number of reasons. First, workaholics grew up in a dysfunctional system, and their role models taught them unhealthy patterns of relating to others. Conditional love is all they know. Second, their need to feel dominant makes them less comfortable relating to people on a peer level. They feel more at ease with younger or older people, and with people of a lower age, status, or socio-economic level. Their friends are often equally troubled individuals. Third, workaholics must maintain their own sense of control or else risk anxiety. Wishing to be respected and to be seen to be in charge is an equally powerful motivator for keeping up controlling behaviour. Fourth, workaholics who are introverted tend to stay on the edge of groups, remaining objective, aloof, and uninvolved. Fifth, workaholics who are thinking types tend to value things, ideas, and accomplishments above all else. Even feeling types learn to repress feelings to win approval and success. Performance goals, not people and relationships, become a top priority. For all of these reasons, workaholics are hesitant to share power, or stop controlling others. We will now see how power struggles result in family dysfunction.

UNEQUAL BALANCE OF POWER

Although equal pay for equal work is a goal today, man's work still usually takes precedence in two-parent families. Even today, men hold on to the image of themselves as the "providers" in the family, even if, in reality, this is not the case. It is Mom who takes off work to look after sick kids. Employers are more likely to be supportive if a wife is away attending to family responsibilities. Men, for the most part, are reluctant to ask for the time off in family crises. The "indispensable provider" role, so important to the male ego, thus remains protected.

Although men are now taking much more personal responsibility for their children, the stories of the clients I see reflect the old bias that father's work is sacrosanct, and his needs and wishes come first. Many marriages still reflect this bias. However, the reality of the 1990s is that many couples want to share power and personal responsibility. The emotional well-being of the family is just as important as financial security. The family suffers if there is trouble in either sphere. In order to understand these old influences on present families, let's look at a couple who married in the 1950s. Many readers will identify with this family's story.

Cynthia

After her marriage, Cynthia worked as a secretary in a law firm until her first child was born. She regretted her loss of financial independence, but compensated by being super-supportive of her husband's medical career. Cynthia was going to be the "perfect" wife. She tried hard not to complain about Jack's long hours, his frayed temper, and eventually his chronic fatigue. When he came home looking grey and drawn, she fussed over his health and was always there to support him. Cynthia, without realizing what was happening, became the nurturing Mother figure, protecting Jack from burdening himself with fix-it jobs, unpaid bills, and patients who called him at home when there was no emergency. Cynthia screened these calls and smoothed over all the irritants to cushion Jack in a "wrinkle-free" home environment.

As more children were born, Cynthia needed more support and help from Jack, but both accepted that the status quo of unequal home responsibility was necessary for the time being. "It's for both of us and our future to build up a base of security," they colluded. Jack's obligation to his home was a financial one, and increasingly his energies went into building his academic and professional image. Since Jack felt he owed any leftover time to his family, he had no time to see his old friends. He stopped playing the sports he used to enjoy. Cynthia was left totally responsible for intimacy, socializing, wiping the children's tears, keeping track of activities and birthdays, and planning all the get-togethers for both sets of family relatives. The whole family's schedule revolved around Jack's work schedule, and they had to fit into whatever time was left. More and more, family time was sacrificed.

Cynthia, of necessity, was left to play the central "hub" role around which the children's lives revolved. They came to her to help them solve problems, to share their adventures, to get love and attention. Jack was either rushing out the door late for an eight o'clock meeting or arriving home very late for dinner. Initially, the family all waited for Dad, but eventually the kids would get too hungry and irritable, so Mom went ahead without her husband. This long, drawn-out dinner scene was a constant theme in the couple's arguments. Jack, to avoid any more trauma, finally made a rule that if he wasn't home by seven o'clock, they were to go ahead. It's significant that a lot of Jack's "rules" let him opt out of parental responsibility. As Jack became more self-centred, he just "did his own thing," totally absorbed in his frantic schedule.

Cynthia later was able to see her own involvement in keeping workaholism alive. "I'm unaware when the realization that my husband was a workaholic dawned on me. I was well aware that I was taking the majority of the responsibility at home. My reasoning was that it made it easier to get the job done. I was always saying, do this, do that — I was always there, but I was also controlling everyone and fighting for my own power base!" Then Cynthia digressed to avoid the pain from her own insight: "All my life I wondered why he didn't have a social life of his own that I could join."

Periodically, Cynthia would grow very lonely and feel so taken for granted that she would stage a brief rebellion. For a few weeks there was talk of cutting down work hours, getting off some committees, and spending Saturdays with the family. Then excuses for maintaining the status quo would be found, and Jack's push for autonomy would re-emerge. As Jack's breakdown symptoms became more severe, any brief attempts at a more normal lifestyle only made his anxiety soar. "I can't stand my office being in such a mess. The piles of papers are driving me nuts! I've got no choice, Cynthia. I'll just have to go down there on Saturdays again." Jack had lost all sense of fun. Because problems were swept under the proverbial rug and never resolved, pent-up anger meant that moods and blow-ups became the norm. No wonder their sex life was almost non-existent. Cynthia's nagging only caused her to slip into a depression, and she became disillusioned and bitter.

A year later, a stronger and healthier Cynthia reflected: "I think the family all learned early on that doctors are always late. It seemed to be expected that he would be late, and gradually he got later and later. He would tell the children he would do such-and-such. And I do think he meant it, but something would come up, or he was too exhausted. Any request to do something was tempered with 'if I get my work done,' and of course the work was never done. I think his favourite phrase is 'I have so much work to do.' In a way he was a guest! He came to things, but never helped create them. We all just learned to work around this. If he was there, great. If not, we understood. His presence was always very important to all of us. He seemed to add the icing on the cake to many family things. They never seemed to be quite as good without him. The children were disappointed, but seemed to accept that because he was a doctor he couldn't be there."

The family dynamics in this case study get played out, with variations, in most workaholic families. Today's younger version of Cynthia might work full-time outside the home, but still be bent on trying to be Superwoman at home. Today's Jack would try to balance housekeeping duties with expanding work schedules, and try to assume the responsibility for changing diapers, getting kids to day care, and cooking dinner. Yet the partners collude to make the job the focus of this merry-go-round. These Superpersons are the advertising world's dream. As Carol Orsborn, in *Enough Is Enough: Exploding the Myth of Having It All*, explained, everywhere you look, in newspapers, magazines, and television, you are given helpful advice. "For improved self-esteem, manicure your nails. For stress, try the B vitamins. But for God's sake, your family's sake, and your credit card company's sake — keep coping, keep going, keep your upper lip so stiff you end up looking like a camel." Confessing you can't juggle anything else, you're too exhausted, you can't see or think straight is a no-no. After all, the role models in the media do it, and their hair and their outfits are always perfect. Your next-door neighbour runs her house like clockwork, and she even looks happy! The real truth — that your fatigue comes simply from doing too much and not getting enough sleep — is ignored. To these perfectionists, a cry of help is a sign of failure.

THE SKEWED FAMILY

Parents in workaholic families not only have an unequal balance of personal responsibility for the children, but help create another dynamic that leads to dysfunctional parenting and to potentially severe problems for the children. Workaholics eventually find themselves living on the peripheral edge of the family circle. "I was spending some time with my wife and children, but doing it grudgingly, as if they were depriving me of my valuable time — time I could be working or recovering from work," says one recovering client. He later came to understand the effects of his own workaholism on his family: "The major impact is on my wife, who has been feeling ignored, taken for granted, unwanted for a long time. The frustration, sadness, and anger that have developed have a very negative impact on the kids, and on our family atmosphere in general." Then, he adds: "There are also lots of incidents where I have taken out my work stress and frustration on the children, especially on our son." This skewed pattern where father is outside on the periphery of the circle and mother is in the middle, closest to the children, creates emotional and communication problems that, once established, become very difficult to undo.

Although, in the modern family, often both parents and the nanny, or a series of homemakers, vie for a place in the family circle, in this chapter I will examine only the situation of the peripheral father since more long-term study is required to understand the complex situation as it is played out in today's yuppiedom.

Unhealthy Triangles

Once the workaholic's career peaks and he is well established, or once a long-sought-after goal is reached, he can let down his guard enough to think about where he has been and where he is going. These questions can create a crisis as feelings of emptiness and loneliness force a search within for a deeper meaning to life. Depression and anxiety attacks also force such questioning. One hopes that this person will recognize many of the reasons for his own unhappiness and plug back into the family to make up for the time that he has stayed emotionally on the periphery of the family circle, overinvolved in his work. Tragically, the realization that he has missed half of life's wealth of relationships often dawns on him only after he has lost his family through separation and divorce.

Because workaholism encourages a competitive and envious nature, workaholics often become jealous of the spouse's close relationship with the children. In our example, it is the husband who wishes to re-establish himself as a powerful figure in the family. This means that the mother and the children must now adjust their comfortable intimacy to accommodate his new needs. Unfortunately, family patterns are strong and highly resistant to change. Alas, the family has learned to function without him. Unhealthy triangles thus begin to form to shake up the status quo. A covert alliance may be formed where a parent and a child will collude to undermine the power and authority of the other central parent. Resulting power struggles can tear the family apart.

Indirect communication — where one person acts as the messenger between two others — is the key to how this dynamic gets played out in the workaholic family. When Mom is in the "hub" role, she tends to give messages to Dad from the children, or Dad discusses things with her and she tells the children. If father has been having rages or temper tantrums, no one dares confront him directly as he may lash back or work longer hours to avoid the family. Mothers in this situation tend to become the scapegoat when any communication goes awry.

When love and energy are sacrificed to the "work god," the husband–wife bond loosens, and control and power struggles form that threaten to destroy the marriage. The parental bond becomes stronger than the marital bond because true love and healthy communication have broken down. The workaholic neglects to affirm and appreciate the spouse who becomes disenchanted with having to compete with work for time and attention.

I believe that the marriages that survive workaholism intact are the ones in which workaholics have remembered to honour the spouses and their different roles. They support their spouses, especially in front of the children, remain faithful, celebrate family birthdays, and remind the children to treat the spouse with love and respect. The workaholics remember to let the spouses know they are needed and appreciated. In turn, their spouses do not resent the workaholic's job because they are kept informed and share in the social gatherings. They are in a partnership where both accord work its proper place in their lives.

In the healthy family, the generation lines are kept clear and are respected. No triangles form across the generations. Husband and wife have separate relationships with each of the children, and speak directly to each child and to each other.

Husband and Wife

—————————————————————————————— Generation Line

Children   X   Y   Z

If you want to give your children the gift of security and love, you must honour and nourish the marital bond and keep it separate and distinct from the parental bond. Each partner must develop a special relationship with each of the children.

In the unhealthy family, the generation line is blurred and crossed over. Parenting becomes more important than the marital bond. Competition between the husband and wife is set up as one parent aligns with a child or children and the other parent is excluded. Or, both parents overindulge the children and vicariously live out their lives as a substitute for establishing an independent life as a couple.

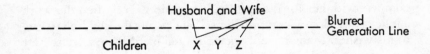

There are many variations of these triangles. "I made my children an obsession. I always took them places, but to the detriment of Monique. She was never my priority, it was always the kids," says Michel. As his insight developed, he realized that the obsession was "good for the kids, but bad for my wife. Now I'd rather spend time with Monique and the children. We're planning family things versus taking the kids alone — but this is only recent."

"Our family life was affected because Bruce didn't seem to enjoy anything that we did as a family. As a result, I would do things with the kids or he would take them places, but not together. I must add that this may have been normal for Bruce as it was the way his family did things. My parents both enjoyed vacationing with us all together," says one wife whose husband felt comfortable only when he could relate to his children alone and be in complete charge.

In the extreme case, the peripheral parent opts out of parenting altogether and leaves the partner solely responsible for the children's well-being. This is one absentee father's response to how workaholism affected his family: "When the children were young, and even now, most of the parenting came from my wife. As the children grew and needed less attention, my wife felt estranged from the real world and shut out of my world — the company, business, business relationships, etc. Overall, I think they may have been affected by my inability at times to relax and enjoy life and do recreational things with them. I was too busy playing golf and curling. I'm afraid some of my children show signs of being obsessive about their school, social life, and their work."

THE PERIPHERAL FATHER

When a father who has been emotionally distant and overinvolved with work suddenly decides to become more involved with his family, he can be welcomed if he respects the role of his wife and does not compete with her for the children's attention. Too often the work-aholic needs a lot of attention himself and wants the children to cater to his wishes. Many male workaholics tell me that they are secretly very jealous of their wives' close relationship with the children. In such cases, the father will try to compete or control and will meet resistance in the form of an established status quo. Change is threaten-ing. Unhealthy triangles often form as the balance of power shifts to allow for father's emotional re-entry.

The timing of this re-entry is crucial to the family's survival. The older the children are, the more patterns of communication and power are rigidly set. As well, if re-entry occurs around the time of the children's puberty, it is likely to interfere with the individuation process, where children stand up to their parents' control and test their own powers. A child in a healthy family will push up against the same-sex parent in a quest for a separate identity. The individuation process is necessary for autonomy and maturity.

A worst-case scenario occurs when the Oedipus complex gets played out. Freudian theory suggests that, around the time of puberty, boys' erotic feelings are directed towards the feminine opposite, the mother figure, and girls' towards the masculine, the father figure. In the fantasied identification with father and mother, the children establish their own primary self-identification. Their future complex male and female social and sexual identifications are formed at this time. Complications in the course of the sexual identification process may lead to the development of an overidentification with the op-posite-sex parent. A girl identifies with her father instead of her mother, and her masculine side dominates her personality. Sexual-identity problems may lead to the rejection of socially approved masculine and feminine roles, and gender confusion. Problems with authority figures also emerge in these troubled teens.

Sons in workaholic families often have not had Father around much to act as a masculine role model, especially in the important pre-adolescent years. When a father is chronically unavailable, the son lacks a proper role model. If he is fortunate, he may become involved with a nurturing Cub leader or baseball coach who becomes an important figure in the boy's life and provides the missing warmth. These volunteers offer firm discipline and guidance, and act as healthy role models. Many clients tell me their fathers did not attend their sports events, but their coach was great. Such fathers don't respect their own playful side and want their children to appreciate their own importance in the working world. One man justified his absence at his son's baseball game by saying that he was "helping the kid learn that the adult world is one of responsibility, success, and personal sacrifice."

A workaholic father may re-enter the family in different ways. He can come in as the strict, authoritarian father to re-establish his power base in the family. Or he can compete with the mother by being the easy-going, laissez-faire Mr. Nice Guy who indulges the children, and thus undermines his wife's discipline as he courts their favour. In doing so, he takes power away from his wife, who is left to play the heavy.

Some fathers can remain emotionally aloof and even negligent, and largely abandon their responsibilities to the family. The negligent father can become completely engrossed in his work, seek out other addictions such as alcohol or drugs, have infidelities, or play the jock role with his buddies and work at his play.

Let's look at each of these three types of fathers and the effects they have on their children.

The Authoritarian Father

The workaholic authoritarian father, closed off from his own sensitivity, adheres to the ideals of responsibility, discipline, objectivity, and rationality. He exercises order by dictating rules and regulations, or by teaching and preaching to the children. Under his proud exterior, however, lies an increasingly powerful inferiority complex built up as denial defences repress more and more negative feelings. In time, strong insecurity means the father must struggle even harder to maintain a dominant position in the family. Growing inefficiency at work and rebellious feelings at home further undermine his confidence. Inferiority fosters jealousy and envy of the wife's power in the family, and the competitive spirit causes these fathers to exercise their "superiority" by putting down other family members. Control tactics can be overt and obvious, or covert, such as in passive–aggressive anger. These men are often the Controller-type workaholics who are used to making rules and regulations and to having others jump into action to implement their work ideas. The children either withdraw in fear, or intense power struggles develop.

One power struggle resulted in impacted bowels for one young son. "I was having severe toileting issues with my three-year-old. I was controlling everyone and everything! Our family activities revolved around my work schedule, and that meant cancelling events at the last minute." Then this enlightened father adds: "Our life had become incredibly intense, but also unpredictable! No wonder poor Billy was always upset and afraid to let go. My rigid face was probably enough to stop a train in its tracks!"

Since these fathers usually have difficulty establishing and maintaining peer relationships because of their need to control, the parent–child relationship is naturally appealing. Narcissistic controllers, especially, will see children as extensions of themselves or as possessions. Their own ideal or perfect image is projected onto the child. The child is seen only from their own viewpoint, in their own image. Children who are radically different in personality are therefore a puzzle, even a threat. These children are thus treated with caution and distrust, and are certainly not accepted unconditionally.

The timing of re-entry is everything here. When the children are still young, and not yet resentful of father's absence, the authoritarian tactics may work. Children want to please their parents to gain approval and positive affirmation. Mother, weary of disciplining the children alone, may welcome the added discipline, and so relinquish some of her own authority, and be able to slip back into her appropriate nurturing, feminine role.

Trouble arises when the children are near puberty's rebellious stage, and Father starts telling them what they should and should not be doing. The more frequent appearances of Father as an active "heavy" activates the children's anger and resentment at his former absenteeism. As one son wrote: "My father got into cycles where he was sarcastic and derogatory towards everyone. He was obsessed with his routines, and if any of us interrupted his momentum, then there was hell to pay! He ran himself into exhaustion at work, and roared home so hyper he nit-picked about the most inane things. He had us running in all directions, picking up things, going off to the store for his newspapers, or looking for his glasses. Boy, his memory was like a sieve. He was forever losing his glasses!"

The message the authoritarian father gives the child is that work is more important than play, and that productivity and the achievement of some external standard are the measuring sticks of success. Personal self-worth and satisfaction gained from being a truly nice human being who is thoughtful and sensitive to others are undervalued because the father's own feeling function does not work. The disillusioned child, to be accepted, must gain his or her identification through performing and doing serious "work." Unless he or she is the best on the track team, or is winning awards, the workaholic tends not to show enthusiasm. Winners are a different story because the child's accomplishments are seen as an extension of the parent's own ambition — a "feather in his cap." Many adolescent sports heroes "work" hard at their play so the workaholic parent will support them. The kids who goof around and play just for fun, or who don't care about competition or who wins, are chastised and encouraged to take their sport seriously and "be successful in whatever you do!"

Rebellious Sons of Authoritarian Fathers

When fathers are unavailable or preoccupied with their own world, young boys often will seek nurturing and identify with female role models, such as teachers or entertainment stars, and reject their own more masculine traits. If the authoritarian father suddenly begins to devote more energy to the family at a time when the pre-adolescent or adolescent needs to establish his own identity, resentment about unmet needs, coupled with a natural longing to be accepted, may lead to confusion. The authoritarian father faced with such ambivalence will feel rejected. The rage from this loss of control over others can create further havoc. One minute his son responds well to some new rules and direction, and the next he is openly rebellious and resents this sudden correction from this "stranger" who is upsetting the established way things are done.

Such power struggles and battles of will often produce violent rages if the son fights back to establish his own control. Scenes of physical abuse are commonly reported. Ken told me that, when he was eighteen, he had gone downstairs to take a break from cramming for his exams. His father asked him to go to the store for a pack of cigarettes, and he refused. "Dad turned a ghostly chalk white, and his eyes narrowed to slits of steel. He ordered me to go, or else, and then picked up a chair and pushed me across the room. I slammed into the wall, hit my head, and then slumped to the floor stunned. I will never forget that look of intense hatred in his eyes — it haunts me to this day!" Ken shuddered at the memory. When the explosion of rage ends up in physical acts of violence, these fathers, barely coping as it is with their own chaotic world, cannot take responsibility for their actions. Some simply withdraw even more, which creates further damage. Sons with a highly developed feeling side can be devastated by such shows of power, and can reject their own masculine side even more, seeking refuge with nurturing peers and adults. These sons often have many girl friends, and are close to their sisters and mothers or other female relatives.

Homosexuality or bisexuality is one outcome of confused role states. The authors of *The Workaholic and His Family* describe one family where the father, in his own eyes and in the eyes of society, is the epitome of human dedication. He is a scientist "who spends seven days (and nights) a week in the lab in order to save mankind from various diseases while his wife suffers from loneliness and his sons become homosexuals and eventually commit suicide." This man becomes furious when his family puts any demands on him and calls him a selfish husband and father. The authors go on: "But he has such a strong selfish need to compensate for his inferiority feelings that he blinds himself to the truth. In reality, his wife and children are correct, and they are suffering severely because of his subtle selfishness. This is precisely the reason why so many of the children of pastors, missionaries, and doctors turn out to be rebellious." Either their children follow their role models and become workaholics themselves, or opt out and seek jobs where competition and ladder-climbing are not emphasized. They suffer extreme ambivalence around valuing play and leisure and experience underlying feelings of guilt for not sharing the values of the parent or parents.

Rebellious children often leave home early to avoid the power struggles and the negative tension there. The parents feel embarrassment and loss of control. The children are fighting for their survival and their right to formulate their own value systems. For workaholic fathers, not used to people saying no or arguing back, being challenged by their offspring is too hard to bear. Mothers are placed in the middle, trying to be supportive to both the husband and son, but they are unable to condone the fathers' inappropriate outbursts or passive-aggressive withdrawal. Quarrels around parenting and discipline problems are frequent in these families as power struggles grow more pathological. The mother's respect for the husband is diminished, and trust issues become a crucial factor in the possible breakdown of this marriage at a later stage.

Authoritarian Fathers' Daughters

In a patriarchal authoritarian society, men define femininity consciously through their culturally conditioned views of what women's roles should be, and unconsciously through their own projections onto women of what they want them to be. Women, in turn, struggle to assert their own femininity, to establish their own values and ways of being, their own emotional responses to their feelings. Linda Leonard, in *The Wounded Woman: Healing the Father–Daughter Relationship*, says: "Whenever there is a patriarchal authoritarian attitude which devalues the feminine by reducing it to a number of roles or qualities which come, not from women's own experience, but from an abstract view of her — there one finds the collective father overpowering the daughter, not allowing her to grow creatively from her own essence."

Cassie found herself in such a position. "My Dad had a thing about my going to be a pharmacist. He thought this was the ideal profession for a woman because she could work part-time while the kids were in school, and still be home in time to get the family meals. I tried to explain why I wanted to go to law school, but he just covered his ears and refused to listen. His mind was already made up, and heaven help us if we challenged him!" The Controller authoritarian father often is narcissistic, and believes his daughter is just like him, an extension of himself. Empathy is not developed well enough in him to allow him to recognize her differences.

Daughters with such authoritarian fathers often grow up believing that they exist, not in their own right, but only in relation to a man's needs. Such daughters sacrifice their own feminine side and identify, not with the mother's feminine qualities, but with the all-powerful, controlling father. He, in turn, projects his split-off feeling, feminine side onto his daughter and views her as an extension of his own personality. Her masculine traits are thus encouraged and idealized. Security, stability, duty, obedience, and rationality are viewed as important. His daughter, not his sons, will follow in his footsteps. Often these girls choose the same career path as the father, and the father acts as a mentor to encourage their success in his field. These girls can be very aggressive, ambitious, and overachieving. Their fathers do not honour their own feminine tender side and are devoid of true empathy, passion, spontaneity, and gentleness. Because these fathers must be "right," require obedience, and make the rules, they are able to justify and rationalize their actions. They tend not to be aware of the damage they do to their daughter's development. They usually keep a tight rein on money matters, so keep the power to influence career decisions. Their wives and children remain in a submissive, dependent position. Any efforts at independence are often met with vindictive punishment, which is meted out to those who dare to challenge.

Workaholic fathers who fall out of romantic love with their wives because the women are becoming more demanding of attention and critical of the lack of affection and empathy often project an unconscious wish for a flirtatious involvement with one or more of their daughters. Guilt feelings surface at times, but are quickly justified as "wanting the best" for the daughter. Denial covers any shame that surfaces. Like a teenager, Michelle, her father's pet, has remained obsessed with guys. Her talk is peppered with anecdotes about her endless search for the ideal man. She knows exactly what he should look like. He must be witty, wealthy, and come from a cultured home. She rejects the overtures of anyone falling short of this dream guy, and quiet, thoughtful, sensitive young men are dismissed as boring. Her man is going to stand out in a crowd. Unconsciously, Michelle is terrified of intimacy, and her constant quest keeps her safe from commitment and a deeper sexuality, which she lacks.

In such situations, the "father's daughter," according to Marion Woodman, in *Addiction to Perfection*, wishes to please the father, to share his intellectual pursuits and meet his perfectionistic standards. "In the dynamics of such a relationship, the mother is experienced either as absent or as a rival. While the daughter experiences herself as the beloved of the father, consciously she knows she dare not share his bed, yet instinctively her energies remain incestuous. Thus her love is split off from her sexuality. In fantasy she dreams of her spiritual lover; in reality, she remains unconscious of her sexuality, acts it out without love, or fears it as some explosive power that can destroy her." Tragically, this dynamic gets played out in many workaholic families.

Marion Woodman suggests that there is serious long-term damage done to these daughters. They often fall in love with men who cannot marry them, then create around these men an idealized world in which they are either adored or rejected. They fantasize their emotions, but lack a sense of self that would allow true feelings to develop. They mirror men, but remain merely a reflection, and fail to develop a persona of their own. Like Marilyn Monroe, such a woman "is her father's walking doll, yet sweet and erotic as she unconsciously may be, she has a pseudo-male psychology." They are often quick, smart-alecky, witty people who attract men initially by their cleverness. Often these girls are not asked out more than once or twice because their brittleness offends as they compete with the male's masculine side.

The "father's daughter's" inner soft feminine is not developed well enough to bring out her gentle, nurturing attributes, and men are turned off sexually. These girls can be a buddy or a friend to their husbands, and tend to sacrifice their life to serve him. The corporate wife who willing sacrifices her own personal life to play out the role of husband's help-mate and business ally is an example. Often these daughters never marry, however, as they are locked into a fantasy in which the father is their true love.

If this daughter's husband matures, he will be bored with his wife's lack of an independent self and frustrated when she remains out of reach emotionally. As well, when a husband is unable to live up to the wife's idealized projection of him as a god-like figure, he will begin to deny the rejection of his own true personality and recognize that he cannot live up to her excessive demands. Marriage breakdown is inevitable as the illusions crack around the couple.

Marion Woodman warns that these women are at great psychological risk. The strength that the "father's daughter" projects onto her man is not available to her. Her projections can drain her and leave her physically and emotionally fragile. Failure in their relationships, for these idealistic perfectionists, leads to depression and feelings of helplessness. In the most extreme cases, a profound doubt that they even exist forces a crisis, and suicide is a potential outcome if psychological help is not sought soon enough.

The Indulgent Father

The indulgent workaholic father is often the *puer aeternus*, or eternal boy, who has never established an inner sense of responsibility, discipline, and authority. He remains naive and does not wish to own his negative shadow side. Ironically, he is ruled by his unconscious and by his instinctive drives. He fears true commitment, and likes to keep his options open. Self-indulgent and self-absorbed, the *puer* acts instinctively out of his feelings of the moment, which may change at any time. He is out of touch with his true feelings. These fathers dream of possibilities of what might be, of what they could accomplish, but their plans fail to come to fruition. They avoid conflicts and, often, responsibility, and lack the inner strength to implement or carry through and actualize their potential. Narcissistic Controller workaholics are usually indulgent fathers who are too weak to discipline, and too self-absorbed to truly love another, other than as an extension of themselves.

Pedestal Daughters of Indulgent Fathers

Such narcissistic men often seduce their daughters by romanticizing them. These fathers treat their daughters like a wife or love object. They make subtle flirtations, involve themselves in the daughter's world of clothes and gossip. They use their charm and Nice Guy image to win the daughter's attention and approval away from the mother. The wife is pushed aside when she tries to be a mother to her daughter, and she is forced to compete to gain her daughter's attention. The narcissist cares little for what is truly in his daughter's best interests because he is intent, instead, on satisfying his own instinctual needs.

If this dynamic occurs around adolescence, it can lead to tragedy. When the daughter begins to establish her independence from her female role model, these fathers will side with the daughter against the mother. In healthy family dynamics, it is quite natural at the beginning of this process for daughters to become very critical of their mothers and lash out at them. Suddenly nothing Mother does is right, and she becomes a target for criticism as the daughter searches for the differences between herself and her role model. "Why don't you ever wear nail polish?" she demands. Or, "Esther's mother bakes cookies for them all the time!" Meanwhile, father is seen as attractive because of his daughter's new interest in the opposite sex. If the father is healthy, he will support the mother to help her withstand the daughter's rebellion. Mother can then maintain her acceptance of the daughter, in spite of the daughter's often obnoxious behaviour. Emotionally, the daughter recognizes that the mother still loves her, in spite of her behaviour, so eventually she too learns to accept herself unconditionally, warts and all. She comes to terms with her real mother, not the idealized one she longs for. Together they work towards a more equal relationship as a resolution of the sexual identification process.

In the dysfunctional workaholic family, the narcissistic father will choose to side with the daughter in an argument, and unconsciously use the daughter's anger to get back at his wife and triumph over her. This is one of the unhealthiest uses of the vindictive triumph. The put-down gives the father temporary satisfaction, but forces the daughter into a position of rivalry with her mother for father's attention, and the Oedipus complex gets played out in a pathological way. The daughter feels idealized and special. She, in turn, idealizes her father, which makes it extremely difficult for her to relate to other men, especially sexually. Adolescent boys, being awkward, self-conscious, and insecure, cannot compete with these narcissistic fathers. These men are young-looking, young-acting, often charming, romantic, witty, and polite, and they inspire their daughters through their talk of endless possibilities and of "what might be."

"The daughters of these eternal boys grow up without an adequate model of self-discipline, limit, and authority, quite often suffering from feelings of insecurity, instability, lack of self-confidence, anxiety, frigidity, and in general, a weak ego." Linda Leonard, in *The Wounded Woman: Healing the Father–Daughter Relationship*, goes on to suggest that the emotional and spiritual growth of these girls is deeply affected by their view of the father figure. The "eternal boy" is thought of by the daughter as someone her own age. The pedestal girl feels powerful because she can manipulate her father through the fascination he has for her. If you can manipulate the "god" in your world, then can you also manipulate God the Father?

Children who can manipulate their parents, and therefore feel "powerful," become extremely anxious and insecure adolescents. After all, if you can "con" the people who are ultimately responsible for your well-being, then you have no real emotional security. These children, in turn, are likely to get trapped at the adolescent level of development and become narcissists themselves because they never work through and complete their own identity separate from those of their parents. Daughters who are rivals with their mothers are robbed of the normal resolution of the mother–daughter struggle. They are caught up in an Oedipal triangle, which leaves them traumatized with guilt and fearful of their own sexuality. Sexuality is blocked from expression with the father. With other men, the daughter can "perform" sexually, but is cut off from her own feminine sexual instincts. Her mother often has had to assume the masculine roles of her weak and indulgent husband. Mother is left to be the strong one who establishes the values, authority, discipline, and structure for the family. The pedestal daughter is left confused about the roles of father and mother, of husband and wife. She learns how to play her parents off against each other, but is caught in an always-lose outcome. In later years, her own relationships will be deeply affected by this power play.

The pedestal daughter's fate is to remain psychologically the "eternal girl," or *puella*, who remains dependent and accepts the identity others project onto her. She sacrifices the direction for her own life, and gives her strength as well as the responsibility for shaping her identity to others. Linda Leonard further sums up her fate: "Quite often she marries a rigidly authoritarian man and becomes the image of woman he wants. Often she looks and acts innocent, helpless, and passive. Or she may rebel, but in her rebellion remains the helpless victim caught in feelings of self-pity, depression, and inertia."

Pedestal Sons of Indulgent Fathers

Sons of narcissistic, indulgent workaholics grow up with a passive, ineffectual father who suffers from a "mother complex." John Sanford, in *The Invisible Partners*, explains: "A man who always avoids emotionally toned encounters with other people is contained within the Mother. One way for him to get out of his Mother complex is to express himself in relationship. If he fails to do so he remains emotionally a little boy who is afraid of women, who resents them if they don't keep him happy, and who is out of touch with his own masculine strength."

When the workaholic suffers the symptoms of the breakdown resulting from job and personal burn-out, he loses his confidence and becomes more and more emotionally dependent on his nurturing wife. He wants her to "fix things up." At the same time, he resents his own dependency and projects his anger and frustration out onto his nurturing, "helpful" wife. The son of this father has as a role model a man who neglects to bring up unpleasant things as they occur, and fails to address problems of relationship because he is afraid of his own anger and his wife's rejection and disapproval. Instead, the son witnesses moodiness, smouldering resentment, and occasionally explosive rages coupled with long periods of Mr. Nice Guy and indulgent generosity. Dr. Jekyll one day, Mr. Hyde the next. Such unpredictable behaviour causes anxiety in children, and many sons experience an ever-present low level of anxiety that results in obsessive–compulsive symptoms. Other sons suffer depressive symptoms of helplessness because they cannot control their unpredictable environment.

Some sons deal with their confusion by compensating for the emotional instability at home. They become overly responsible achievers who seek emotional security in their work outside the home. Many go on to develop workaholism, and the cycle repeats itself in the next generation.

Other sons opt out of responsibility. They take advantage of the narcissistic father's need to gain approval through establishing high performance standards, thus presenting a successful persona to the world. As Dr. Jay Rohrlich, in *Work and Love: The Crucial Balance*, points out, his wife and children must "have the best," he must not be in debt to anyone or ask for favours. It is a weakness to ask for help because the narcissist refuses to recognize his own unconscious desire to be dependent. Their indulged spoiled sons, if they are at all lazy, will be tempted into becoming "takers" themselves. The best way to stay on Dad's side, they learn, is to let him control and solve problems for you. "Go with the flow," accept what Dad provides so that his "generosity" is not questioned.

Because the narcissistic father lacks an awareness of other people's needs, Dr. Rohrlich adds, intimacy, sharing, and an easy give-and-take with his sons is too threatening. Ironically, the narcissistic father complains that other people just take from him, but, in fact, any form of giving leaves the narcissist depleted and drained. Jim, a Narcissistic Controller, had become increasingly cheap about spending money as his denial system became challenged. He couldn't hold back the flood of events that broadcast his failures. His wife had left him, his job was in jeopardy, and he feared the auditors would discover a serious error he had made. At home, Jim became incensed at his sixteen-year-old son. Gary had worked hard to save enough money for a computer camp, but was two hundred dollars short. He knew his father would be upset if he asked for help, but he mustered up his nerve. Jim exploded in fury and accused Gary of being "a selfish bugger who never thought about anybody else but himself." He humiliated Gary by attacking his character, called him a "wimp" and "taker of the first degree." Devastated, Gary fled from the house, sobbing. His world had fallen apart, too, when his mom left, and now his computer dreams were shattered.

These sons are often emotionally crippled unless the mother is strong enough to provide the real love needed for healthy emotional development. An inner void and lack of identity often result because of the lack of identification with the workaholic father. The emotional stability of the mother is a key to the fate of these sons. If the wife's loneliness and anger at not getting any of her needs met lead to depression, alcohol or drug abuse, or other addictive co-dependent behaviours, then the children are left with no healthy role models. Many mothers are so preoccupied with trying to survive without financial backing that they are temporarily out of commission as a nurturer to others. Many sons never become responsible adults, and drop out of school, shift from job to job, and relationship to relationship. These are the "lost" figures who never quite cope with the realities of life.

The Negligent Father

Workaholic fathers may show negligence by being psychologically and often physically unavailable to their children. Especially as the children get older and demand more time and energy, the workaholic is unable or unwilling to adjust and change his schedule. He wants his family to appreciate and value his work because, in his eyes, he is indispensable, and no one can do what he does. Looking back, one recovering negligent father says: "My family was not seeing the me that I thought and hoped I was! Our relationship as a unit was threatened, though I did not realize the severity or ramifications of the effects on them at the time. I suppose that I was short-changing myself, as well, in terms of losing valuable time, time which you cannot get back, creating and developing the kind of relationship with my family that we all needed and now want."

These fathers fail to take an active role in their children's development and growth. Some justify their long absences by rationalizing that "quality" time is what is important. When they are with the children, time is often spent making sure the child comes up to their unrealistic, perfectionistic standards. They want their kids to ski well, swim well, and perform well at school, but give little or sometimes no time to help the child achieve a level of expertise. It is Mom who drives the children to lessons and encourages them. Often a skill is learned to please the absent parent, and is never really "owned" as the child's own unique gift. Woe if the child is a slow learner, dyslexic, or withdrawn and socially inept. Patience is not one of the workaholic's strengths. When the children fail to meet their father's unrealistic expectations, they tend to internalize the failure, and feel like klutzes, incompetent and unworthy of self-esteem. Something is surely wrong with them because they cannot meet their parent's expectations. The children are left confused, frustrated, and discontented with their lot. These children must take the blame because society values the adult's hard work and perfectionistic standards.

The wives of these negligent fathers often totally immerse themselves in the children's lives to compensate. Or they compete with their husbands by spending a great deal of time away from home as well. They plunge into frantic activities or devote excessive energy to friends or causes. The partners spend little time together and pass like ships in the night, living separate lives. When wives work outside the home, they often lead parallel, equally busy lives. Money is rarely a problem. However, no time is left for discussing and sharing the stresses of everyday conflicts within the family, and the wife is usually left to deal alone with all the emotional issues. Because workaholics become very narcissistic as the sickness grows, their children are left emotionally deprived and lonely.

The Detached Daughters of Negligent Fathers

Often the workaholic father will show the same emotional unavailability and aloof detachment to his daughters that he shows his wife. In order to seek affirmation, the daughter has no option left but to prove her own worth and thus seek his attention. She can aspire to a superior level of performance, or go the rebellious route and become involved in drugs or sexual misconduct.

The ambitious daughter who craves success is self-contained, and seeks her identity and sense of accomplishment in her outer world of work and achievements. Independence, power, and a drive to succeed push her to excel in her line of work. She values being in control, efficient, well organized, and productive. One such daughter, who was still struggling with denial, intellectualized: "What does 'obsession' mean? I have a 'preference' for work because it permits development of traits more easily accessible to me. I have no family of my own. This I attribute more to alienation from my femininity/fertility than an 'obsession with work.' "

When the workaholic father is absent a great deal and does not offer adequate fathering, daughters often react by identifying with their masculine side as a compensation. Rather than face the pain of rejection and deep feelings of abandonment, they build a protective armour around themselves. They become successful in a "man's world" where independence, financial rewards, and power are the criteria for success. Outwardly these daughters are confident and in command, but inwardly they have abandoned their feminine feelings and creativity. They are split off from their sensitive, empathic, vulnerable side. Instead, they plan and control their lives, and fear showing weaknesses or appearing lazy or bored. Relaxation is very difficult for these women because they are cut off from the feminine feeling functions which allow them to enjoy being still and reflective.

Overwork and overachievement lead these daughters into their own workaholism, and eventually to a total loss of feeling and instinctive sources of strength. Depression is common, as well as existential crises where nothing she does and achieves gives meaning to her life. She is left cynical and cold, and detached from others. The fear of rejection follows her throughout her life. These daughters desperately need to reconnect with their feminine feeling values, and to seek a spiritual centre, which will place work in its proper place.

The "acting-out" daughter also sacrifices her true feminine, which would nurture and protect her from evils. Instead, she escapes to the world of alcohol, drugs, or sexual promiscuity because her self-worth is minimal and her sense of self is confused. The workaholic father has seen her only in terms of her productivity and her achievements. Nothing she does is quite good enough. Her school grades could always be better. She has no model for successful masculine interpersonal relationships because her father is too busy to worry about friends. She has not learned to communicate her needs and wishes appropriately. Even if she did, it would do no good. Father is too preoccupied to hear, or too uninvolved emotionally to care. The extreme rebellion for such daughters may be to live unproductive and marginal lives. Some involve themselves in prostitution, drug abuse, or cults. Jill, dressed like a model in some far-out fashion magazine, told me that she had tried yoga, meditation, gurus — the whole works — and nothing had helped. Her father was a typical absentee workaholic who paid lip-service to parenting, but was available to her only when his schedule allowed. Jill, searching for the love she had missed, had become quite promiscuous with a series of men ten to twenty years older than herself. She was always under financial stress, and hated her job and the superficial fashion world she was trapped in. She was skirting around her own spirituality, but going off in all directions rather than centering on finding her true self.

The Detached Sons of Negligent Fathers

If the father is absent a great deal, or emotionally unavailable, his sons follow an elusive role model. They grow up trying to win his attention and approval. It's hard to "get blood from a stone" though, so these sons must make their mark in society, make a loud statement that they are successful and okay. Or they may opt out of the rat race and seek solace in worlds where competition and success are not part of life.

The ambitious sons seek power outside themselves in the world of competition where they can win or score points that tell them they are all right. They seek a place in business or in a profession where titles, promotions, and position help define who they are. Winning the game, accomplishing a task, seeking a prize or goal absorb all their energy. Lacking personal warmth from their fathers, these sons can become concerned only with reaching goals and acquiring the trappings of wealth and security. Some become cut-throat and corrupt and lose their integrity on the climb up the corporate ladder. Few are good at people-related problems because they remain impersonal and objective about the end-product. How one gets to one's goal, or at what cost to others, is not a priority. Driven, determined, and even ruthless, these sons quickly become workaholics themselves, and thus model after the missing father.

Sons who "act out" become the misfits of society. These sons have never been unconditionally accepted by their fathers, or valued for who they are. Many drop out of school. Some get involved with drugs and crime. Although many misfits are the victims of alcoholic families, I suspect, a growing number are victims of workaholic families as well. Emotionally crippled workaholics have little of themselves to give to their sons because their energies are drained by work and worry. Because workaholics are afraid of intimacy and touch, their children rarely see their father showing any loving behaviour. These detached sons may perform sexually, but they do not love themselves enough to be able to be truly sexual with others.

THE SAD SIDE OF WORKAHOLISM

Children see only the sad side of workaholism. The glamorous, fascinating world where workaholic parents spend most of their time and energy is outside the children's experience. What they do see is a parent who is bushed or beat, hiding behind the newspaper or slumped in front of the television. "Don't bother your father. He's exhausted!" says Mom, helping make the walls around the father even higher for the kids.

Workaholics are like sponges, soaking up all the family's love, but unable to give of themselves because of exhaustion and worry. Drained, self-absorbed, and more and more narcissistic, workaholics do not like it when other family members become selfish, self-centred, and demanding in an effort to nourish themselves and preserve their sanity.

Spouses often worry that the workaholic is working to get away from them and the children. It's a great way of abdicating responsibility for the children and avoiding sharing intimacy responsibilities with the spouse. Children, very aware of their parents' reactions to each other, soak up the tension and become highly anxious themselves.

Many children understand and do not question that their workaholic parent works weekends, but they do remember the times when the other parent got upset because of it. They take late dinners and broken appointments for granted because it becomes a way of life. Many kids wait until Father comes home to start their homework, and develop tricks to get him involved in projects and sports. Even young children learn to consult calendars and ask for appointments to see Father, but gradually lose enthusiasm for this. The five-and-a-half-year-old son of minister Wayne Oates, author of *Confessions of a Workaholic*, asked for an appointment with his father in his office because he had a "problem" he wanted to talk about. When Wayne offered to discuss it there and then, his son refused. A specific time was arranged, and "to my surprise, he arrived on time at my office. The problem he wanted to discuss was the Resurrection — how could this really happen and what is Jesus like 'right now'? . . . From this rather sobering experience, I learned that I had scheduled time for everyone except my own sons."

Because denial is such an important factor in workaholism, most workaholics avoid acknowledging how little time and energy are spent with their children. This precious time can never be made up in a child's life, and the damage to the children must be severe before some workaholics wake up to their addiction. It often takes a crisis in the child's life to force the parent to see what he or she has done to the family. "If it weren't for my son's near-fatal accident last summer, I would still be going along doing my own thing! God really does work in mysterious ways. At least I've finally got my priorities straight, if nothing else!" said Roger with a grin. He was well on his way along the recovery road because of these insights.

THE HYSTERICAL MARRIAGE

A typical workaholic family seen in my office often has a non-expressive, thinking-type husband who has become remote and obsessive, and a warm, affectionate, feeling-type wife who becomes desperately frustrated, depressed, and hysterical because she alone carries the responsibility for true intimacy in the marriage. The feeling partner remains superficially warm and charming, but when her needs remain unmet, she too can become self-centred and indulgent, demanding constant reassurance of affection and romantic love. These roles can be reversed if the workaholic is a woman.

The remote partner is usually quiet, introverted, shy, and uncomfortable with the opposite sex. Often, before they "fell in love" with their wife, such men dated only a few women because their fear of rejection was so strong. They are taciturn, rarely express affection, but appear well adapted and respectful. They value order and control of their emotional environment, so are usually somewhat inflexible and lacking in spontaneity. Outward signs of affection, such as holding hands in public, are abhorrent to them. Even formal kissing as a form of greeting is uncomfortable. These people are self-contained, have modest emotional needs, and are unable to give without great cost. Hostility is not expressed, but simmers well below the surface. Needs are rarely acknowledged or communicated. Their autonomy is sacrosanct.

The histrionic person lacks adequate impulse control and tends to say and do things without judging the impact on others. These people are emotionally expansive and enthusiastic, and often attract attention. Public displays of affection are easy for them. This overly emotional mate is left in charge of intimacy and closeness, but is often criticized for being too emotional. Maggie Scarf, in *Intimate Partners*, describes their see-saw pursuer–distancer relationship: "The intimacy seeker has promised to chase but never to overtake the partner, just as the autonomy seeker has promised to run but never to get too distant from her breathless, dissatisfied pursuer." The intimacy carrier bears the guilt and responsibility when frustration and unmet needs erupt into hostility and aggression. The emotional partner expresses or acts out the anger for them both, and then is seen as "hysterical" by the aloof, critical partner. It is a check-mate situation where no one wins, and the workaholic family suffers as no solutions are found to alleviate the loneliness and alienation of the couple.

HOPE FOR WORKAHOLIC FAMILIES

A number of surveys have found that a change is coming that will restore the importance of the family. In a survey of one thousand men and women in the United States by Robert Half International (*Office Equipment and Methods*, September 1989), "nearly eight out of ten men and women would sacrifice rapid career advancement in order to spend more time with their families." If given a choice of two career paths, 78 percent chose one with flexible full-time work hours and more family time but slower career advancement. The remaining group opted for inflexible work hours but with faster career advancement. Two-thirds were willing to reduce hours and salaries an average of 13 percent in order to gain personal and family time. One-third only would accept a position that required less family time. Creative options that re-examine the "9 to 5 syndrome" are suggested because the "fast track" is losing out to greater personal fulfilment. One such option would be a career path that would allow employees who are parents to work flexible work hours.

The Conference Board of Canada (*Toronto Star*, September 28, 1989) surveyed 11,000 workers and found that 80 percent of the respondents were having difficulty coping with the pressures of juggling the responsibilities at work and at home. People arrived at work late, left early, or called in sick. Job performance was affected, and strained interpersonal relationships at work compounded the stress level. When both partners work, who gets to work late? Who will pick up the kids? Whose job is more important? Whose fatigue level and stamina are greater? These are common quarrels as people try to accommodate their work and family needs.

We can only hope that the high divorce rate and concern for the health of today's family will force an examination of workaholism's effect on the family. Business is gradually becoming more aware that workaholics are not good workers after all, and more companies are paying for psychotherapy for their employees so that the workaholic and the spouse can collaborate to overcome this modern problem.

The key concepts of workaholism have now been presented. We looked at why denial, control, and power are crucial dynamics that keep workaholism growing. We examined how perfectionism can lead to obsession, which can lead to narcissism in the potential workaholic, and how loss of feelings, fears, guilt, and chronic fatigue all play into some significant losses that change the workaholic's personality and actions. Dysfunctional dynamics in the workaholic family illustrate why the spouse and children suffer so much from this addiction. Now it is time to find out what you and your spouse and children can do to start the recovery process and bring health and happiness to your family.

7.
The Road to Recovery:
Restoring the Inner Balance

"How can I recover from workaholism?" That's a question I'm often asked. My answer, in a nutshell, is that you will be well on your way to recovery when the power of love in you becomes stronger than the power of anger and greed. Before any psychological healing can take place, however, each person must confront his own personal denial and addiction. As I kid my clients: "Workaholics are my greatest challenge because they're so bright, quick, creative, and sometimes witty. The real dilemma is that they have yet to learn that humility is true wisdom!"

AWARENESS OF THE INNER SPLITS

Awareness is the first task in the recovery process. Until we really know "who we are" and have learned to love ourselves unconditionally, we cannot be truly intimate with others. Overcoming any addiction requires insight and strong discipline. The workaholic needs this and more. One cannot trust oneself or others when one's own image is built on arrogance and denial, and one's work is done for self-aggrandizement.

The workaholic must become aware of three inner splits: Being/ Doing, Feeling/Thinking, and Love/Anger. The anxiety created by these splits can cripple a person emotionally, or be channelled into a positive search for solutions that will restore inner harmony and peace. Growth, unfortunately, comes only through painful confrontation!

The Being/Doing Split

Carol, a young client of mine who was a remarkably successful businesswoman, had relentlessly pushed herself up the corporate ladder. Her sales figures were never high enough for her, and each year she drove herself until she lost track of who she was. She had become a machine, outperforming her reputation of the previous year until, at the age of twenty-nine, she was barely able to function. High anxiety coupled with severe depression left her totally drained and chronically fatigued. One day Carol would come flying into my office and talk a mile a minute, and the next week, she would drag herself in and sit slumped in one of my chairs, hardly able to drum up the energy to talk at all.

After Carol's moods had moderated, and she was making good progress towards self-understanding, she still used a lot of "shoulds" in her conversation. "Shoulds" are typically a sign of a clash between the ideas and values passed onto the child by authority figures, parents, or significant others, and the individual's own instinctual needs and wishes. Gestalt techniques are useful for creating a dialogue between the two conflicting sides. The therapist identifies and names the split, and the client is instructed to go back and forth between two chairs, each of which represents one side of the split. I suggested Carol try this technique to understand why she gets anxious on weekends when there is little structure in her days. Our conversation went like this:

CAROL: I always have to be doing something. I keep driving myself. But the world is passing me by. There's no reason for existence!
BARB: You have to perform or you're not okay? Let's do some chair work. Sit in that chair and be your Doing side. What is your Being side like? What would you like to call her?

CAROL: Dumb Diana! (laughs) The Being side is quiet and withdrawn. She doesn't need to talk to anyone. She sits and looks at the river or the view. She's the watcher — slow, not with it, selfish, self-centred. She's not interested in sharing.

BARB: What would you like to tell that side?

CAROL: Get off your fat ass and do something!

BARB: Change chairs, and be Dumb Diana. Tell the Doing side what you think of her!

CAROL: You're bossy, overcontrolling, domineering, and inflexible. You need to relax more and have some fun. Just leave me alone! I just want to sit.

BARB: What would you call her?

CAROL: Irritating Irene! (laughs) I used to have a friend like that. (Long pause) The Doing side works at the office.

BARB: What is she going to do when she gets back there today?

CAROL: Well, she's going to have to close the door. She has to get lots of things done. She's going to be away for two weeks. There's hell to pay. She's got to get eight hours' work into four, and she can do it as long as no one interrupts her. She hates being interrupted, especially now that her concentration isn't that good.

BARB: Does the Doing side need Diana? Switch chairs now and have Irene answer back.

CAROL: Without you I'd burn out, and everyone else would be concerned. I'm too serious. You're funny, easy-going, less sarcastic, more jovial. You buy flowers and write nice thoughtful notes. Walk along fantasizing and even get lost. It's dangerous. Lately your hay fever's bad.

BARB: (Laughs) She's the one with hay fever? She's an air head? Sounds to me like she's your wise part! Your intuitive part. Your Doing side is sailing around without wisdom! (Both laugh). That Being side anchors her!

CAROL: She's interesting. Curious mind. Great person for doughnuts and coffee. But she's not allowed doughnuts and coffee, except once a week. I'm her conscience. Both of us nag. I have big arguments with myself. (Laughs)

BARB: That Doing side is much bigger. When you're in that chair, your voice is strong and forceful.

CAROL: Very dominant. Way bigger. My Being side is having trouble spreading out. This side puts her in a box. She's never really developed. She's so small because I give her only Saturday mornings.
BARB: When Irene orders you around, how do you feel?
CAROL: Inferior, smaller. I don't like arguing. I resist. You have to give me more time. You're a workaholic! You've got two weeks off. You've never done this before! That will give me time to do reading, shopping, sit in cafes, and eat cake. You only live once, you know.
BARB: What will Irene do at the office if you leave her there while you are gone?
CAROL: She'll be ordering them all around. Start to meddle. Be bored. My old friend, Irene, was stiff and had a shrill voice. I never wanted to be like her. Two weeks — long enough to get her out of my system.
BARB: What will happen to your Being side?
CAROL: She will be bigger because the balance will be there. I still need Irene, but she doesn't need to be so big. It's economics at this stage. She has a career, up and coming — whatever that means! She's building up freedom for the future; she can do other things then. She doesn't realize that she doesn't need the effort from two years ago. She needs to get hit over the head. She has put a box around herself. (Pause) Feels great sitting here. (Carol is smiling and her voice has lost its thin, squeaky quality.)
BARB: Can you own that Being side, and say "I"?
CAROL: I'm going to have fun!
BARB: That part needs Saturday and Sunday.
CAROL: Old Irene will have to be more effective. But I don't really need any more money. More money causes more problems.
BARB: That Doing part looks heavy.
CAROL: That part is fat. It doesn't really know what it wants. Or why it is doing things. It's that scary. It's really weird. Irene has proven everything. She's succeeded beyond anyone's expectations. Doesn't need to do that any more. This part is caught in a circle — goes around and around. She sets unrealistic goals, achieves them, and then gets depressed.
BARB: Why?
CAROL: Another $5,000 doesn't buy happiness. She sets unrealistic goals, feels she is going to be happy, then finds out she isn't. Money

doesn't create happiness. It might be a tool to create happiness, but if she doesn't let her other half go and enjoy it, there's no point!

She and I talked about the need to validate both parts of herself, and to stop either side from putting the other down. There had been no balance between Carol's Being and Doing sides. There was a bad split, and a need for integration and harmony. "It's got a lot to do with value systems and success," Carol said. "You don't realize what is happening to you. It evolves so slowly. The Being side gets smaller and smaller until it disappears!"

The Doing/Being struggle is a continuing one for recovering workaholics who must battle constantly to free their shrivelled, playful, joyous, spontaneous self. Too often workaholics allow their perfectionistic work ethic to overpower their weaker love ethic. This situation will change only when they develop their Feeling values.

How strong is your Being side in comparison to your Doing side? Think of a balancing scale, and weigh the influence each side has on your life. Your challenge is to find the healthy balance! Your Being side is more receptive and open to experiencing and appreciating things for their own sake. Playing with a baby, watching a sunset, or sauntering through the woods and stopping to look at a tree or smell the flowers are ways of appreciating and valuing something. Your Doing side is more purposeful or goal-directed, and involves performing. You teach a baby a word, you try to figure out the cycles of the moon, or you walk very fast as a way of staying fit. Both sides are valuable, and both have a time and place where they are most useful. Workaholics have overemphasized their Doing and their Thinking functions. They often feel it is a waste of time just to go for a walk. They want to end up somewhere, to do something for a purpose. Their growth will come through developing their Being and their Feeling functions. In Chapter 8, we will learn some practical steps for developing the Feeling–Being side of the person.

The Feeling/Thinking Split

If workaholics are to recover fully, they have to restore their repressed Feeling function. We have both Thinking and Feeling functions, but one is naturally more dominant and comfortable. If one of the functions is continually repressed, it ceases to function effectively. As one client said, "My old self was very distant, and I kept my feelings in check. I was so good at pretending I had no feelings my wife had begun to treat me as if I really had none." Thinking and Feeling are ways of making decisions, and both are equally valuable. Thinking decisions follow a logical process aimed at an impersonal finding. Feeling decisions are based on what one values or appreciates. Feeling bestows on things a personal, subjective value.

The Feeling part of us values openness and receptivity. It is the part of us that waits, watches, and wonders. Thoughtfulness, sensitivity, empathy, harmony, tact, grace, loyalty, sharing, intimacy, devotion are part of the Feeling side. They all consider the other person. The Feeling side enjoys showing appreciation, being enthusiastic, sharing ideas and experiences. It makes decisions in the context of their effect on people, and considers what the other person values and appreciates. The Thinking function is used to check for possible flaws and errors in decisions made based on emotion and intuition. Feelings are important in family life and in all social contacts. Teaching, selling, acting, singing, and dancing capture our feelings. Clergy minister with compassion, therapists counsel with empathy, and doctors use their expertise to take care of their patients. People in whom Feeling is dominant tend to be curious and other-directed, so they question, listen, and solicit feedback on their ideas.

The Feeling side processes information through a diffuse awareness that is directed outwards to include not only the person's own thoughts, but also cues and feedback from the environment and other people. People whose Feeling side is dominant are open to and watch for others' reactions, and often solicit feedback to help them confirm their own ideas and gain approval for their position. Harmony is all-important to them. When these people become workaholics, their best function, Feeling, ceases to be effective, and they make decisions from their less-developed Thinking side. It is little wonder that their judgment often becomes poor.

In contrast, people whose naturally dominant side is Thinking have a focused awareness that permits them to concentrate on an idea. They are concerned with organizing and clarifying their own ideas and thoughts. They enjoy the intensity and thoroughness of working through a problem. These people zero in on some thought that interests them, take it inside and process it, form a subjective point of view, and personalize it. External factors — other people, situations, or events — can have little importance and be intrusive to the real work of thinking an idea through.

Because these people process information within themselves, their explanation of ideas may not be too clear to others. They may not give enough information, or may seem blunt, curt, and abrupt. He may take too long or be too intense about his idea, and not focus on the relationship with the other. She may bore the listener by lecturing and not exchanging views, or fail to personalize what she is saying and talk in generalities or use theoretical arguments. When these people become workaholics, their Thinking function becomes even more developed, and their weaker Feeling function is repressed even more. These workaholics often do not take the time to think through how they do feel, especially if the feeling is a negative one. Instead, they grow restless and impulsively rush on to the next idea or start to solve the next problem.

The core of my practice is to teach people who are predominantly Thinkers to develop and refine the Feeling–Being side of their personality. Psychotherapy gives them an opportunity for self-discovery and growth, a time to develop their opposites. Workaholics, because of their strong denial defences, must also gain insight into what is wrong, what is missing, and why their feelings are flat and constricted. Their major task is to develop their repressed Feeling function so that it will support their strong Thinking function.

The following instructions may help you nurture and develop your own feelings. If you exercise your Feeling muscles, the awkwardness you experience in the expression of feeling will disappear, replaced by a more natural and genuine expression. Remember, the key concepts of feeling are openness, receptivity, and reaching out to others.

1. *Try to be more open and receptive to others*. Become a watcher, not just a talker. Be curious, question, and listen. Wait, watch, and wonder are the three skills required for openness.

2. *Go beyond your own subjective point of view*, and the way you personally perceive information, to consider openly the viewpoints of others. For example: "I didn't see it that way, but tell me more about why you got so upset at what Bill said."

3. *Increase awareness and develop diffuse awareness,* in addition to your Thinking's focused and subjective viewpoint. Make an effort to do the following:

   a) *Open up your awareness* by watching other people's reactions and facial expressions, and watch for feedback on your ideas. If you see loss of interest, restlessness, boredom, confusion, blank expression, no understanding, loss of eye contact, try to curb your naturally skeptical Thinking side and realize *you* may not be communicating clearly. Remember that humility is a virtue!

   b) *Comment on* the possibility that your communication may not be clear. Say, "Sometimes I get carried away with my ideas," or "I may not be making myself clear."

   c) *Ask for feedback* from other people: "Am I making any sense?" or "Is this something that interests you?"

   d) *Listen* to the feedback, and then invite others to share their views. For example: "Enough about my ideas, what do *you* think about this?" Or, "I tend to be narrow-minded sometimes, so please be patient if I'm not the best listener!"

Reaching out and involving other people fosters sensitivity, empathy, and diplomacy. It encourages discussion rather than arguments. A sharing of ideas and experiences requires good listening *and* real communication where feedback for your ideas is sought and received.

4. *Express yourself.*

   a) *Do not just state an idea* with no preamble or introduction.

   b) *Lead into an idea* and preface it with added information: "The other day something happened that I thought was interesting." Remember that your ideas may be clear to you because you have thought them out beforehand, but other people may not have sufficient information to follow your line of thinking.

   c) *Add a feeling component* to engage other people's interest and to reveal your own emotional involvement in your idea. For example: "I had an idea the other day that really got me excited!" People are more likely to try to understand what you are saying if they realize your idea is important to you.

   d) *Avoid bluntness,* or opinionated, sharp delivery, which suggests that your way is the *only* way to see this. For example: "Nonsense, that's ridiculous!" becomes "That's a far-out idea for me, but I'm willing to listen."

A blunt, sharp delivery shuts other people out and suggests that there is no point in challenging your "superiority." Your voice may be louder and your words more intense, although you may not be aware of this. Others will be be left angry, and will feel put down, uncomfortable, or rejected. Even if you are polite and amiable, others may sense that you want to disarm, pacify, or placate them so that they will not interfere with your wishes. Think of a dishonest used-car salesman. He is the prototype for a person to whom winning the sale is more important than anything else.

5. *Encourage discussion.*
   a) *Seek harmony* through a sharing and exchange of views.
   b) *Share your ideas* and invite others to do the same. Say, for example, "Now, that's my critique! What did you get out of that play, Mary?" Try not to worry about how your opinion will be received or you will inhibit yourself. Risking and openness are important here, as are diplomacy and sensitivity.
   c) *Do not use closure statements* like "This makes sense to me," or "That's what I think!" Such statements suggest that there is only one way to see things and make the assumption that others agree. If others don't, they must counter your definitive statement, and this frequently leads to arguments about who is "right."
   d) *Leave the subject open-ended* and solicit other people's opinions. Also build in a waiting period during which you can form an opinion that considers the other person's point of view. Say, "I need to think about this some more. Let's talk again soon."

6. *Give up control.*
   a) *Try to be more spontaneous* when stating your ideas.
   b) *Try not to "script-write"* ahead of time what you plan to say. Don't think: "If he says he won't go to the theatre, then I'm going to say . . ." Risk being more spontaneous.
   c) *Do not second-guess* what others will say or do. Free yourself to be more open and trusting.
   d) *Do not project your subjective view onto others.* Don't say, "I think you should take that business course. It would be good for you."

Try to explain your thoughts without telling someone else what to do, and be content to have your ideas understood. Try to be fair and non-judgmental, and trust that others must decide what is best for them. This will help you avoid being arrogant and controlling.

e) *Ask instead of tell.* Don't say, "I think you should wear the red dress tonight." Telling other people what to do, think, or feel is not helpful and can be destructive. What is right for you is not necessarily suitable for others. Instead, ask others what they think about something, or how they feel about so-and-so, or what they plan to do about a situation.

7. *Be generous.*

a) *Learn to show appreciation.* People need affirmation and appreciation. Counterbalance your naturally critical nature and focus on the positives. Consider "half-full" instead of "half-empty."

b) *Show enthusiasm and interest* in other people's ideas, thoughts, and deeds. Praise, encourage, and support what others do and say. For example: "I really appreciate all the effort you've put into this."

c) *Strive to be genuine* and mean what you are saying. "I'm really a lucky guy to have you as my wife" may be awkward to say, but the attempt to show caring will be appreciated.

d) *Notice how others look*, and say so. "You look great today! That colour really suits you." Or, "It's so nice to see you smiling and happy."

8. *Be appreciative.*

a) *Be receptive to what others have to give.* It is often difficult to receive what others give us because we are not in control at such times. Giving to others is much easier because we call the shots.

b) *Develop your sensitivity to the positive reasons* people act as they do. Try to see the generous motive behind the gift even if you do not like the gift itself. Constant skepticism and suspicion of others' motivation can inhibit your gracious acceptance of gifts.

c) *Comment on the feeling behind the gift.* For example, "What a great idea this is!" Or, "What a nice thing to do!" Or, "Thanks so much for your thoughtful gift."

9. *If you want to make changes.*

a) *Avoid criticizing other people.* Talk about the value you wish to support instead.

b) *Describe the desired change* so that the other feels supported rather than criticized. For example, say: "I love it when you are polite and thoughtful," rather than "Why are you always so rude?"

c) *Emphasize the values you wish to share*, not what is lacking in the other person. Say, "It's important to me that *we* are honest with each other," rather than "Why don't you ever tell me the truth?"

10. *Give constructive criticism.*

a) *When criticism is in order, soften it* by confirming a positive aspect first, and then lead into the criticism. Present a balanced point of view with as much diplomacy and grace as possible.

b) *Try not to be curt, blunt, and sharp.* Say, "You're often very thoughtful, so I'm having some trouble understanding this," instead of "That's a rotten thing you did!"

c) *Share your own foibles and weaknesses* as well if it is appropriate. "I'm probably not the best judge of this because I have a hard time being patient myself."

d) *Invite* other people to tell you what bothers them about your behaviour: "I'd really welcome your being honest and straight with me, too. I need all the help I can get!"

11. *Foster harmony.*

a) *Learn to apologize.* Apologies are difficult, especially when you are not used to making them.

b) *Acknowledge that you have heard* the other's point of view, even when you do not agree with it. "Let me paraphrase what I've heard so far to see if I've understood you."

c) *Stop yourself* if you get too heavy-handed: "Sorry! So caught up in my own ideas, guess I was a little overpowering there!"

The Thinking side causes us to be seen as very intense and we may not be aware of the insensitivity being conveyed. Swear words and derogatory adjectives used to prove a point are especially difficult to listen to without getting defensive.

12. *Be a friend.*

a) *Strive for a peer relationship* with other people. Treat them as equals. Try not to be arrogant or feel superior. When you try to "help" others, you put them in an inferior position and they feel helpless to help themselves.

b) *Try not to help.* Listen instead.

c) *Be humble* and acknowledge your own weaknesses, as well as your strengths: "I'm great at jumping in and problem-solving for others, but I know it's not too helpful."

d) *Do not lecture or preach.*

13. *Smile!*

a) *Be aware of your own facial expressions.* When the Feeling side is not well developed, a person's face is often rigid. The jaw is set, and the cheeks are hollowed out. The eyes can look expressionless and cold.

b) *Try to loosen up facial tension.* Relax your face and chin. Try yawning or singing to stretch away some of the stress.

c) *Open up your mind; relax and be receptive; try to smile more.* Occasionally try to catch your reflection in a mirror to see how others see you.

d) *Let your feelings show,* both positive and negative ones!

Review these instructions every month for a while to see how you are progressing. Is it getting more natural to say and do Feeling things? Are you remembering to consider others as well as yourself? Have you been apologizing if you slip and go back to the old ways? Are you asking your family for feedback on whether you really are changing? Do you feel like a nicer person? All these questions need to be asked for a while until your new behaviour becomes established and comfortable. Remember that attitudes can change quickly, but behaviour changes take time and effort.

Every now and then a client will come in and I'll notice that something looks different about him. Then, over the next few weeks, I'll become aware that his face is softer and more gentle. Cheeks appear fuller, the jaw is relaxed, and often his sense of humour is heightened, and he is smiling more often. These clients are a joy to behold when their Feeling function is working. They no longer need to translate, to think about how they feel. They just are! When the pain and the hard work of changing behaviour finally turn to joy and laughter, the struggle all seems worthwhile.

The Love/Anger Split

Workaholics are angry, frustrated people who live on the edge of rage. This anger at times may be well hidden to protect the persona they show the world, but often it bubbles up to the surface or explodes suddenly — especially when others challenge them in some way. The Controllers channel their anger into the pursuit of power to avoid becoming vulnerable victims of a system or boss. Their impatience and impulsiveness show up in their irritability, their use of sarcasm, and general intolerance for those who threaten their control. Pleasers absorb anger passively rather than risk the displeasure of standing up to the boss or other employees. Instead, they relinquish control and suffer black moods, or sabotage others in passive–aggressive ways. Such negative behaviour doesn't solve problems, but only adds to them. Feelings of hopelessness leave them bitter and resentful.

Recognizing Anger

How angry are you? Many clients don't recognize their own anger, let alone know where it comes from. Anger is a strong emotion of displeasure or antagonism that stems from a sense that we have been insulted or injured in some way. When obsessive drives are thwarted or frustrated, then hostility and destructive rage build up. The work-aholic directs this anger outwards, onto others, or turns it inwards, onto the self.

Hostility wraps itself in many disguises. Did you know that the following words are substitute words for anger? "I'm really *upset* with George." "I've been *hurt* badly by my husband." "I'm *jealous* of her promotion." People *cry* when they are angry, and feel *sadness* rather than own their hostility. They *lash out* in hurtful behaviour. When you are obsessive, negative feelings flood up from the unconscious, so you need to really listen to yourself and ask yourself how often you feel this way. Other words for anger are: cool, cross, grouchy, cranky, annoyed, bitter, mean, exasperated, frustrated, disgusted, touchy, moody, huffy, furious, uptight, and so on. Realize that suppressed anger underlies depression and feelings of hopelessness, that suicide is the ultimate cry of rage.

Anger arises out of our present fears and our past inner resent-ments. In Chapter 4, we saw how the fears of failure, laziness, boredom, discovery, self-discovery, and paranoia increase as the breakdown process escalates in the workaholic. Anger in the work-place has always been commonplace, but today the fear of lay-offs and dismissal, or redundancy in the wake of corporate take-overs, causes understandable anxieties. As businesses have grown into larger and larger corporations and into global conglomerates, competition for fewer jobs creates further fear and anger. Lines of communication are no longer clear in the bureaucracy of expansion, and misunderstand-ings are frequent. Companies cannot offer the long-term security of guaranteed steady employment, and employees sacrifice loyalty to the boss to self-centred survival concerns. Loyalty, empathy, and com-passion lose out in all of this.

Has the race for the almighty dollar left you disillusioned and angry? Did you sacrifice seeing your children when they were little to reach a coveted position? Did you have to yank up family stakes and move the kids across the country because you were promised greater rewards and prestige? Have you had to face cost cuts, or retrain to fit into diversification tactics? How much job security have you got after all this? Are the politics at your university or hospital driving you crazy? Do your staff or clients put pressure on you too often? No wonder a general paranoia envelopes the psyche of the company employee!

If you recognize some of the sources of anger in your experience, how have they affected you? Have you held on to this anger and let it eat away at you? Are you even aware that you are angry deep inside? How do you show your anger? Do you lash out at others? Or are you fighting depression or suffering from anxiety attacks because you have suppressed anger? It is important to recognize the level of anger you are now living with. Many workaholics live with depression and anxiety for years without recognizing the symptoms. They are numbed to their real feelings. Doesn't everyone feel like this? they ask.

Resentment over Lost Childhoods or Lost Opportunities

Resentment is anger that lies beneath the surface until it erupts into consciousness at unexpected times. It builds up when anger persists because the problems causing it remain unresolved. As a child, the workaholic may have been asked to do housework every Saturday morning when he wanted to play ball instead. The inner resentments often have their roots in childhood, but are fed by daily experiences.

When his wife asks him to help her by scrubbing a floor or washing the walls, he may react with indignant fury. Few workaholics enjoyed a carefree adolescence. Did you, too, become overly responsible early in life? Were you a budding entrepreneur as a child? Did you work long hours while you were still attending school? There are sometimes practical reasons that children must work, but others just want the independence that the extra money provides. You may have wanted your own car, or stereo, or did you start a small business to get an early start at success? Were you following in a workaholic parent's footsteps because the work ethic had been drilled into you? If you had an alcoholic parent, you may have made a conscious decision not to follow your parent's example. Without realizing it, you may have slipped into an equally dangerous addiction!

Where Did You Miss Out?

What are the early sources of your anger?

1. *Did you establish independence too early?* Controller workaholics typically push for independence as early as two years of age. Their parents often were strong, controlling people who had definite ideas and schedules. Were there power struggles over your toilet training? Did you have a strong need to do your own thing, in your own way, in your own time? Independence so early often means that these children deprive themselves of the nurturing and coddling that would be naturally given by a parent. These children often do not like to be touched, and resist physical affection, yet carry resentment that their parents were cool and reserved.

2. *Did you feel as loved as you would like to be?* Pleasers usually seek approval throughout their lives. These children want to be accepted and appreciated, and need to be affirmed by others in order to feel good about themselves. If these needs aren't met, these children can be left with a deep craving to be loved and appreciated in order to fill up the emptiness inside. Did you experience sibling rivalry, or were you jealous of older, more accomplished siblings? Did you compete with one parent for the other parent's affection? Work and accomplishment can become a substitute for missed love and affection. Desperately seeking admiration, Pleasers are often the Nice Guys and Gals of

the workplace. They go out of their way to do things for others, neglect their own work, and end up exhausted and resentful because they are way behind. At least at work their efforts are noticed. At home, the ongoing demands of personal relationships are too much added stress. Personal problems don't go away, and their procrastination or inaction at home only makes things worse. Ironically, they rob their spouses and children of what they themselves missed out on. The pattern repeats itself because, not having received, they do not know how to give.

3. *Did you miss out on adolescence?* Childhood means being free to do nothing, relax, enjoy the sun, watch clouds and the journeys of bugs. It is about wasting time and being free from responsibility and cares to wonder about nature, sort out the questions of God and the universe, and explore nooks and crannies — these are the joys of childhood. Incidentally, it is also where you learn just to be, and to wonder who and what you are. Were you too busy trying out for teams, practising, competing, winning? Did pleasure come only if you won, performed correctly, or did it right? Did you harbour a grudge if you didn't win, or get mad if you made a mistake and spoiled the fun? Goofing off and playing just for fun may not have filled up that empty space inside that cried out for external confirmation that you were a worthwhile person whether you performed or not.

4. *Have you experienced a major failure?* We all hate to fail, but failure is particularly devastating to perfectionists because they play to win, to be the best, often at great personal cost to themselves and others. Have you been passed over for promotions or denied the salary increase you deserved? Have you been left out of meetings; not been chosen for clubs, awards, or merit points; or failed an exam? Did you take these slights or failures personally? Rejection can produce serious slides in self-confidence. Such crises can also, however, get people to reach for help and support. But first they have to overcome their desire to keep their problems secret to protect their positive persona. Pride is all important to workaholics!

5. *Have you lost control of your anger often?* If so, ensuing guilt places you in a vulnerable role that can become intolerable if it goes on for any length of time. The longer it lasts, the more anxiety escalates. Is

your guilt the corrective type? Do you eventually apologize and try to make amends? Or is your guilt the repressed type that makes you push once again to establish your "superiority"? The "vindictive triumph," we have learned, is a way to accomplish this reversal, and when someone dominates, someone else must assume the submissive role. No one wins, but revenge and anger result.

Expressions of Anger

Just what does your anger look like? It can be directed outwards to punish others overtly, or be more subtle and punish others through withdrawal and moodiness. Challenge yourself to examine how you express anger.

Outward Expressions. Do you express anger overtly by putting others down through insults, sarcasm, innuendo, stinging remarks, poisonous jabs, snarls, or rage? Do you react impulsively and too quickly because anxiety creates impatience, irritability, and dissatisfaction with the status quo? Does your voice get peevish, bitchy, whiny, high-pitched, or louder as you act more aggressively? Do you reproach others by lashing out, or do you patronize, preach, and lecture in an attempt to exert control? Do you distort communication by exaggerating, falsifying, and magnifying information?

Inward Expressions. Do you act out your anger in a passive–aggressive manner? Do you become self-centred and judgmental? Is your anger absorbed? Do you express it inwardly? Do you become passive and lethargic, and feel hopeless, helpless, overwhelmed, or useless? Do you generalize your anger, and think of all the things that are wrong, or that you have done poorly? Do you feel sorry for yourself, and think, "Poor me," "Isn't it awful," "This always happens to me"? Do you become self-absorbed, and shut yourself off from the world? Do you withdraw and become silent, and sigh? Did you realize that eye contact and relatedness are lost when you look down and get caught in negative feelings? Physically, do you slump forward, hold in your breath, and feel heavy and fatigued? Do you experience an empty, sick feeling in your stomach? When nothing seems funny, does life take on a tragic gloom?

The Victims of Anger

Nobody wins with anger! When you are experiencing anger, you are caught in your own emotions and are unavailable to others. Your judgment is poor because your thinking and feeling functions don't work properly. If your anger takes the form of a passive–aggressive moodiness, your withdrawal means that other people must approach and connect with you if there is to be any immediate resolution of the conflict. This type of anger is a move away from intimacy. Overt anger, on the other hand, can be an expression of intimacy since we seldom get really angry at people we don't care about or who don't affect our lives. Remember that it is indifference that destroys marriages, not the healthy kind of anger that motivates us to solve problems!

Co-dependents often unwittingly encourage unhealthy situations. If your spouse (or secretary or child) accepts the expressions of your anger, it becomes his or her anger, and therefore his or her problem too. As one client recalls: "I was often angry, especially at work. Every morning we had to attend a meeting with my boss. I would come out excessively mad because I felt he was incompetent. Everything he did was wrong. Although others were upset with him, I was the most upset. He poisoned my day, from eight in the morning until eight at night. All my energy was wasted on him. All my energy was anger. I did not like myself that way." Collusion of this kind keeps workaholism and dysfunctional family patterns strong. If co-dependents ignore or dismiss your anger, then they too learn to dissociate feelings, or to become indifferent and uncaring. Loneliness, isolation, and alienation are the outcome of destructive anger.

Why do spouses give in to angry disapproval, rejection, or avoidance? Do they fear independence and separation because they feel insecure and unloved, and their self-esteem is poor? Have they been badly damaged by emotionally abusive behaviour? Are they trying to "get blood from a stone" by seeking approval and confirmation from a negative source? Do they choose to collude to keep the peace rather than face the break-up of your family?

Co-dependents often accept or ignore the expressions of a workaholic's anger because they feel they are responsible for the anger. These problems are not the fault of the spouse or other co-dependents, and they will continue until workaholics acknowledge their addiction. Meanwhile, partners do have a choice. They do not have to be willing participants in the addictive system. (Ways to avoid co-dependency are discussed in Chapter 8.)

Now that you understand some of the sources of anger, and can recognize the ones that apply to you, the big question becomes, what next?

TRANSFORMING ANGER WITH LOVE

Anger is a choice. Anger arises out of the aggressive instinct and, not coincidentally, so does work. Work is, after all, about mastery and skilful organization, but also about manipulation and control. Anger, too, manipulates and controls! Aggression can be useful if a goal or product is to be marketed effectively in the spirit of competition. Relationships and love, however, suffer and are destroyed by aggression and competition. It is important to note that *no one makes you angry unless you give over your own power and lose control yourself.* Healthy anger motivates you to find solutions to achieve harmony. You have a choice to continue to carry the other's projected anger or to try to be compassionate and forgiving, and to eventually let go of your own anger.

Love grows out of the sexual instincts, and is the experience of emotional and sensory union with another. When we truly love someone, we wish to be with them, not to dominate them. We can never own or possess another person. Intimacy brings people together, but each person must be responsible for his or her own autonomy and own growth. We bring our differences and strengths, and are willing to share ourselves the more we love. Trust and respect provide the climate for true growth.

Blaming others comes from neediness, irresponsibility, fear, guilt, or self-anger. When we take responsibility for our own lives and deal with our own problems as best we can, we will not blame others for who we are, or what we have done. Do you get impatient, irritable, and short when you feel needy or don't get your own way? Do you expect something or someone outside yourself to make you feel better? If so, such dependency will lead you to expect that someone else will cater to your needs; forgive you when you err; and unquestionably allow you to keep doing your own thing, in your own time, in your own way. Do you demand mothering from those who try to love you unconditionally, but do you fail to nurture them? If workaholics are honest with themselves, the answers to these questions will be yes.

Maturity comes when we grow to accept adult responsibility and we are able to love another person selflessly. If we don't know where our ego boundaries are, the fear of losing our own separateness will inhibit us from taking the risk of merging and fusing our self with the other in an intimate relationship. Unfortunately, the self is often sacrificed to ego-building when the workaholic stubbornly pursues outside approval and worldly success.

In summary, recovery comes when you make a conscious decision to grow and to develop your capacity for true intimacy and love. We've looked at two of the tasks that lead to recovery: *learning to be* and *developing our feelings*. Loving ourselves and feeling worthy of another's love are the next steps.

RESTORING A LOVING RELATIONSHIP

Respect and trust are the foundation of real love. Let's now explore how expressions of anger can be transformed by love. *Honesty* must replace denial, *fairness* must prevent the projection of destructive moods, and *forgiveness* must be allowed to dissipate self-anger and guilt.

Honesty

Dishonesty is the workaholic's major stumbling block to recovery. Workaholics, especially Controllers, will boldly lie, or, by omission, neglect to tell the truth to themselves and others. Their "Nice Guy" or "Nice Gal" persona ensures approval outside the family, whereas within the family, Dr. Jekyll becomes Mr. Hyde. Some call the absence of truth "diplomacy"; others rationalize that it is "kindness"; still others label it "pragmatism."

These questions may help you uncover your own dishonesty. Some dishonesty is blatant and obviously controlling, while other ways of being dishonest hide behind the cloak of "meaning well," and the controlling is covert.

Overt Dishonesty

1. *Do you say yes when you mean no,* and agree to requests with no intention of following through? Do you say, "Yeah, Pete, I'll probably come to your game Saturday morning. Mom tells me your team is winning! Way to go!" and then not make it?

2. *Do you second-guess what others want and assume you know* instead of respectfully asking them? Do you say, "I'm going to give Theresa a party. That will cheer her up. She's been depressed too long"?

3. *Do you develop "expertise" in knowing what response is needed* for each situation? Are you good at smooth talking and manipulating others to get what you want? "Oh, don't worry about old George. I know how to get him on board ship. We'll get the deal signed, no problem!"

4. *Do you stubbornly procrastinate if you don't get your own way?* Do you do nothing, then wait it out to wear others down? "If I ignore what Pat is saying long enough, she always gives in!"

5. *Do you rarely take direct responsibility for getting what you want?* Do you instead use others as an excuse for doing your own thing? "Order those baseball tickets for Harry and me, will you, Grace? I'm just swamped at work, and you've got lots of free time. Harry wants to go to the game on Saturday and then out for drinks!"

Controllers tend to use this type of dishonesty. It protects their autonomy and independence, and their privacy and secrecy. The welfare of others is not their concern, and it allows them to stay aloof and distant. How much do you use overt dishonesty to control others?

Covert Dishonesty

1. *Do you say and do the "nice" thing, instead of saying what you really feel or think?* "No, Adele, of course I don't mind if you smoke during dinner!"

2. *Do you not tell others what you would like to do, or go to see?* "Lyle should know I don't like violent movies like that. What's wrong with him?"

3. *Do you give in and agree to do what others want to do just to keep the peace, and then sabotage the evening?* "I'll go to the symphony, Lillian, but on one condition. I'm going to bring my briefcase with some papers I have to read before tomorrow."

4. *Do you pick up subtle cues, and second-guess what others want from you, but fail to check out your presumptions?* "I know Stewart would want me to get the blue one."

5. *Do you set yourself up for confrontation and rejection?* "Anyone who has a white carpet and teenagers, that's a neat freak! My mother's just begging for a test!"

Pleasers and "good" co-dependent spouses and children use this more subtle form of dishonesty, which leaves the impression that they are loving, giving people who are nice and generous, with a wonderful capacity for understanding or listening. In reality, they may be passive, vague, irresponsible, and manipulative. How often do you use this type of dishonesty?

In response to my questions on dishonesty, Alice, a bright young workaholic producer who is used to being manipulative to get her own way, replied: "You must have been watching me with my staff this morning. The very thing I did, you face me with an hour later. You know, that devious dishonesty sounds horrid! That's my Shadow. That's why I'm here, right? I'm going to have to put a curl in the middle of my forehead. When I am good, I am very, very good. When I am bad, I am horrid! And I certainly can be!" Alice had recognized that her own behaviour was self-serving, but she could laugh at her Shadow and accept that knowing about her faults allowed her to change.

Another client, an artist who was recovering from a nervous breakdown caused by chronic fatigue and immobilizing insecurity, had this insight: "In my job, I was Mom. I felt I had to anticipate their moods and cater to them. Just everyone — that was my role. It is my job, to a certain extent, but I sure went overboard. You know, once last year I was up to midnight cooking a cake in the shape of a musical note! That kind of stuff is way above what is necessary. When it comes right down to it, I wore myself out for nothing. I could have given them doughnuts, and they would have been just as happy."

When Pleasers and co-dependents who support the workaholic system practise dishonesty, they avoid responsibility to themselves and risk the loss of self. Do you volunteer to "take care" of others by serving, helping, or fixing? Do you set aside your own needs, and put your boss or your spouse and children first? Do you complain a lot, but when help is offered, refuse? Do you not wish to burden others, but prefer to do it yourself, simply to keep control and have things done *your* way? Do you refuse to delegate, and feel only you can do the job properly?

Pleasers are the martyrs in the family or the organization. Since they want to keep control, they burden themselves unnecessarily and refuse to share power. They are unrealistic about what they are able to do because they are trying so hard to please. Sometimes they are rewarded for their thoughtfulness and giving, but more often, no one else really notices or even cares. So they burn out and feel resentful. Then they take responsibility when things go wrong, and suffer guilt and self-rebuke. Society sees them as Nice Guys or Gals, yet underneath they are angry, bitter, and depressed because they have tried so hard to be liked and appreciated.

The insights of some recovering workaholics may be of help. Timothy, a chartered accountant, came to this awareness: "It was lucky I had a rough time. I was getting nowhere trying to please people. It wasn't my fault the company was losing money. I was only the CA. I finally got it through my thick skull that I was just preparing the financial statement. Yet I would feel so awful when things went wrong, and I'd go home at the end of the day feeling sick." Timothy was really unclear about his ego boundaries, about where his real responsibility stopped and started.

Judith, a legal secretary, confessed: "My boss asks how long the project will take, two or four days. Because I want to please, I pick the deadline that I think he would like, rather than being realistic. When I say yes, I have every intention of making the deadline. I've been totally unrealistic though, and I can't go back and discuss my promise and lose face. I simply can't admit I was wrong. There's no malicious intent, but there's no way I can fulfil those obligations in just two days." Judith sheepishly added: "I avoid my boss for the next week and scuttle around the halls like a rat! That's how I feel. Meanwhile, our receptionist says: 'I haven't seen her. I'll ring through to her office. She's not at her desk right now.' "

Almost any behaviour can be rationalized or explained away to "protect" others, or make you "look good," and others "bad." Ask yourself these questions again and again over a period of time, because once denial begins to break down, more truths will reveal themselves to your new-found conscious self. Being humble and realistic really isn't so bad! It's important to learn to love your Shadow so that you can nurture and protect your weaknesses, instead of letting unconscious evils sabotage your healthy instincts.

Fairness

A fair person is considerate and does not burden others with his negative moods or her angry projections. Moods are a complex of emotions welling up in the person to reflect present feelings and past associations connected to what the person is experiencing. Moods are a sign from the unconscious that something in the person's psyche is troubled. It is difficult to be rational and logical under such circumstances, and decisions should be put off until one feels in control again. Try to be responsible for catching your mood before it escalates, so that the mood does not control you.

Moods and Quasi-Logical Communication

A mood is a flooding of emotions that, once entrenched, leaves us with no power to feel or think or be creative. It is a denial of feelings, a withdrawal inwards that leaves no capacity for relationship with others and no objectivity for judging and evaluating things. Once a mood takes possession, we are out of commission, ineffective, and paralysed until it runs its course.

When we are caught in a mood, our communication tends to become quasi-logical. We become critical and come out with opinionated thoughts or absolute, rigid attitudes. These autonomous statements are received as blunt, critical judgments of an unpleasant, even destructive type. They don't invite discussion but, rather, set the scene for argumentative disagreements.

To support our judgments or criticisms, we may use authoritative sources such as books or our parents or teachers. Sweeping generalizations delivered in a preachy tone often disregard facts and history. Relationships can only suffer as a consequence of such controlling tactics. Logic becomes distorted, and it is difficult to know what is true and what is false.

Triggers of a Mood

Moods can be caused by a number of triggers. These triggers are our Achilles' heel, the hooks that catch our moods and cause us to overreact out of proportion to our normal level of response. Here is a checklist I give my clients. See if you can recognize what tends to trigger your moods.

1. Do you feel *personally hurt* by
   — a chance remark?
   — a slight?
   — a rude statement?
   — a sarcastic remark?
   —a general remark taken personally?
2. Do you experience an *unnoticed disappointment* when
   — plans are cancelled by others or by weather?
   — your expectations are not met?
3. Do you feel *rejected or abandoned or in pain* because:
   — someone is not listening, not understanding, not remembering?
   — someone is ignoring you by looking off and away?
   — someone is leaving you out of a conversation?
   — someone is avoiding you physically?
   — you are feeling lonely?
4. Do you feel *frustrated or hopeless* about
   — the situation you are in?
   — another's feelings towards you?
   — your lack of skills to improve a situation?
   — your own guilt, i.e., self-anger?
5. Do you *lose control* when you are angry, or when someone else is?

6. Are you *disappointed in yourself* because of
   — your poor performance?
   — your immature behaviour?
7. Does *illness or fatigue* almost always leave you subject to moods, more vulnerable generally?

   I, for example, can get very upset when people cancel plans at the last minute. I know I don't handle that very well, and in the past it has triggered a mood that has spoiled my whole day. Once we know our triggers, and recognize their onset, what do we do?

Signs of a Mood Beginning

It is important to take control of a mood before it possesses us. Earlier in the chapter we looked at the outward expressions that signify overt anger, and the inward expressions of anger that tend to be passive, but can be equally hostile and destructive. Check back to identify the *earliest* reaction you tend to have when one of your triggers is set off. Your awareness will be heightened each time you check to see how each mood began. At the first sign that you are starting to get moody, act quickly to intervene.

How to Gain Control of a Mood

Timing is crucial here. As soon as you recognize the earliest outward or inward expression of anger beginning, take the following steps to catch the mood before it runs out of control and leaves you immobilized, or you lash out at others in an angry projection.

1. *Own your mood.* It is *your* problem, and your job to get out of your mood, the sooner the better. You don't have to succumb to its destructive powers. You do have a choice!

2. *Fight for control.* Try to remain in focus and stay with your negative feelings. Name the feeling, and recognize what you are doing that doesn't feel good. "Boy, am I getting cranky. I can just hear the whine in my voice!" Know your mood will pass!

3. *Use your self-discipline.* Will can control the mind and, through it, the emotions. You have a choice now to focus on all the negatives, or to search for positives in a situation. "I'm really hurt that they

cancelled our plans, but I can use the extra time to work out in the garden. That always makes me feel better!"

4. *Reframe what has happened*. Change your focus from a negative thought to a more positive view. "This situation presents me with a challenge to learn more about myself, and to exercise my positive thinking so that I avoid any tragic outcomes. I can win this one, or lose to self-indulgence and feel despair."

5. *"I can handle it!"* Concentrate on the problem-solving aspects of getting out of a mood. Try not to worry about the outcome, or to write scripts about what you will say to others and what they will say back to you. You will be disappointed when no one else knows the lines to your play!

6. *Resume eye contact with the other person immediately*. Relatedness is the way out of a mood. Your eyes automatically turn downwards when you are caught in a mood.

7. *Give an honest expression of genuine feelings*. Say what is upsetting you, what the problem is. Then *stop*. "I'm so mad! That man was incredibly rude, and I hate that!"

8. *Directly express your hurt, anger, or bewilderment*. Use "I" instead of generalizing. It is you who is talking, not people in general or authority sources. "I'm in a bad mood! It's not your fault. Just leave me alone for a while." By expressing your anger, using "I feel . . .," you move towards intimacy because something is happening in the relationship when you share your feelings. Moods, kept inside, lead you towards autonomy and alienation. Relating frees you up to be responsible and adult, instead of giving way to the petulant child in you. If the other person is not available, write out what is so troubling to you and describe your own feelings about the situation. Share your thoughts later, if it will make you feel better.

9. *Take time to nurture yourself.* Be related to yourself and your vulnerability at this time. Tune in to your feelings, and listen to them chattering away inside.

    a) *Sit up*, open up the chest area so that you can breathe and give your brain some added oxygen so that you may think more clearly.

b) *Take time out* to look after your wounded ego.

c) *Simplify* your plans, eliminate anything that is not absolutely necessary to do.

d) *Relax, rest, or exercise*, take it easy.

e) *Do something interesting* you like to do. Get absorbed in a project or hobby, if this would be fun.

How to Handle Someone Else's Mood

DON'T. Their mood is their problem!

1. *Offer empathy only.* Do not problem-solve or get involved. Do not lash back. "You seem to be upset. I hope it's not something I've done."

2. *Stop feeling guilty or anxious.* Allow the other person to remain in their mood and work it out. Respect the other person's feelings. Remember that guilt is really self-anger.

3. *Avoid any judgments, comments, or criticism.* This is the time to go about your own business. Leave any discussions until later if you choose to follow-up to gain a better understanding. Since one's mood is one's problem, you may decide to drop the matter.

4. *Share your own feelings at a later date.* Use an "I" message to describe your own feelings only, so that you do not project blame and induce guilt feelings in the other person. Two wrongs don't add up to a right! "I feel helpless when you get so down! I really would like to understand what you are going through."

Being fair to yourself and others by handling your own moods and not feeling responsible for other's moods will leave you feeling more tranquil within. A comfortable feeling about ourselves leaves us free to be available to others. Workaholics, often dragged down by more frequent periods of moodiness as the breakdown progresses, cannot be emotionally there for their families. They are barely coping as they struggle to keep performing publicly.

Forgiveness

Forgiveness is not possible if denial is present. "If I don't think I've hurt you, then why should I apologize?" is a familiar response from a workaholic. Denial covers a multitude of sins, and as long as the workaholic is able to repress the Shadow aspects he or she wishes to disown, or dissociates and pretends people or things don't exist, self-forgiveness is not necessary either.

The essential work of recovery is the gradual breaking down of the walls of self-deception. When this happens, denial no longer covers the pain the workaholic has been working so hard to choke down. Recovering workaholics, feeling their real distress for the first time, are often in incredible pain. My client Murray, his eyes brimming with tears, shared his new-found feelings. "I never could cry before, you know. It hurt too much because I had everything so tightly bottled up inside. On the rare occasion when I did cry, it would rack my insides, but there were no tears. Now if I'm upset, I cry real tears. I feel things so strongly now. I was watching something on TV the other night, and tears were just splashing down my cheeks!" He grinned. "You know, it felt good. I'm finally joining the human race again."

Unfortunately, the day of reckoning also means that the workaholic has to face his past misdemeanours or her thoughtless deeds. The workaholics who sought out affairs because, they rationalized, their spouses were not reacting favourably to their increasing absences and indifference must face the real truth. Workaholics are often caught in the dilemma of hurting both the spouse and the new lover as some solution must be sought to end the cruelty to both parties. Recovering workaholics have to come to terms with their own hurtful or irresponsible behaviour and realize how unfair and cruel they have been in the past. To do this, they must experience their own pain. Only then can they begin to understand how others felt as the recipients of their anger and vindictive punishments.

Many of my clients, beginning to take responsibility for their rages for the first time, see what these outbursts have done to their spouses and children. It's as if the scales have dropped from their eyes and they can now see the wounds they have inflicted because of this crazy-making addiction called workaholism. Unhealthy guilt used to be exorcised by putting others down, by regaining the dominant position. But now true guilt must be faced. "What have I done to my poor family?" is a common question at such a moment. Sandy, still in the transitional stage of having to question his behaviour constantly, said:

"I don't feel any better about myself. Worse actually. Guilt that I did not see what was going on in my marriage haunts me. There's a strong element of denial in my nature. I always had trouble trying to resolve any problems with my wife, so after a while we just stopped trying." Then this ambitious executive added: "I'm not through healing yet. I hope when I'm through, I'll feel positive about myself in the real sense. I still feel confused about a lot of things. I haven't replaced the arrogance, the swelled head, with a 'real' confidence in life. There's a void there that is leading to lots of concerns and questioning and a loss of confidence in my roles of husband and executive. If I'm not what I thought I once was, then what am I? I'm not sure yet."

What makes the pain bearable is the new-found joy that surfaces when the workaholic begins to be a truly nice person, instead of the irresponsible Nice Guy or Gal. At one end of the spectrum of full feelings is pain; at the other, joy. Apologizing now becomes the order of the day. Asking for help from their families to change behaviour, and finally being fair and honest have positive rewards. And these fuel the fires and provide the extra energy necessary for rebirth and renewal. Chronic fatigue has left the workaholic drained, with little energy for growth. The positive feedback from others as behaviour changes for the better often provides a spark of encouragement and renewed energy. The workaholic often feels as if he or she is on a roller-coaster during this period. Self-disgust, even self-hatred, is alleviated by excitement as adult responsibility is faced.

The Goal of Forgiveness

The goal of forgiveness is to restore relatedness and to reconcile with others. Reconciliation is the proof that forgiveness is complete. Unfortunately, it comes only when a person repents and is truly sorry. Attitudes must change, behaviour must be altered, and, eventually, a changed lifestyle must be considered.

The real work of forgiving cannot be accomplished alone. True forgiveness can come only if all parties are receptive and share the responsibility for reconciliation. Otherwise, one party will be self-sacrificing in trying to adjust and give unconditional love where that love is not deserved or accepted graciously. Temporarily, there may be a surface politeness and more cordial formal relationship, but the active forgiver will end up more frustrated, lonelier, and more isolated than before. Narcissists, especially, will soak up love and rarely give any in return. They are like bottomless pits, empty and in need of constant refilling, or they may sulk and project their moods onto others and drag them down too. Forgiveness, for these individuals, is foreign as they do not have enough insight to recognize what they do to others, and guilt is tightly repressed.

While it takes two people to reconcile, it is important for one's own sake to become a loving and forgiving person, someone who at least tries to understand others. To this end, here are some steps to take towards self-love:

1. *Come to terms with what real love is.* Distinguish it from conditional, self-serving love, which gives only so that others will meet one's needs in return. Unconditional love places no conditions on the other; it is freely offered by a warm, giving, and loving person. Self-love will come only to a person who is worthy of being truly lovable.

2. *Appreciate and value your own good qualities.* Workaholics can be very critical, judgmental, and "half-empty" pessimistic people, but they do possess the qualities of determination, perseverance, and boundless nervous energy. These can be redirected into reshaping a more balanced, loving, feeling personality.

3. *Communicate your confused, mixed-up feelings to others.* When you do this, you are reaching out towards intimacy. Ask for others' support and guidance as you try to formulate and discover new facets of feelings. New-found humility will allow you to delegate and share responsibility. Journeys made together are less lonely, and less likely to detour off the path to recovery.

4. *Ask for forgiveness.* Try to perform healing acts to amend for your mistakes and indifference. They will aid you in restoring your own sense of goodness and will help make you feel better about yourself.

5. *Ask for patience and understanding.* Self-love does not come overnight. It took years to get into this mess called workaholism, and your behaviour will change very slowly. Attitudes can topple more easily, but, without accompanying behavioural changes, nothing of real sub-

stance will be sustained. You will just revert back to your old controlling ways.

6. *Invite real dialogue* where each person struggles to be more honest and direct. Manipulation and control brought you only misery in relationships. Risk honesty and being *real* instead. It's more fun not to have to be perfect!

The most important thing to understand about self-forgiveness is that it is not a one-time thing. Each time you repeat old destructive behaviour, you must renew the process and ask for and seek forgiveness once more. There is a learning curve, though, that accompanies this process. The quicker you catch yourself being manipulative or controlling, the less damage will be done. You will take the steps towards self-forgiveness sooner, and your recovery will be faster and more secure. Strength comes from using positive forces within yourself to heal old wounds through forgiveness.

Spiritual Forgiveness

Reconciliation comes through re-establishing your love for family members and friends, and making peace with any of your colleagues from whom you are alienated. People will forgive almost anything if they see you are trying, although some people do not have the strength to forgive or have been too badly damaged. Recovering workaholics must, therefore, be prepared for partial forgiveness from others. It is painful, and it is a wound they carry forever; that is, unless they have enough faith, belief, and self-compassion to ask a Higher Being to help them carry such a burden. "Letting Go Unto God" is a difficult concept for workaholics because they have fought for control all their lives. Recovering workaholics must come to terms with their missing spirituality in their search for the new self. God comes only when they are open and receptive, when they "wait, watch, and wonder" — when they are centred in their Feeling side.

It is a rare privilege to watch and share my clients' struggles towards a closer connection with their personal experience of God. Several clients have told me that a Presence has appeared in their dreams, or at moments in their personal awareness, God is experienced as present in the room with them. At such moments, my clients and I experience the recognition that we are not just journeying along together on the road to recovery. We are accompanied and supported by a higher Being who knows the road ahead, and can light the way on the path to understanding and self-acceptance.

Self-love comes when we seek forgiveness for ourselves. Forgiveness releases love, so that we can learn to truly love others for themselves.

In summary, the inner balance can be restored by re-establishing your Feeling values, and devoting more time and energy to your Being side. Take the time to think more often about how you feel about what is happening to you. Self-love will thrive in an atmosphere of honesty, fairness, and self-forgiveness. Soon you will have enough love within to be able to reach out to others. Remember where the power of greed led you, and set your path towards establishing love as the power in your life.

Resistance always accompanies us on this search for the real self hidden behind the persona. One of Gary Larson's "Far Side" cartoons shows a number of men and women trudging along towards a fork in a road. All take the branch marked "The Beaten Path" except one lone man, accompanied by his skeptical wife, who follow the "Off" sign. "I don't know if this is such a wise thing to do, George," she natters. Don't let your fears deter you from this exciting journey.

From the focus on inner balance, let's look now at some practical steps towards replacing the addiction of workaholism with a healthier lifestyle.

8.
Practical Steps to a Healthier Lifestyle at Home and at Work

"You sound like a captain on a ship called *Denial*. The captain is so full of his own importance that he is blind to his course, and is sailing down a river leading to a waterfall. The only alternative he sees is to change direction, but the force of the current traps him on his course. This captain is blind to the heavenly stars above which might reveal his salvation." This was my contribution to a session of Active Imagination, a therapeutic technique that uses metaphors to challenge a client's perceptions.

Paul, the client and a recovering workaholic, responded with his own metaphor: "I am like a person wandering in a beautiful park with a concrete path sliced through the middle. I'm afraid to get off the path to touch and experience Nature around me. I may get lost and not find my way out. Now I see all the damage that I have done to my family, my company, and all the employees I had to let go. My beliefs and self-confidence are breaking down all around me. The picture in my own mirror is so distressing! The crazy part is that since I've started being so honest, I'm not worried any more about where this journey I've begun is headed. I think this sea captain might be following a star after all!"

Paul had been caught in his own selfish world of work and, like Narcissus, had become fascinated with his own persona. Self-aggrandizement had been the driving force propelling him forward into workaholism. Now, through his refreshing self-honesty, Paul was beginning to trust the process of discovery. "I know I'm going to be up and down like a toilet seat. My good days are terrific and there are lots more of them these days, thank goodness. My bad ones are the pits, but it's okay! I'm getting there, slow but sure."

Steps to Behavioural Changes

We looked at the inner changes necessary for recovery in Chapter 7. Here are some reminders. Just for fun, place *Honesty* stickers on your bathroom mirror, your telephone, or your fridge to remind you that denial is your worst enemy. *Keep Reality Testing* through your self-confrontations and checking with others, instead of using your defences of avoidance, procrastination, and rationalization. *Be Generous* with your love. A reciprocal give-and-take is more fun than self-centred preoccupation. *Be Responsible* in the way you affect others' lives. Controllers, try thinking we instead of just I. Pleasers, try thinking about I, not just you. *Celebrate your marriage*, and your children will feel happy and secure. Make your family your number-one priority.

Here's a list (yes, another list!) of steps to take that will change your behaviour and guide your actions on the road back to health.

1. *Own your workaholism.* The sooner you admit that you are addicted the better! Learn as much as you can about this addiction by reading the books listed in the Bibliography, especially those marked with an asterisk. Ask others, particularly your family, for feedback on your behaviour. You may be able to provide your family with material support, but they can give you emotional support only if you open yourself up to receive their love and concern.

2. *Be extremely patient.* Don't expect miracles! Your impulsive need to see results immediately will work against you. Don't expect to change overnight. Remember, workaholism took years to wreak havoc on your life. The longer you remain in the transitional period in which you confront and question who you are, the more Shadow aspects of your personality will become clear.

The sources of anxiety that feed your obsession with work must be discovered. Only when these anxieties are understood and resolved will the need for addictive abuse be eliminated. Lucy explained her greatest anxiety: "New situations or new areas that I can't readily control or get a handle on always set me off. I get overcontrolled and expect too much of myself and others. I can't admit I need help or I don't understand. I work myself into a frenzy and get totally obsessed with conquering the problem. Nothing else matters!" Your need for control and power have roots in your childhood, so it is important to delve into family history. Each step in this exploration will add to your self-knowledge. Lucy discovered her excessive need to control everything related to the collapse of her small world when her father suddenly left his family when she was seven. Welcome your Shadow side into consciousness because you will be much safer if you can recognize your faults and accept them as yours. Only then can the transformation that enables you to change and challenge your weaknesses take place.

Think of recovery as a gradual removal of the "wall" of denial you have built around yourself. Celebrate each step, and reward yourself with enthusiastic praise when another hurdle has been met and conquered. A client told me one day that he wanted to boast about a few things, then described his new-found pride and successes in being a good husband and father. He went on to tell me that he is making up with his "arch enemy," a man at work who got a promotion that he wanted badly, and the reconciliation was bringing him a great deal of peace. The "new you" will be a realist rather than a perfectionistic idealist. Humility will replace arrogance, and sensitivity, thoughtfulness, and graciousness will grow as time goes by. Life becomes an adventure when personal growth is sought. Be prepared for a roller-coaster of chaotic feelings along the way. Peace and self-love are hard-won rewards!

3. *Recognize the anger in yourself.* As we have learned, workaholics are angry people, and the rage rushes up from deep inside. Learn to distinguish your passive–aggressive anger from your overt expressions of it, and recognize when and with whom you use each type. Educate yourself by reading about anger in the books listed in the Bibliography. Count to ten, or take time out to breathe deeply and

long when you first recognize anger. *Wait* until you can express how you feel in a calm and dignified fashion. Temper tantrums are the realm of spoilt brats! Instead, decide *not* to do anything until you have gone away to think about your feelings. Never try to solve problems when you are trapped in a mood. Remember, both Thinking and Feeling functions are needed to problem-solve with others — Thinking, to be logical, rational, and fair; Feeling, to be considerate, sensitive, and empathic.

State your position clearly, then *listen* to the other person's position. Try to *negotiate* a solution through mediation and compromise. The object is reaching an agreement, not putting others down. *Now* is the time to problem-solve, but only when you are back in control of your emotions. Withdrawing solves nothing, unless you decide to let go of your anger because the issue just isn't that important. Happiness and bitterness are mutually exclusive. Go for happiness! Getting back at people is self-destructive. Withholding your services, pretending nothing happened, and avoiding commitments lead away from adult maturity.

Impulsive action usually leads to contentious confrontation. Before acting, identify what it is you are reacting to. Is it the situation or someone else's personality? Is one of your "rules" or values being threatened? Is someone using unfair tactics? Are you really angry, or might it be that you are feeling rejected, passed over, threatened, or hurt?

Develop a plan for problem-solving that works for you and your spouse. Think through the problem, ask yourself if you have made a mistake, and change what can be changed. When you acknowledge your mistakes, ask for feedback and be open to a fresh perspective on reality. Mistakes can be turned into opportunities for personal growth!

4. *Develop effective listening skills.* Most workaholics are notoriously poor listeners. They get bored and restless easily, and often look for openings in the conversation that will bring the conversation back to their own interests. As the teenaged daughter of a workaholic phrased it: "Dad never really focused his attention on me. His mind always seemed to be somewhere else. Mom had to point things out to him — like when I went off food for three weeks and lost twenty-five

pounds. He never remembered things, like my birthday. I'm not even sure he heard me at all when I chattered on about what I was doing. The little things I told him went right out the window! He never seemed to remember where I said I was going either, and Mom had to keep telling him the same things over and over."

Loved ones need to be listened to. Information is more likely to be stored in long-term memory if you repeat what has been said, or review the information in your mind. We remember things that are interesting to us, so make a real effort to move away from your narrow self-centred focus and learn to be curious about how other people see the world. Your children and spouse will be forever grateful.

Many children of workaholics act out in a desperate plea for attention, trying to "fill up" their emptiness with drugs, alcohol, shoplifting, or sexual misconduct. The damage done by dysfunctioning parents is not measurable, but therapists' offices are filled with victims of all ages who have suffered greatly. Good listening skills can go a long way towards correcting the damage. Be prepared to not like what you hear, but *listen* anyway!

5. *Strive for intimacy and being "real."* Only when you have a strong sense of self and a well-developed ego boundary can you allow yourself to be vulnerable and join with another in intimacy. It is likely you haven't taken the time to define your own clear sense of self separate from others, but have been dependent on work for self-definition. The selfish interests of the workaholic leave little room for true intimacy. You may be highly dependent on your spouse to take the major responsibility for intimacy, while you hold onto your autonomous position.

Learn to share responsibility for intimacy and for your own needs. Recognize that while your attention and energy were diverted to your obsession with work, you unconsciously depended on a nurturing figure to meet your physical and emotional needs. As a recovering workaholic husband, Sydney, explained: "I realize now that my wife didn't have a chance to be happy. My needs totally dominated our life. She was frantically trying to cater to my whims, deal with my parents, be gardener and cleaning lady, and care for three little kids with almost no help from me. I imagine she was frightened and overwhelmed with so much responsibility. To add insult to injury, I blamed her for all her complaining and nagging. I accused her of making my life miserable! Wow, how am I ever going to make up for all of that?"

Your spouse, too, needs help to stop playing the nurturing "fixer" and to start to expect a reciprocal give-and-take. Together as a team, work towards a peer relationship where you share in a mutually satisfying way. This way, the dominance–submission game gives way to a flexible sharing of power where the key is mutuality, an easy shifting back and forth between dominance and vulnerability. Humility allows you to be comfortable in either role, because you can reveal your weaknesses and admit to problems as well as celebrate victories and good news. You won't feel guilty or anxious if someone else is leading you or looking after you.

More generally, try to relax and let other people be in charge for a change. Expose yourself to recreational groups where someone else is the leader. Organized tours and ski or tennis weeks are good places to experiment. If you talk all the time, you won't learn anything. Adrian, a young physician, was feeling totally swamped by all the committee work she had become involved in. On questioning, it became clear that since she was very opinionated and always wanted to get her "right" views across to colleagues, she often dominated discussions. I asked her if she was aware that the person who talks the most in a group is usually elected the task leader. She was surprised at this aspect of group dynamics, and I proposed she try out some new behaviour. "Why don't you go to that meeting this afternoon, and keep quiet for a change. Practise your listening skills, and see if you can't learn something new!"

That afternoon was a turning-point for Adrian. Her arrogance was gradually turning to humility as she learned to appreciate the strengths and wisdom of her colleagues. She eventually gave up the committee work, which was so draining for her. Mediation and delegation were not her natural strengths, and these meetings had sapped all her energies and left her frustrated and angry. The distress she caused in others by "grandstanding" was finally registering on a conscious level. Adrian had justified her controlling tactics to herself by her belief that her ideas were the "right" ones.

If you are a caretaker, especially a physician, minister, or counsellor, risk slipping out of your protective, safe roles. Try to be honest about your own fears, self-doubts, and negative experiences. Talking about your own Shadow qualities will move you into peer relationships with your patients, clients, or parishioners. Playing God and remaining in a "superior" position leads to arrogance, loneliness, and self-deception.

One recovering workaholic used the checklist of Nice Gal and Ms. Real qualities to measure how she was progressing towards being more honest and more capable of intimacy. She drew a line between the two columns, and used numbers to estimate her progress from 1 to 10. Occasionally, she gets out the list and reviews where she is for each item. "It is a way of keeping myself on course because I definitely like Ms. Real a whole lot better!" she adds. If you can truly be yourself, you will free yourself up from the stresses of "impression management." The more you are willing to let others know you, the more whole you will be in your own eyes as well. Self-acceptance is self-healing.

6. *Search for your spirituality.* Disbelievers in my office scoff at the thought that on the road to recovery you might just meet your soul! Without a centred self, people commonly feel empty. Has work really enriched your life, and left you fulfilled and content? Or does a sense of meaninglessness prevail because work has drained you of all energy and creativity? Have you reached the stage in workaholism where you hate your work? How can spirituality help you fill this emptiness deep inside?

First, learn to celebrate life's rituals. Spirituality is a celebration of life. Family traditions, such as Sunday dinners, birthdays, anniversaries, reunions, also celebrate life. Tradition helps keep family members coming together and honouring one another in a meaningful way. Make a point not to work on such occasions, or on national holidays. Instead, relax, play, and have fun together. Risk leaving the briefcase at the office, where the work belongs. Work will always be there, but your family may not. That sixteenth birthday party or that Thanksgiving dinner will never happen again for that child at that special stage of his or her life. Get personally involved in the preparations for the celebration. Cook a special dish, plan a toast, or play an instrument to contribute to the occasion in a personal way. Inviting other families to join your own may increase the fun and excitement of the celebration.

Second, search for your spiritual roots. In the early stages of the recovery, I often recommend inspirational readings, such as Scott Peck's *The Road Less Traveled* or Matthew Fox's *A Spirituality Named Compassion and the Healing of the Global Village.* These books will provide guidance for your pilgrimage into unexplored territory. In addition, you may want to seek a spiritual home by attending a place of worship with your family, or return to regular attendance at worship and participate more fully. Counselling with your spiritual adviser can enrich your self-knowledge. You will find that others have struggled as you do, and they share some of the same self-doubts. Our greedy materialistic and hectic world has left many people bereft of a spiritual centre. Meditation and thoughtful prayer can lead to a closer union with a Higher Being. Risk surrendering your control, and ask for guidance back to health.

Third, recognize that spirituality and compassion are closely connected. Where self-centred compulsions and irresponsible immature behaviour ignore others' feelings and needs, compassion moves us to share our feelings of pleasure and joy, as well as pain. Compassion means that we are genuinely concerned and connected with others. It moves you from the inner experience of loving and forgiving yourself outwards so that you can love and relate to other people in your life. True love is a sharing of the simple, everyday experiences — earning a living, raising children, and doing daily chores. Try to be appreciative of these simple things. Your fast-paced lifestyle may have been full of excitement, frantic activities, or chaotic relationships, but it has drained you. Try not to yield to the temptation of always wanting more.

Friendship is the essence of a good, lasting marriage. Are you a good friend to your spouse? Do you resist dwelling on each other's weaknesses, and instead respect each other's differences? Do you support each other's spiritual and psychological growth? Do you refrain from imposing impossibly high standards on your spouse? Are you kind, considerate, generous, and interesting and fun to be with? Do you handle your own moods and frustrations? Are you able to forgive your spouse when he or she slips up?

Such love is spiritual in nature because it is God-like. Sexuality can flourish and be mutually satisfying only in such a climate of true love. Rediscover your sexually repressed feelings as you open up your self-awareness, and become more sensitive to others' needs and wishes. Performing sex is not loving behaviour! Put people first in your life, and special things will happen. Express love, and by saying lovely things, your capacity to love will expand. You may feel awkward at first, but it will become more natural each time.

7. *Get professional help.* In addition to the work you do by yourself, I recommend that you see a well-trained and experienced psychotherapist. He or she can help you chip away at your strong denial system and can test your view of reality with his or her professional knowledge and expertise. Since the disturbances spill over into the family system, many therapists work with the spouses as well right away. You will establish healthier patterns of behaviour faster if there is a "team" family approach. The therapist may wish to involve your children at some later point to disentangle the unhealthy triangles, and re-establish the marital bond as the most important to the family's well-being. However, once the parents' relationship has begun to improve, the children's problems often disappear on their own.

Initially, one of the biggest headaches you will have is finding the time in your busy schedule to commit yourself to regular psychotherapy sessions. The clients who do well have given their recovery first priority, and their bosses or companies are well aware of the problem and are supportive in granting the necessary time off. Explore whether your company has employee-benefits programs that might cover the cost. Your company will be more than reimbursed when you once again can be effective and make wise decisions. New people skills in the workplace will be welcomed by management, as so often workaholics have alienated other staff by irritability, impatience, or angry rages. Be aware that lack of insight still may be blinding you to the damage you have done to others.

LIFESTYLE CHANGES AT HOME AND AT WORK

There are a number of things you can do to look after yourself better, and to improve your well-being.

1. *Free yourself now.* Break free from your fears of failure, boredom, laziness, and discovery. Stop sacrificing today's joy for tomorrow's

ambitious desires. A frequent excuse I hear in my office is "I'm working so hard now in my forties so I can retire early in my fifties. Then I'm really going to make up for lost time!" Meanwhile, the person neglects his health so badly, he is in rough shape by the time he reaches "early" retirement. Or she sacrifices her own and her family's happiness, and creates a climate of resentment and bitterness that is extremely difficult to undo.

Give yourself the freedom to live each day well. Make sure people are given a high priority in your day. People skills take time, so stop rushing. Give up some of your "efficiency." Keep a healthy balance between getting the work done and treating people with respect and concerned caring.

Revitalize your psyche by purposefully exploring your less-developed functions to balance your naturally stronger ones. Introverts might join a small interest group. Extroverts might stay home and read more. Why not reacquire some of the skills that appealed to you earlier in life? Would piano lessons be fun, or would you be interested in joining a group of amateur photographers on photo outings? What about joining the company's baseball or volleyball team and rooting for your teammates and sharing in their enthusiasm while you're at it!

People with high levels of intuition need to learn to be less restless and to see more detail. Take time to sniff the roses, right up close. Let colour wash over you as you sit in front of a painting at an art gallery. Enjoy the artistic presentation of your food instead of wolfing it down in thirty seconds! Listen for birds, and watch them entertain at your feeder! Clouds are especially fascinating if you only take the time to look up and let your imagination go wild. Savour the sensations of touch, taste, sight, hearing, and smell. Free yourself, and the emptiness within will be replaced with some satisfying soul food.

2. *Stop rushing.* Free yourself from the tyranny of the clock. Hurrying can become an unhealthy habit! Everything doesn't have to be done in the shortest possible time. Doing two or three things at once is compulsive. When you talk on the phone, are you also shuffling papers? Stop what you are doing, and really tune in to what someone else thinks is important. Don't rush anybody or anything, except in a dire emergency! *Slow down* to a leisurely pace, preferably starting with

the way you begin your day. Remember breakfast; it's one of the most important meals of the day. Try *courtesy* on your way down to work. Let people get into the line of traffic. If traffic is terrible, *shrug*. There is no point dodging in and out. Think of your car as a quiet haven where you can be alone with your thoughts. Listen to your favourite tapes, say thank you for all the good things that happened yesterday, and watch your fellow drivers to guess which ones are frustrated Type As. Do you *really* need that car phone? Sanctuaries, after all, are about peace, not work.

3. *Get in touch with your body*. Instead of functioning only from the neck up, where your intellect dominates and obsessions boil, integrate body with mind. Become aware of the wonders of your body. Take time out each day to exercise. Take a walk with the kids before or after supper. Take your lunch to a park, then go for a brisk walk before heading back to the office. How long has it been since you and your husband or wife went dancing? Ask one of your neighbours to jog with you on a regular basis so that you don't keep putting it off. Friends can keep you in line sometimes! If you have back problems, a typical workaholic's complaint, walk at a fast pace instead.

Chronic fatigue is no excuse! If you exercise for twenty minutes three or four times a week, your energy will be noticeably improved after six to eight weeks. Twice a week is not enough. *Non-stop* cardiovascular exercises — fast walking, jogging, or swimming — are recommended for total fitness. You want to increase your lung capacity so that more oxygen will be pumped into your system naturally. Nature's tranquillizers, the endorphins, come with that extra oxygen, and a feeling of well-being will be your reward for such discipline. Body awareness is aided by exercise, aerobics, or dance exercises, which help you move into your body, out of your head.

Look after your total health. See your doctor once a year for a regular checkup. Let your family doctor keep tabs on your physical and mental health, and make sure your health records are up-to-date. Only then can changes in blood pressure, cholesterol, and sugar levels be noticed and treatment started in time to prevent serious illness. Remember that workaholism can be a killer, and you have to counteract the damage already done to your body.

Listen to your body. It tells you what your soul is up to! Your chronic fatigue is a loud message telling you to *stop and look* at what you are doing! Those chest pains and panic attacks are a *cry for help* from your wounded psyche and oxygen-deprived brain. Your breathing gets choked by rigid, uptight facial and throat muscles, and your chest caves in if you slump in your chair, bent over with fatigue and worry. Your depression signals a sense of *hopelessness and helplessness*. The way you are living your life is lopsided and out of harmony with your natural self. Nature's alarm bells are going off left, right, and centre!

Addictions are also warning signals that you are sabotaging your chance for health. Just how many cigarettes did you smoke today? Did you take a drink when you came home to "relax" you? Are you overweight? Watch for these distress signals, and recognize that other addictions often accompany the obsession with work. Workaholics have addictive personality traits. *Be honest* with yourself, and seek help to overcome all your addictions. Self-punishing behaviours, often unconscious, are part of the vindictive-triumph phenomenon in which guilt leads to self-destructive actions.

Discipline yourself so that chronic fatigue does not turn you into a couch potato! The fear of laziness and boredom may lead to a self-fulfilling prophecy where what you fear really happens if you don't check these tendencies. Your life can become an adventure when you rediscover the curious child within who has lost the ability to play and entertain. Protect Saturdays and Sundays from work, so that those days are mini-holidays. Plan outings and events with friends. And encourage them to get on your case if you sacrifice yourself to the folly of excessive ambition.

4. *Play is supposed to be fun, and recreation a source of pleasure.* You may jog or swim for health reasons, but unless you really enjoy it, it isn't play. "Play is what happens when you laugh and cry and share and leap and dance and celebrate and feel light and happy," Lee Morical reminds us in *Where's My Happy Ending?* When was the last time you really laughed at anything but put-down humour? What was your most enjoyable moment yesterday? Where did you go and what did you do for a fun evening this month? What do you still like to do that was fun in your childhood? When was the last time you did it? What activities provide you with relaxation and pleasure, and leave you

feeling content and revitalized? Reassess some of the routines you and your family have got locked into, and ask yourself if they are still fun. If not, find new adventures.

Play can open up many facets of your personality. Play, Morical reminds us, is like a friend who introduces us to new experiences and draws us out of our shell. Play helps us realize that we are valuable for something other than our work and accomplishments. Play and humour can provide objectivity and distance, and offer a fresh new perspective on our problems. Play loosens up rigid ways of doing and seeing things. Play absorbs emotional energy, and tempts us away from frantic busyness and the serious side of life. Play and holiday experiences can be precious treasures we store up to carry and sustain us through stressful and tiring periods of work. Playfulness should be experienced as joyful, amusing, fun, and an effortless celebration of life. If we make play an integral part of each day or week, then our other activities, too, may be touched by a sense of fun and zest for living. Beware, joy is contagious!

5. *Learn to say no.* Saying no when you have nothing to give and are feeling overloaded and exhausted is what I call *healthy selfishness.* Your energy must be renewed with rest and relaxation if you are to function well. Make sure your giving comes from a generous spirit, not because you want to please or impress somebody, or manipulate them into owing you something in return. Say yes when you can follow through cheerfully. Otherwise decline, or promise to reconsider at a later time when you honestly do have something to give and are up to the challenge. Save enough energy at the end of each day to take some home to your family.

6. *Put energy into a wide variety of baskets.* A person's "work" basket should be kept in proportion with other baskets. Draw a diagram that shows the areas your energy flows into now — work, family, friends, hobbies, outside interests, sports, spirituality, community, etc. Indicate the size of each area. As you strive to regain control of your life, your work basket will gradually become a healthier size. Make some major decisions to establish new priorities about which basket your newly released energy should flow into for a healthy, balanced life.

Fill up your people basket. When your feelings are developed, your values will naturally shift towards a people orientation. You will have more empathy and compassion to give to others. Look up old friends, and get back into entertaining them and renewing your mutual interests. New friendships will keep you stimulated and lively. Try to enter social networks outside your line of work. People from different backgrounds and socio-economic levels can be stimulating, and can help you to be more objective about your particular area of work. New friends expose you to fresh interests, and you can introduce each other to favourite haunts. Don't forget to articulate positive feeling to your friends, and focus your energy on harmony, not on arguing and being "right."

7. *Make a date with your spouse on a regular basis.* Encourage the romance in your marriage by planning special evenings or events together. Sunday evening is a good time to sit down together to review the week's activities, meetings, and responsibilities, and to plan your week to allow for some *We* time. Honour promises to each other, and do your best to protect this reserved time together from interruptions and others' demands. Punctuality is a sign of politeness and respect, so arrive on time and don't keep your "date" waiting. Incidentally, you will be good role models for your children on how wives and husbands should treat one another. Some day you will see them behaving in the same thoughtful and loving ways with their spouses.

8. *Share the planning of a special outing with each of your children.* Some children need one-on-one conversations, and others are content when the whole gang does things together. Recognize their unique qualities and gifts, and spend this time fostering or sharing their natural interests or talents. Shared sports activities, fishing, boating, theatre, dancing, and amusement-park outings provide memories that will last forever. No car-phone messages on the way, please! Office worries belong at the office. Kids need undivided attention on a regular basis to affirm that they are all-important in your life. I remember one day, on my way home, feeling so upset for a sad-faced little boy staring out the back window of his father's car while Dad was obviously en-

grossed in a call on his car phone. Ask yourself what you are teaching your kids by your behaviour.

9. *Family conferences are important to healthy functioning.* Tense times, short tempers, and stressed-out parents mean uptight, anxious, and often angry children. Provide a regular outlet for the family's anger and frustrations. Let each member of the family have "air time" to vent his or her feelings, or offer suggestions. Wait until after dinner, when everyone is fed and energy is restored. *Listening* is all important! Problem-solving for others is *not* to be encouraged, but unfortunately it is one of the most difficult things to give up when you are used to being in charge. Children need to be consulted and respected for their ideas and wishes. Give them time to experiment with solutions and to try out new behaviour. Making mistakes is part of not being perfect, and no more perfectionists are needed in your family! *Let go of control and share the power of love.*

WORK-RELATED ISSUES

This list will ask some important questions, and give you some tips on how to reorganize your job.

1. *Are you honest on the job?* Take full responsibility for being completely truthful, up front, and straightforward with your colleagues and support staff. Admit your problem with workaholism, and ask for others' support to help you be more realistic about what you can handle. When you replace phony arrogance with humility, you will be more approachable, and will receive the support that is there for you. *Be receptive.*

2. *Are you in the right job? Step back and re-evaluate your work environment.* As one client advised: "If it seems crazy, then it probably is. You are part of it and you are affected by it. You might be controlled by it, you might even have created it. Examine the impact of your work both physically and emotionally." Is your work still interesting and fun? Was it ever really fun? As Stan, a vice-president of a small manufacturing firm, put it: "Here I've been killing myself to get this company out of the red, and I'm so bogged down with administrative drivel that

I've lost sight of why I went into business in the first place. What I'm good at is developing theoretical system models, but I'm no good at the nuts and bolts of getting things to fly. Right now I'm drowning in paper, and feeling no good at anything!"

Have you, too, been trying so hard because you are a square peg in a round hole? Is this the right career for your talents? Be honest about the reasons you went into this line of work in the first place. Was it something Mom had always wished she had gone into, or was it a way to get Father's attention and have something to talk to him about? Did you fall into your job because it seemed to be the easiest way to make a fast buck? Did your father's best friend's initial offer to get you a summer job in his firm lead you into working for him again when you graduated? Are you on the right corporate ladder? Did this job have the glamour and prestige you always dreamed you wanted?

Has the Peter Principle promoted you above your competence? Did your last promotion move you to a job you can't handle, and therefore don't enjoy? Did the shift of duties forced on you when the company had to reorganize move you away from people contact? Are you isolated in your ivory-tower office? Or are people driving you crazy because you're much better working with computers and software?

It is traumatic to leave a profession or job you have trained for and worked so hard in for many years. Maybe you don't need to. Instead, can you slant the emphasis of your job so that you can focus on the tasks that tap into your strengths? Could you begin to delegate the onerous tasks to others who do them so effortlessly and efficiently? Could you take on some special projects geared to your talents, which would be fun and, at the same time, would win management acclaim? Covering up your deficiencies exhausts all your resources.

One recovering workaholic gave the following advice: "If you want to get out of the rat race, try to take less responsibility in business, but most of all, give up your power *over* people." Most of the recovering workaholics I work with eventually get around to eliminating excess responsibility in their jobs, or try to concentrate on what they do best, so they can leave enough time and energy for their families and interests outside work. Sadly, more and more workaholics no longer have an intact family to make the efforts of work meaningful. Others are finding satisfaction in their jobs again because they are no longer chronically fatigued and have found fresh motivation.

Let yourself get excited about some of the pet projects you have secretly wanted to do. Offer your enthusiasm to others' special tasks. Try to battle the fear that others might compete with you for your job if you share your knowledge and talent. That's called paranoia! Your writing skills can be offered to company publications or bulletins on subjects that fascinate you. Teaching skills can open doors to offering lectures to others on your pet theories. By reaching out and assisting others, you will work against the self-centred and narcissistic tendencies of your past. Be enthusiastic, but watch for obsessive fanaticism. *Stop* if you start to feel the chronic fatigue returning. You may not be ready yet to spread out. Go back to reducing your responsibilities to a manageable level until you feel healthy again.

When anxiety is high, workaholics tend to be restless and have short attention spans. A change of activities can be as good as a rest at such times because it forces you to interrupt driven and obsessive thinking. Even unwelcome interruptions may be just what is needed to help you step back and be more objective about what you are absorbed in. Variety feeds your need for stimulation and counteracts your fear of boredom. However, be aware that your short attention span is signalling high anxiety and fatigue levels. Rest and relaxation are in order, the sooner the better.

3. *Are you being scapegoated?* Workaholics tend to hire other workaholics, so if you have lost your job or are about to be transferred because your functioning has been poor, *be careful*. Be sure the degree of involvement you now wish to have fits the demands of the new position you are considering. Remember, workaholic bosses lack empathy and compassion, and your needs will not be paramount in their scheme of things.

Pleasers, usually found in middle-management jobs, are often caught in the unfortunate dilemma of being swamped with work because their workaholic boss is unable to function and make decisions. Is the boss's overload funnelling down to your desk? Do you end up looking bad instead of your boss? Executive assistants and secretaries often get caught in this trap. Being such a "nice" person, you keep covering up for your boss's inadequacies and overload yourself with added top-management responsibilities. You also tend to get overinvolved with the boss's personal life and his or her responsibilities to his or her spouse and children. You may find yourself making personal family travel arrangements, typing letters for the spouse or children, or trying to match schedules of business meetings to allow for the family's various commitments such as parent-teacher meetings. When these arrangements don't work out, you have to listen to the spouses' anger and resentment. It's like choreographing a three-ring circus that you never wanted to be in. The workaholic's chaotic state spills into your life, and leaves you harried and overloaded. No one warned you that you would be on the receiving end of the Terrible Twist, and that the boss's rage would be directed at you. Watch for signs of depression and feelings of being trapped in a bad situation. *Awareness* is your best protection so that you can confront the situation before you too become a dysfunctional workaholic.

4. *Do you set time limits?* Decide the length of day that you can work effectively and comfortably. Announce the hours that you plan to keep from now on, but keep flexible until you are comfortable with your new schedule. If you become consistent, then others can fit into your timetable easier. Don't try to cram six hours of work into a four-hour morning. Don't put artificial deadlines on projects, but keep a small range of acceptable times. "I'll finish that paper some time between Wednesday and Friday." Think of a tube of toothpaste. If the lid is screwed on tight and you squeeze the tube, you have bottled-up pressure. Leave the lid slightly loose, and you have a safety valve if pressure builds.

During the shorter day, commit yourself to being fully there. When your concentration begins to wander, or you begin to be obsessive about small details, take a few minutes to breathe deeply and relax or stretch out your limbs, and then refocus. Be responsible, but not overly responsible. Stop overnurturing and worrying unnecessarily about things over which you have no power. *Worry about things you yourself can do something about today.* Otherwise, delegate responsibility, and then let others seek independent solutions to what is now *their* problem.

5. *Do you pace yourself?* Use your time wisely. Workaholics usually get up and get going early in the day. Underlying anxiety makes them hyper-alert, so relaxing or resting is difficult. Figure out if you're more effective in the morning or afternoon. Schedule your difficult tasks when your energy level is highest, and don't waste this time on obsessive trivialities, or avoidance or procrastinations, such as reading the paper or shifting through junk mail. Know your rhythms, and do routine jobs during your slack time. You may find it best to have your secretary hold calls during a set time each day to allow you to focus when your productivity is high.

6. *Do you waste time?* Reassess the essential tasks of your job. Are you performing routines that are no longer relevant to your job? Could you use memos instead of letters, or create form letters for specific purposes? Are your letters rambling? Do they reflect the present state of confusion you feel? Do you schedule meetings when others are missing lunch and running on empty? You may not think you need time out for coffee or lunch, but your staff will.

Your time is very valuable. Do you protect it? Do you really need to be on that planning committee any longer? Is it accomplishing things that are pertinent to your present job? Are you the best person to represent your division, or is somebody else more suited to team decision-making? Don't be afraid to resign and give up some of your control. Why overload yourself by always taking on new challenges, and neglecting to give up the old ones?

Business lunches are bad for your health because you continue to pump adrenalin throughout the day. It is an inefficient way to conduct business because there are so many distractions. If alcohol is involved, you will have a depressive reaction about an hour and a half later, and your afternoon inefficiency will be curtailed as well. Try having lunch with a personal friend, preferably one who works in an unrelated field, once a week. This will revitalize you instead of draining all your energies. Try eating by yourself sometimes — it can be quite peaceful — or go for a walk after a short lunch. Above all else, make time for lunch — don't skip it!

7. *Are you decisive? Do you delegate?* You may have worked yourself into such a state of perpetual anxiety that making even simple deci-

sions has become a monumental task. Your time and energy are precious commodities. Don't waste them seesawing back and forth between alternatives. Consult with others, or get others to help you brainstorm other possibilities or solutions. Then pick the one that feels best, carry it out, and *live with it*!

Delegating is not just giving up control, it is smart behaviour. It is letting others do things for you that they are better trained or equipped to perform. Controller workaholics, notoriously poor about sharing decision-making, exhaust themselves keeping tabs on every detail of an operation. Ask yourself why your employees are so dependent on your approval and act like children sometimes. Could it be because they feel patronized, checked-up on, and rebuked if their way is different from your "right" course of action? No wonder frayed nerves and fragile egos collide, and emotionality stalls effective resolution of the dilemma. You have set yourself up for failure, and once again you can utter the famous words: "If I want anything done right, I have to do it myself." *Give up control, and keep your sanity instead!* Instead, praise your staff to instil confidence when the job is done, even if it is not the way you would have done it.

8. *Have you isolated yourself?* You will need all the support you can muster to conquer workaholism, so do not try to do it alone. Keep communication going between management and yourself. Arrange feedback sessions to monitor your progress, and seek support to improve your judgment and decision-making skills. Remind yourself that if you were recovering from a heart attack, you would probably have no trouble with working shorter hours or going home early when you were exhausted.

Work on a buddy system. Ask one of your colleagues to alert you when you do things in the old way. Letting off steam with an understanding friend will prevent rages later.

9. *Have you lost your sense of humour?* "Boy, had I ever got to be a real drag." Joe laughed. "The Grinch that stole Christmas had nothing on me!" Intensity will work against you if everything that happens to you is perceived as super-serious. Humility comes from realizing you are quite dispensable, and that if you dropped dead tomorrow from a heart attack, the company would quickly recruit a replacement or find other

ways to carry on. However, do humour yourself along by appreciating the skills you do have. Try to develop a quiet pride that acknowledges these special gifts without having to have others applaud or confirm that you are okay. Some of your gifts admittedly have been temporarily "stored in mothballs" while your addiction got the better of you! Tease yourself about being human after all, and give up all claim to perfectionism. *Laugh and be silly and have fun instead.*

10. *Are you well rested, well nourished, and well groomed?* Feel comfortable, and then forget about your persona and your ideal image. It is arrogance to imagine that others are that interested or concerned with your image. Instead of "looking in other people's mirrors to see yourself," focus on feeling good inside about who you are as a person. Be nice to people. Obsession and narcissism drive many workaholics to be overly neat, formal, and super-polite. They are sticklers for details no one else notices, let alone cares about. Your body is frankly tired out from excess adrenalin and going without much sleep. *Stop* rushing through meals, eating too fast, or too much, so that you can begin to appreciate the sights and smells always present, but unseen. Chronic fatigue is Nature's warning. Become *wise*, and *slow down*. Get off the endless spiral downwards towards self-destruction.

11. *Do you take time out to meditate or relax?* If you feel tension building up, whether at work or at home, here are some quick and easy exercises to counteract stress.
Shoulders — Close your eyes, hang your head, and allow your arms to hang down at the sides of your chair. Concentrate on the feeling that a great weight is stretching your arms down farther and farther, and they are becoming heavier and heavier. When your fingers start to tingle, be aware of whether your shoulder muscles are releasing and lengthening out to a more relaxed state. Enjoy the sensation, and then look up and around you without moving your arms from their hanging position. Concentrate on a picture in your office or the view out your window, and breathe slowly and deeply. Later, you can achieve the same numbing sensation and relaxed shoulders without having to close your eyes first. Eventually, the tingling in your fingers will occur sooner, and you will be able to continue talking and do the

relaxation at the same time without any special concentration being required.

If you are alone in your office, try standing up and bending over from the waist in a Raggedy-Ann position. Hang your head, and let your arms go naturally and freely in a circling motion. This will relax the whole upper body.

Arms — Raise your arms up over your head, and then make a series of circles as you gradually lower them down to your side. This motion opens up your chest area, and helps you breathe more deeply. Extra oxygen is important when you are under stress as it releases endorphins into your system. Repeat the process upwards to strengthen your arm muscles and get your circulation moving.

Extend your arms at shoulder height, and rotate them back and forth, and then in small circles in both directions, to release the tension in your upper body and arms. Clench your fists, and then shake them out.

Make graceful, loose circular waving motions in the air, conduct your own symphony, or let your arms dance out some of the stress that has been tying you up in knots.

Legs — To release leg tension, raise one foot off the ground while you remain sitting in your chair with your back supported. Rotate the ankle in a circular position, first clockwise, and then in reverse. Cover all the points on the circumference as you rotate. Repeat with the other foot, until you feel your circulation improve.

Stomach — Stomach muscles can be exercised at work. Sit up straight, hold on to the arms of your chair or the edge of your desk, and then lift both of your knees towards your chest. Start small, and work higher as your muscles get stronger. Make sure you breathe normally and deeply.

11. *What are other people doing to solve work problems?* Your choices and opportunities for change have expanded greatly. Some employees are refusing to move at the company's whim. They choose to move laterally in the hierarchy, refuse promotions, or take demotions instead. Many two-career families find it difficult to relocate. The upheavals, hassles, and personal sacrifice cause too much resentment. Others have freed themselves to make job changes, as it no longer carries the stigma of instability that it once did. Many change careers a

number of times in their lifetime. Industry has less power to dictate or threaten its employees into succumbing to corporate wishes.

People are retiring earlier. Incentives to retire early have left many people free to start new businesses, do volunteer work, and enjoy leisure at a time in their lives when they are still active and in good health. Many employees are returning to volunteer work. The frantic workaholic had no time or energy to volunteer. Such jobs have been scaled down to adjust to work schedules, and business meetings are held in off-hours convenient to the worker. Volunteering leads to good feelings of warmth and belonging, and there is no comparable experience in the workplace where you are paid to help others and satisfaction comes from performance and productivity. The joy of giving time and energy to others is fulfilling a need for meaningful experiences in people's lives.

Many men and women are choosing to work part-time, or they are job-sharing. More people are also working at home as fax machines and computers make their presence at the office unnecessary. The opening up of previously sex-stereotyped jobs has provided new opportunities. Equal-pay-for-equal-work legislation is slowly changing the workplace. Workaholics have a wide scope of options should they choose to change jobs or the circumstances of their present position.

SOME HELPFUL HINTS FOR THE SPOUSE

Co-dependents need to stop playing the martyr–victim role and realize that they must lead the way towards re-establishing a healthier relationship. This does not mean "fixing" the workaholic — that is his or her personal journey. Instead, concentrate on your own happiness, and on protecting yourself and the children.

Expect to be treated well, and make sure you honour your own values, and do not lose them in the fray. Let your spouse know what your values and needs are. Don't be afraid to talk about how you like to be loved. "I want us both to be sensitive people. . . . I really want to share decisions and be a team. . . . It's important that we try to work through our differences together so that our family will be a happy one."

Get angry at unhealthy behaviour, not at the person. Personality attacks are unfair and lethal! The message "Be crazy, but not in front of me" means that you emotionally distance or remove yourself physically when the workaholic has a temper tantrum or gets in a rage. Don't play the workaholic "game."

Don't get sucked into the *dominance–submission–punishment* game. Competition or power struggles take two participants, so try not to participate in one-upmanship talk. "I don't see that the same way you do, but let me think about what you are saying. . . . I don't enjoy us being in competition with each other, so I'd rather not comment." Or, "I would appreciate it if you could be more positive with me. Our marriage is more important to me than who is 'right.' "

Don't let yourself be caught in the "Terrible Twist" victim role. The fact that you are angry is not your "fault." Try to remind the workaholic that the reason you were upset in the first place seems to be forgotten. Repeat your views once more, and then *Stop*! "I would appreciate it if you would take time to think about why I was so devastated by what you said. Maybe we could talk about it when we aren't both so upset." Or, "We're both pretty defensive right now. I know it's not much fun to be criticized. It's important, though, that I let you know how I react to things that affect me deeply. Otherwise we won't understand each other." If the discussion isn't getting anywhere: "Let's call time-out and go for a long walk. I think we both need to think about the good things between us."

Know that *dishonesty* is the most difficult problem to cope with because one can feel outrage when someone is being irresponsible by avoiding the truth or lying. Reality testing is about all you can do, and it will be your reality versus theirs. Diplomacy is essential here, as pride is at stake. "You neglected to mention that you went to your office on Saturday when you told me you were going off to do some shopping. It's so important to be honest with me, and I'll try to understand your explanation." Or, when the workaholic is in trouble at work, but has not let you know: "I'm hurt that you would tell me everything at work is just fine. It's embarrassing for me to hear from your secretary about the cut-backs that are threatening your job. It leaves me feeling betrayed and alienated from you. I hope you trust me enough to listen, and not to try to solve anything for you. I want to be as supportive as I can, but I have to know you are in trouble first."

HANG IN THERE —
PAIN IS THE GROWING EDGE OF GROWTH

It's painful but necessary for workaholics to bring their Shadow into consciousness where they can recognize their own shortcomings instead of projecting and seeing their faults only in others. Only weaknesses that are brought into awareness can be improved upon. Problems must be recognized before solutions are sought. Pain cannot be avoided if there is true self-confrontation!

Because workaholics grow up with conditional love, the suggestion that they try to love themselves unconditionally is often met with surprise. As one client exclaimed: "I love my wife and my child unconditionally. No matter what they do or say, I still love them. But you're saying to love myself that way. Well, I'll have to spend some time thinking about that!"

Pain is at the cutting edge of new growth. Unless something faulty dies within and is let go, there is no room for healthier behaviour to emerge. When one of my clients tells me he is in total confusion, and doesn't even know who he is any more, I say, "Good, I know you're in a state of turmoil and feel awful, but now you'll be able to do some growing!"

Although pain cannot be avoided, you are responsible for your own. Try to accept it and learn to live with the discomfort. Use pain as an incentive to motivate yourself to seek new solutions for important problems. Don't wallow in pain or, worse still, lash out at your family, your friends, or even God in retaliation for feeling victimized, overloaded, or overwhelmed. Often your suffering is the result of your own impulsive actions. Unless you take responsibility for your pain and bitterness, anger will fuel the flames of inner rage, and you will become depressed and demoralized — your own worst enemy. *Be your own healer* and give up the curse of perfectionism. Being perfect itself is a real pain! You hurt yourself and others by driving yourself mercilessly towards your goals, trying to control everything and everyone in your path. *Let go of pain, and new energy will let you get on with life!*

Welcome the Shadow

Welcome the Shadow up to consciousness where you can keep an eye on it! It's like Pandora's Box. Within your unconscious lies not only the negative things you do not wish to acknowledge about yourself, but also all your positive, unlived potential. Trapped within, the wisdom of the ages awaits release as well. Honesty, your strongest ally in the battle to free hidden strengths, will enable you to transform the envy, greed, jealousy, and selfishness you discover there. As denial breaks down, you need sensitivity and compassion to correct what you have done to others and to yourself.

Beneath their arrogance, workaholics are very insecure and are terrified of the Shadow and what it will reveal. They feel overwhelmed enough without adding any more negatives! Donna, a very ambitious, driven executive, had come far enough along in her recovery to admit her fears. One day, she and I had an Active Imagination session. The conversation went this way:

DONNA: I'm afraid to face the negative aspects of my personality, of my Self. My Shadow is distant. It is not close to me. I am honestly frightened of it. Not that it will hurt me, although I now know it is capable of hurting others. I am more afraid of what I will feel about it when I see it or confront it. Repulsion is what I don't want to feel.

BARB: It sounds like your Nice Gal is firmly entrenched in a bed of sand, like a wooden Indian stubbornly rooted to the spot. Is she standing in quicksand?

DONNA: Quicksand implies sinking and disappearing eventually. I don't see it as a sinking, but rather stopped. I don't want to go any farther.

BARB: It's as if you fear a grotesque mask covers her face. I wonder if she remains wooden, will the mask become even more hideous? Has she really a choice to postpone the revelation?

DONNA: Yes, but at the cost of destroying those around her, and eventually herself. So, therefore, the mask will become hideous if it remains wooden. The trick is to soften the mask. (Pause) Not the mask, the heart, so that it can look at the Shadow, and forgive, and love. I think this whole fear thing is related to my inability to sustain intimacy.

BARB: The direction you are trying to find intimacy in sounds confused. It's like a signpost that the painter forgot to write the street names on. What names will you give the street signs in order to know where to go at the fork in the road?

DONNA: Tolerance and love, I think. Love is many things, but I've decided my definition is to nurture or promote the growth of another at some cost or sacrifice that will sometimes involve suffering. Tolerance is much smaller in scope, but essential because it is the first door to open to permit one to begin loving. I am afraid to suffer!

BARB: That's the workaholic's nightmare! Escaping pain at all costs traps the curious child within. How can that person with the mask let this child at least live so that the inner child will not be sacrificed and stillborn?

DONNA: "He that keepeth his life shall lose it!" Selfishness is at the root of my fear of suffering, because suffering is much broader than pain. Suffering is multidimensional, and perhaps is better understood as self-sacrificing. If that's the case, what is there to be afraid of? Hmmm. So to the extent that I am prepared to give of myself, my time, my caring, my emotional support, my ears to listen, my mind — everything that I have been given — then I will provide life to that child.

BARB: It sounds like the travails of childbirth will expose the Shadow, but also the newborn child. Joy and pain will be born together as twins. Do you think she is brave enough to bear the pain if there is enough joy in this new creation?

DONNA: The signpost, the direction to meet my Shadow, is towards other people, and to learn to love the Shadow in them. While my direction gets clearer, my bravery's still in the neophyte stage! (Laughs)

Donna had conceptualized her Shadow as a powerful shaman figure that might overwhelm her. The analogy of the "child within, waiting to be born" was an image she could accept more easily as it was one over which she might exercise some control. Donna's growing self-acceptance and willingness to reach out to others mean that each time she confronts facets of her personality that disturb her, she also opens herself to hidden strengths that will emerge to help her handle her insight. New growth requires both sun and rain. Her journey will follow a zig-zag course, with periods of progress mixed with regressive slips into past behaviour. It takes faith to persevere, especially when events rain on your parade!

Birthing always hurts, but as every new mother knows, you soon forget the pains when you see the face of your newborn.

THE TIME FOR YOUR JOURNEY IS NOW

In discussing the process of recovery with Alexander, he explained, "Progressively work has become less important. I don't recall how it happened or what I've done to change it. I just know I'm not obsessed with it anymore. I can handle situations and problems better. I'm in control of myself again, and much more open to others' opinions and needs. The biggest change is in my attitude towards people. I'm more compassionate and I try to understand others more instead of judging them. I'm simply more interested in people than before."

"What advice would you offer fellow workaholics?" I asked. Alexander thought for a moment: "The best advice I can give is that it just isn't worth it! Too much work reduces the value of every day, every week, month, year of life. Discover that people and relationships are the keys to happiness, that relationships founder in the workaholic world. Finally, fight arrogance! Remember you are only one of many people on earth. Don't swell up, come down to earth, and, above all, get your priorities straight."

Arrogance took on a new meaning as well for Harvey Oxenhorn, a Ph. D. in literature. In a review of *Tuning the Rig: A Journey to the Arctic* in the *Globe and Mail* (August 29, 1990), Laszlo Buhasz tells of the voyage Oxenhorn made as an apprentice seaman on *Regina Maris*, a converted scientific vessel. "When I first came on board, I thought that the whole world owed me. I was ready to make music, damn it. I was disappointed, angry that so little in my life would stay in tune. But tonight . . . I understood such disappointments to be arrogance. It is arrogance to expect that our life always be music. It is false pride to demand to know the score. Harmony, like a following breeze at sea, is the exception. In a world where most things wind up broken or lost, our lot is to tack and tune." His capacity for simply being — with each other, with nature, with ourselves — had been lost. "What I discovered aboard *Regina* is that we have it backward. Freedom, Hegel said, is recognition of necessity. In exercising self-restraint, in accepting the kinds of limits that I had previously squandered so much energy evading, I experienced a sense of purpose and a kind of solidarity I'd never known before. I had gone far off to bring what mattered closer — gone to sea and come back feeling grounded — relieved of the lonely ego, released but also re-engaged."

The captain of *Regina*, a former distinguished doctor, gave Oxenhorn his own father's advice from thirty years earlier: "He said that a lot of folks spend most of their lives doing one thing in order to be able to do another. They are always trying to get through what they are doing to 'make time' for something else, and they wind up resenting both things. But life doesn't work like that. The only way not to resent the expenditure of time and effort is to devote yourself to the one activity you don't want to get **through**. You should choose as your life's work whatever feels most like play."

A playful spirit does not allow itself to be too intense. It permits objectivity, it keeps your life in balance, and it offers wisdom. Workaholics must find this playful spirit within themselves. Wayne, in the process of rediscovering his humour, told me that his life had been a paradox: "I feared celibacy as a teenager, but was celibate till my early twenties. I feared spiritual enlightenment, but have been seeking it for years. I loathed suffering, but, by avoiding the truth, have suffered greatly. I was denied or denied myself material comforts, but now materialism controls my life. I need sensory awareness and the feel of nature, but I sit deskbound, task-oriented in a paper process, surrounded by concrete and the urban environment." Wayne's soul-searching angst had been a painful journey of self-discovery. But slowly, step by step, he was regaining his loving feelings, for his wife, his children, and for himself. Without that self-love, Wayne had gone astray and got lost in workaholism.

The beauty in recovery is that everyone you connect with in a loving way will be touched in some minor or profound way by your transformation. *Don't wait* until the damage is irreparable. Start your journey today.

BIBLIOGRAPHY

* especially recommended

Beattie, M. *Codependent No More*. New York: Harper and Row, 1987.

Birnbaum, J. *Cry Anger: A Cure for Depression*: Don Mills: General Publishing, 1973.

Brennan, A., and J. Brewi. *Mid-life Directions: Praying and Playing Sources of New Dynamism*. New York: Paulist Press, 1985.

Buhasz, L. "Running Away to Sea with a PhD." *The Globe and Mail*, August 29, 1990.

Campbell, R. *Psychiatric Dictionary*. Fifth ed. New York: Oxford University Press, 1981.

* Fox, M. *A Spirituality Named Compassion and the Healing of the Global Village: Humpty Dumpty and Us*. San Francisco: Harper and Row, 1979.

French, W. "Biography Portrays Mead as Arrogant and Domineering." *The Globe and Mail*, July 6, 1989.

Gefen, Pearl. "Making Those Hills Come Alive with the Sound of Music." *The Globe and Mail*, August 18, 1990.

Hall, J. quoted in "Our Shadows, Our Selves." *Chiron*, 10, no. 1 (January 1990): 4.

Horney, K. *Neurosis and Human Growth*. New York: W.W. Norton, 1950.

_____. "Neurotic Competitiveness." *The Neurotic Personality of Our Time*. New York: W.W. Norton, 1937.

Hyder, Q. *The Christian Handbook of Psychiatry*. Old Tappan, NJ: Fleming H. Revell, 1971.

Jeffers, S. *Feel the Fear and Do It Anyway*. New York: Harcourt Brace Jovanovich, 1987.

Johnson, R. *We: Understanding the Psychology of Romantic Love*. San Francisco: Harper and Row, 1983.

Jung, C. *Psychological Types*. Bollingen Series XX. The Collected Works of C.G. Jung, Volume 6. Princeton, NJ: Princeton University Press, 1971.

Kaplan, H. Singer. *Disorders of Sexual Desire: The New Sex Therapy*. New York: Brunner/Mazel, 1979.

Kiersey, D., and M. Bates. *Please Understand Me*. Del Mar, CA: Prometheus Nemesis Books, 1978.

Kohut, H., and E. Wolf. "The Disorders of the Self and Their Treatment: An Outline." *International Journal of Psychoanalysis*, 59, no. 413 (1978): 413–25.

Kroeger, O., and J. Thuesen. *Type Talk. Or How to Determine Your Personality Type and Change Your Life*. New York: Delacorte, 1988.

Lacey, L. "Japanese Flute Player Enjoys Pace of Vancouver's 'Slower Train.' " *The Globe and Mail*, September 23, 1989.

* Lahaye, T., and B. Phillips. *Anger Is a Choice*. Grand Rapids, MI: Zondervan, 1982.

Lautens, G. "Do You Suffer from This Dreaded Disease?" *The Toronto Star*, February 20, 1989.

Laurie, N. "The Strain of 'Suppie' Lifestyle." *The Toronto Star*, September 28, 1989.

Leonard, L. *The Wounded Woman: Healing the Father–Daughter Relationship*. Boston: Shambhala Publications, 1982.

Lewis, M. "Trump Fights Back." *The New York Times Book Review*, September 2, 1990.

Longclaws, Lyle. "First Nations Elder, quoted by Tomson Highway." *The Globe and Mail*, April 24, 1989.

* Machlowitz, M. *Workaholics: Living with Them, Working with Them*. New York: New American Library, 1980.

Masters, W., and Y. Johnson. *The Pleasure Bond*. Toronto: Bantam Books, 1970.

Messer, T. "People Will Give the Competitive Edge in the Future, Says Federal Report." *Office Equipment and Methods*, September 1989.

Miller, A. *Timebends: A Life*. New York: Grove Press, 1987.

Minirth, F., and P. Meir. "Do 'Nice Guys' Finish Last?" *Happiness Is a Choice*. Grand Rapids, MI: Baker Book House, 1978.

Minirth, F., P. Meier, F. Wichern, B. Brewer, and S. Skipper. *The Workaholic and His Family. An Inside Look*. Grand Rapids, MI: Baker Book House, 1981.

Morical, Lee. *Where's My Happy Ending? Women and the Myth of Having It All*. Reading, MI: Addison-Wesley, 1984.

"Morning Smile." *The Globe and Mail*, April 25,1989.

Myers, I., and P. Myers. *Gifts Differing*. Palo Alto, CA: Consulting Psychologists Press, 1980.

* Oates, W. *Confessions of a Workaholic*. Nashville: Abingdon, 1971.

* Osborn, C. *Enough Is Enough. Exploding the Myth of Having It All*. New York: G. P. Putnam's Sons, 1986.

Oxenhorn, H. *Tuning the Rig: A Journey to the Arctic*. New York: Harper and Collins, 1990.

* Peck, S. *The Road Less Traveled*. New York: Simon and Schuster, 1978.

* Robinson, B. *Work Addiction: Hidden Legacies of Adult Children*. Deerfield Beach, FL: Health Communications, 1989.

Rogers, C. In *Psychiatric Dictionary. Fifth Edition*. Ed. R. Campbell. New York: Oxford University Press, 1981.

* Rohrlich, J. *Work and Love: The Crucial Balance*. New York: Harmony, 1980.

Sanford, J. *Evil: The Shadow Side of Reality*. New York: Crossroads, 1984.

_____ . *The Invisible Partners*. New York: Paulist Press, 1980.

Scarf, M. *Intimate Partners: Patterns in Love and Marriage*. New York: Random House, 1987.

Schaef, A. *When Society Becomes an Addict*. San Francisco: Harper and Row, 1987.

Schaef, A., and D. Fassel. *The Addictive Organization*. San Francisco: Harper and Row, 1988.

Schwartz, T. "Acceleration Syndrome." *Vanity Fair*, October 1988.